T0229865

The SIM Guide to
Enterprise Architecture

Enterprise
Architecture

The SIM Guide to Enterprise Architecture
Creating the Information Age Enterprise

Edited by: Leon A. Kappelman, Ph.D.
Chair, SIM Enterprise Architecture Working Group
Professor of Information Systems
Director Emeritus, Information Systems Research Center
Fellow, Texas Center for Digital Knowledge
Information Technology & Decision Sciences Department
College of Business, University of North Texas

Foreword by: Jeanne W. Ross, Ph.D.
Director, Center for IS Research, MIT Sloan School of Management

Managing Editor: Thomas McGinnis, University of North Texas

Contributing Authors, Panelists, Artists & Editors (alphabetically):
Bruce V. Ballengee, Pariveda Solutions
Larry Burgess, Aviall Services
Ed Cannon, New Madison Avenue
Russell Douglas, Aviall Services
Larry R. DeBoever, EAdirections Inc.
Randolph C. Hite, U.S. General Accountability Office
Leon A. Kappelman, University of North Texas
Mark Lane, PNM Resources
Thomas McGinnis, University of North Texas
George S. Paras, EAdirections Inc.
Alex Pettit, University of North Texas
Thiagarajan Ramakrishnan, University of North Texas
Jeanne W. Ross, Center for IS Research at MIT
Brian Salmans, University of North Texas
Anna Sidorova, University of North Texas
Gary F. Simons, SIL International
Kathie Sowell, Custom Enterprise Solutions, LLS
Tim Westbrock, EAdirections Inc.
John A. Zachman, Zachman International

Submission Reviewers (alphabetically):
Keith Andrews, EDS, an HP Company
Bruce Ballengee, Pariveda Solutions
Scott Bernard, Syracuse University
Larry Burgess, Aviall Services
Leon A. Kappelman, University of North Texas
Chang Koh, University of North Texas
Mark Lane, PNM Resources
Thomas McGinnis, University of North Texas
Bill Peterson, LiquidHub, Inc.
Alex Pettit, University of North Texas
Brian Salmans, University of North Texas
Anna Sidorova, University of North Texas
Nancy Wolff, Auxis

This project was sponsored by:
Society for Information Management (SIM)
SIM Enterprise Architecture Working Group
Information Technology and Decision Sciences Department
at the University of North Texas

SIM

**Enterprise
Architecture**

The SIM Guide to Enterprise Architecture

Edited by
Leon Kappelman

CRC Press
Taylor & Francis Group
Boca Raton London New York

CRC Press is an imprint of the
Taylor & Francis Group, an **informa** business

CRC Press
Taylor & Francis Group
6000 Broken Sound Parkway NW, Suite 300
Boca Raton, FL 33487-2742

Printed in the United States of America on acid-free paper
10 9 8 7 6 5 4 3 2 1

International Standard Book Number: 978-1-4398-1113-9 (Hardback)

Library of Congress Cataloging-in-Publication Data

Kappelman, Leon Allan, 1947-
  The SIM guide to enterprise architecture / Leon Kappelman.
    p. cm.
  Includes bibliographical references and index.
  ISBN 978-1-4398-1113-9
    1. Management information systems. 2. Business enterprises-Computer networks.
3. Information technology--Management. 4. Software architecture. I. Society for
Information Management (U.S.) II. Title.

  HD30.213.K37 2010
  658.4'038011--dc22   2009015503

Visit the Taylor & Francis Web site at
http://www.taylorandfrancis.com

and the CRC Press Web site at
http://www.crcpress.com

To my wife, Sheba Kappelman, who makes it all worthwhile. And to our son, Adam Kappelman, for whom I hope this book helps in some small way to make the world a little better than it is today when he is ready to make his contributions to it. (Ed.)

Artwork by Russell Douglas

All we ever know is our models, but never the reality that may or may not exist behind the models. ...Our models may get closer and closer but we will never reach direct perception of reality.

—Stephen Hawking

Contents

List of Figures

List of Tables

List of Charts

Notices

Disclaimer

We have tried our very best to provide useful and accurate information. Nevertheless, our lawyers ask that we advise you that all of the contributors, their employers, the Society for Information Management, the authors and editors, and any and all related entities, make no representations or warranties with respect to the contents hereof and specifically disclaim any implied warranties or merchantability or fitness for any particular purpose. Furthermore, they reserve the right to revise this publication and to make changes from time to time to the content hereof without obligation to notify any person of such revisions.

Proceeds

All author proceeds received (if any) from the publication of this book will go to further the EA-related endeavors of the not-for-profit Society for Information Management's (SIM) Enterprise Architecture Working Group (EAWG). However, if the SIMEAWG ceases to exist, the proceeds will go to further the advocacy, research, and educational activities of SIM.

About the Cover Art

At our September 2008 meeting, the SIM Enterprise Architecture Working Group, preparing for SIM's annual SIMposium conference, decided upon what we hoped would be a catchy phrase or "tag line" to use at the conference. We came up with "Enterprise Architecture is Enterprise Alignment (EA)^2." After the meeting, Mark Lane went to work on a poster for the conference and came up with the idea of using the dominoes metaphor to embody the essence of the alignment between an organization and its information technologies. Rolando Hernandez provided the expertise of his graphic artist Ileanne "Ile" Buigas-Lopez, and the result was a poster for the conference and our cover art.

The dominoes metaphor represents the dynamic alignment of the enterprise and its technologies, as well as the alignment of the conceptualization of the enterprise and its actual manifestation. The enterprise is the bottom half of each domino, the top half the explicit architecture of the enterprise. The enterprise always has an architecture whether it is explicitly represented or not—hence the bottom half of the dominoes is always complete. In the beginning, leftmost domino, the EA is incomplete as represented by the single dot. Over time, the enterprise architecture (EA) becomes explicit, and both the concept and reality of the enterprise can and do become one; and because the EA is now explicit, they can remain as one. As the enterprise and its EA become one over time, so too the enterprise, its technologies, as well as all of its other assets, align to oneness, synchronicity. The use of a six-by-six domino as the end state honors the seminal ontological work of John Zachman in developing his framework for Enterprise Architecture.

The image reminds us to maintain a perspective of EA as a management discipline and enabler of continuous transformation of the enterprise, not merely a tool for managing technology. As the dominoes transform, EA has a mandate—to lead change and manage complexity in order to deliver short-term value through organizational efficiency and long-term value through organizational effectiveness. The inherent instability of a line of dominoes symbolizes the realities of the competitive world—enterprises that fail to manage all the information about themselves (i.e., their architectures) will likely fail or falter in this fast-paced, hyperefficient, convergent Information Age. The probable prescience of this hypothesis surely increases as the enterprise's size, speed, complexity, and rate of change increases. The recent ongoing meltdown of major financial and other institutions supports this premise, as "too big to fail" may really mean "too big to manage" without an EA. And as surely as this applies to commercial enterprises, it applies to governments, nations, and other institutions as well.

Acknowledgments

We would like to acknowledge all those individuals and organizations that have helped to make this document possible. Our sincere apologies to all those who may have been unintentionally omitted.

Organizations

All the Member Organizations of the SIMEAWG

Information Technology & Decision Sciences Department (ITDS), UNT

Institutional Review Board (IRB) at the University of North Texas (UNT)

SIM Year 2000 Working Group

Society for Information Management (SIM)

Individuals

Jennifer Ahringer
Taylor & Francis Group

Dick Burk
U.S. Office of Management & Budget

Mary Barten
University of North Texas

Kevin Campbell
Hunt Consolidated

Tim Biovin
Tech Image®

Patricia Coffey
Allstate

Shelia Bourns
University of North Texas

Leo Collins
Lions Gate Entertainment

Ileanne "Ile" Burgas-Lopez
BizRules.com

Jenna Countryman
Smith Bucklin

Dick Dooley
TDG, Inc.

Nadja English
Taylor & Francis Group

Elisabeth Fisher
University of North Texas

Finley Graves
University of North Texas

Dan Green
Tech Image®

Holt Hackney
Architecture & Governance Magazine

Marsha Hecht
Taylor & Francis Group

Melanie Hirsch
Smith Bucklin

Michael Holland
U.S. General Accountability Office

Andrew Jackson
BravoTech

LaTasha Jones
Univerity of North Texas

Mary Jones
University of North Texas

Joe Lacik
Aviall Services

Jerry Luftman
Stevens Institute of Technology

Jim Luisi
Smith Bucklin

Steven McDevitt
Federal Emergency Management
  Administration

Ephraim McLean
Georgia State University

Edward Meagher
U.S. Department of the Interior

Ruth Gallagher Nelson
Smith Bucklin

John Oglesby
ACH Food Companies

Nicole Pfleeger
Smith Bucklin

Rick Pride
Impact IT

Marty Schulkins
Smith Bucklin

Stacy Suits
University of North Texas

Bob Thomas
Thomas Communications

Peter Whatnell
Sunoco Inc.

John Wyzalek
Taylor & Francis Group

Denny Yost
Align Journal

SIMEAWG Membership Roster (2007–2009)

Keith Andrews
EDS, an HP company

*Arnulfo Antonio
Aviall Services

*Bruce Ballengee
Pariveda Solutions

*John Bartsch
Chateaux Software

*Scott Bernard
Syracuse University

*Ashim Bhayan
JC Penney

*Raymond Bordogna
LiquidHub, Inc.

Scott Braden
NET(net)

Joseph Bradley
University of Idaho

*Larry Burgess
Aviall Services

*Brian Cameron
The Pennsylvania State University

*Keith Carpenter
CIT Group

*Mark Cauwels
Capital One Auto Finance

* Jon Cordas
Purdue University

*Steven Dal Porto
Allstate Insurance

*Ronald de Vries
Atos Origin, Inc.

Larry DeBoever
EAdirections, LLC

*Al Doctor
Microsoft

* Active members 2009 (as of June 30)

*Russell Douglas
Aviall Services

*Christopher Feola
nextPression, Inc.

*Mark Fowler
Pinnacle Technical Resources

Sharma Hanish
University of North Texas

*George Harth
Atos Origin, Inc.

*Rolando Hernandez
BizRules.com

Guy Hoffman
Metallect Corp.

John Hooper
University of North Texas

*Steve Hufford
Portland General Electric

*Jim Humrichouse
Pinnacle Technical Resources

*Mike Janiak
PepsiCo

*James Jennings
nextPression, Inc.

*Dimitra Kane
Allstate Insurance

*Leon A. Kappelman
University of North Texas

*Geoffrey Knoerzer
Diversified Technology Services

*Chang Koh
ITDS Department at UNT

*Mark Lane
PNM Resources

Bih-ru Lea
University of Missouri–Rolla

Maurice Leatherbury
University of North Texas

*Gene Leganza
Forrester Research

*Stan Locke
Zachman International

Haiping Luo
Association of Enterprise Architects

*Curtis Lupton
Auxis

*Hector Martinez
Pariveda Solutions

*Israel Martinez
National Cyber Security Council

*Thomas McGinnis
ITDS Department at UNT

*Neil McMahon
CIT Group

*Aaron Merrill
Aviall Services

*Kim Morris
PNM Resources

*Chrissy Napper
Forrester Research

*Edwin Nassiff
Lockheed Martin Corporation

*Don Nguyen
PepsiCo

*Patrick O'Malley
Pariveda Solutions

*Armando Ortiz
CIT Group

*Valden Paes
PepsiCo

*George Paras
EAdirections, LLC

*Christopher Parker
Texas Instruments

*William (Bill) Peterson
LiquidHub, Inc.

*Alex Pettit
University of North Texas

*Sandep Purao
The Pennsylvania State University

*Mohan Putcha
Allstate Insurance

Thiagarajan Ramakrishnan
ITDS Department at UNT

*Praveen Rao
Interstate Batteries

*Mike Rochelle
Microsoft

*Akhtar Saeed
Capital One Auto Finance

*Doug Safford
Allstate Insurance

*Brian Salmans
ITDS Department at UNT

*Suja Chandra Sekaren
PepsiCo

*Anna Sidorova
ITDS Department at UNT

*Skip Slone
Lockheed Martin Corporation

*Merv Tarde
Interstate Batteries

*Dana Tate
Zale Corporation

Peter Tribulski
Chubb & Son

*Gary Walters
Capital One Auto Finance

*Brian Williams
Aviall Services

*John Windsor
ITDS Department at UNT

*Davis Wise
PepsiCo

*Nancy Wolff
Auxis

Tery Wong
PepsiCo

*John Zachman
Zachman International

*John Zachman Jr.
Zachman International

*Ken Zimmerman
Chateaux Software

Editor and Contributing Authors, Panelists, Artists, and Reviewers

Keith Andrews is an enterprise architect for EDS's Global Architecture Capability. In this role, he collaborates with major clients to identify, define, and lead opportunities resulting in increased business value through targeted placement of innovative architecture, technology governance, and services. His primary expertise is the assessment, derivation, and application of enterprise-wide architectures, models, methods, and processes to measurably increase enterprise efficiency and effectiveness. He holds a BS in industrial technology from Ohio University, an MBA from Southern Illinois University, and an MS in management systems from the University of Texas at Dallas. He is a member of SIM, and also of the Institute of Electrical and Electronic Engineers' Computer Society.

Bruce Ballengee is chief executive officer and cofounder of Pariveda Solutions, Inc. He also serves on the boards of privately held Newfangle Media and 2GO Software, as well as the national board of the American Electronics Association and the Governor's Advisory Board of Aidmatrix. He has led enterprise architecture efforts and teams at several Fortune 50 companies over the past twenty-five years as well as presented and published on enterprise architecture at several symposia.

Scott Bernard, PhD, has over twenty years of experience in IT management in the academic, federal government, military, and private sectors. He has held positions as a CIO, chief enterprise architect, IT management consultant, network operations manager, telecommunications manager, IT security officer, and project manager. Dr. Bernard's areas of research include IT strategic planning, enterprise architecture, security architecture, and capital planning. In 2004, Dr. Bernard wrote the first textbook on enterprise architecture that features the EA3 Cube™ framework and Living Enterprise™ repository design. Dr. Bernard is also the chief editor of the *Journal of Enterprise Architecture.*

Larry Burgess is a chief technology officer with Citigroup. He holds a BBA degree in information systems and a BS in accounting from Harding University. Before joining Citigroup, he worked with Bank of America and JPMorgan in infrastructure security and process maturity. Over the years, Mr. Burgess has worked in the health care and technology industries with a concentration in finance, system development, program management, and enterprise architecture. Mr. Burgess cochairs the Society for Information Management's Enterprise Architecture Working Group and has presented at the Shared Insights Enterprise Architecture Conference.

Ed Cannon is the founder of New Madison Avenue, a specialty consulting company helping senior managers use technology to drive top-line growth. New Madison Avenue offers both strategic and implementation services in e-commerce, social networking, content management, search, and demand chain and supply chain technology. Ed has authored a book on electronic data interchange, was one of the first professionals in the world to implement supply chain technology, and worked with the White House and the U.S. Naval War College on securing cyberspace from terrorist threats. Ed is also a past board member of the New York chapter of Society for Information Managers and has guest lectured at Fordham University's Executive Management Program.

Larry R. DeBoever is a managing director of EAdirections, an EA research and advisory services firm. He holds an MS degree from Purdue University and an MPA from the University of Southern California. He founded DeBoever Architectures (DAI) in 1990, the first consulting firm focused on EA project execution, and published one of the first EA process methodologies in the early 1990s. DAI was acquired by the META Group in October 1996 where Mr. DeBoever started the Enterprise Architecture Strategies (EAS) practice, the first EA research service. In 1997, he started the Enterprise Architectures Conference (EAC) and chaired the event in its early years. One of the industry's most entertaining and insightful analysts, he has twenty years of experience in EA and has worked with hundreds of clients.

Russell Douglas currently serves as director of IS strategy and emerging technologies at Aviall Services, a wholly owned subsidiary of the Boeing Company. Aviall is a technology-based provider of component products and related services to the aviation and marine aftermarket. Russell has lectured on enterprise architecture, SaaS, performance management, and storage implementation in several U.S. cities and abroad in Korea, Singapore, Taiwan, Hong Kong, Malaysia, Indonesia, and Bangkok, and authored several white papers on product integration, performance management, and project implementation methodology. In addition, he has implemented several large software projects including at Philip Morris, Cisco Systems, Sara

Lee, Dayton Hudson, AT&T, Qualcomm, Micron, Xilinx, Prudential Insurance, BHC Securities, Merck, First USA, Queen's Medical Center, Salt River Project, Toys"R"Us, and Greentree Financial. Russell also has deployed enterprise management suites at Whirlpool, Bay Networks, West Group, IMC Global, People's GAS, Petroleum Information Dwight, and Dagens Nyheter (Sweden), and developed and deployed websites at AdvancedRX.com, Aviall.com, CompuCom Connection, and Personnel Portal. After arriving at Aviall Services, Russell completed major SAN and server upgrades for the entire UNIX application infrastructure, and in 2005 co-led the largest technology upgrade project in Aviall's seventy-five-year history, including data migration, new servers, security, load testing, interface testing for warehouse management, planning and forecasting, CRM, EAI, EDI, and various other subsystems. Today Russell is chief architect, leading Aviall's integration into the Boeing Company's Material Management, Jeppesen, and Integrated Defense Systems divisions.

Randolph C. Hite is director of IT architecture and systems issues in the U.S. Government Accountability Office (GAO). He is responsible for GAO's work on IT issues across the government, specifically architecture and systems acquisition, development, operations, and maintenance, as well as GAO's IT work at the Department of Defense (DOD), the Department of Health and Human Services (DHHS), the Department of State, and the Justice Department. During his thirty-year career with GAO, he has directed reviews of many major federal IT investments and has also directed GAO's research and publication of enterprise architecture best practices, as well as its evaluations of federal agencies' development and use of enterprise architectures, and their systems development and acquisition and IT services outsourcing efforts. Hite is a principal author of several information technology management guides, such as GAO's guide on system testing, the federal CIO Counsel guide on enterprise architectures, and GAO's enterprise architecture management maturity framework. He frequently testifies before Congress on these and other topics. Hite has received many awards throughout his career, including GAO's Meritorious Service Award, Distinguished Service Award, multiple Congressional Client Service Awards, the Federal Computer Week Federal 100 Award, and the e-Gov Institute Excellence in Enterprise Architecture Award.

Leon A. Kappelman, PhD, is a researcher, teacher, author, and consultant dedicated to helping organizations better manage their information and technology assets. He is director emeritus of the IS Research Center and professor of IS in the Information Technology and Decision Sciences Department of the College of Business at the University of North Texas, where he is also a Fellow of the Texas Center for Digital Knowledge. Dr. Kappelman is the founder and chair of the Society for Information Management's Enterprise Architecture Working Group and has assisted the Executive Office of the President of the United States and the Department of Veterans Affairs with their EA work, given presentations, written articles, and testified before the U.S. Congress about EA. He has published several books and over one hundred articles in journals such as *MIS Quarterly, Communications of the ACM,* and the *Journal of Management Information Systems.*

Dr. Chang E. Koh is Farrington Professor of Information Systems in the Information Technology and Decision Sciences Department at the University of North Texas, Denton. He also serves as managing director for the Center for Decision and Information Technologies at UNT. His major research interests include business implementation of radio frequency identification (RFID) technology, business Internet practices and strategies, e-government readiness and barriers, and international/cross-cultural issues of IT implementation. His research articles have appeared in such journals as *MIS Quarterly, Information & Management,* and the *International Journal of Electronic Commerce* among others. He holds a PhD from the University of Georgia in information systems.

Mark Lane is an EA practitioner, cofounder and president of CAEAP, and contributor to the EA community with thirty years of IT executive and EA leadership experience. Mark specializes primarily in EA program development, risk management, portfolio management, standard and policy compliance, and strategy development. Mark is an author, speaker, and consultant who is dedicated to moving the EA profession in a consistent and coherent direction. Mark attended Oakland University in Rochester Hills, Michigan, with BA studies in computer science, business, and psychology, and has many professional certifications related to arts and sciences.

Thomas McGinnis is a doctoral student at the University of North Texas. He holds an MS in MIS from Central Michigan University and a BS in CIS from Bentley College. Before pursuing his doctoral studies in information systems, he spent sixteen years in the chemical industry focusing on enterprise information systems and business process reengineering. More recently, he was a consultant for a leading IT consulting firm. His research interests include enterprise resource planning, enterprise architecture, and knowledge management. His research has been published in conference proceedings and in *Information & Management.*

George Paras is a widely recognized speaker, writer, coach, and thought leader in enterprise architecture, strategy and planning, portfolio management, and IT governance. He has coached hundreds of IT leaders in the practical aspects of creating effective and successful EA programs. His insights and perspectives have advanced the EA discipline through his positions as chairman, featured speaker, and EAC Thought Leadership Council member for the Enterprise Architectures Conferences (EACs), and as editor-in-chief of *Architecture and Governance Magazine.* He is currently a managing director at EAdirections, which he founded with Larry R. DeBoever and Tim Westbrock.

William J. Peterson is a principal consultant in LiquidHub's management consulting practice. He holds a BS degree in biochemical engineering from Rutgers University, an MS in computer science from Villanova University, and an MS in organizational dynamics from the University of Pennsylvania. Mr. Peterson's interests and experience are in the area of organizational effectiveness, particularly with respect to IT and technology organizations, and include activities strategic planning, organizational design and development, and organizational alignment and effectiveness. He has authored two research studies for The Conference Board covering best practices for ERP implementations.

Alex Pettit has government, industry, and Big 4 consulting experience, and is a recognized leader in BCP/DRP program development and linkage to civil response emergency plans. His industry experience crosses all industry verticals, with a specialized focus on telecommunication services, financial services, and public sector organizations. He has directed both industry and consulting organizations in diverse roles as a chief technology officer, senior manager and BCP service line leader, and regional director of technology and telecommunications. Alex has received the Best of Texas Award for IT Leadership, the Public Technology Institute IT Leadership Award, and the Society for Information Management Executive of the Year Award for his leadership during a civil emergency response. In addition, Alex is a published author on IT leadership and disaster recovery in *Studies in E-Government, Government Technology Magazine, Texas Technology Magazine,* and the *Journal for Enterprise Architecture.*

Thiagarajan Ramakrishnan is a PhD student at the University of North Texas. He received his bachelor of engineering (BE) degree in industrial electronics engineering from University of Pune, India, and his master of science (MS) degree in information systems from Tarleton State University, Texas. His research interests include business intelligence and data mining, decision making, ERP implementation, and enterprise architecture.

Jeanne W. Ross, PhD, is director and principal research scientist of the Center for Information Systems Research (CISR) at the MIT Sloan School of Management. Ross studies the organizational and performance implications of enterprise initiatives related to enterprise architecture, governance, and new IT management practices. Ross shares her research in lectures, executive education courses, articles, and books. Her work has appeared in the *Sloan Management Review, Harvard Business Review,* the *Wall Street Journal, CIO Magazine, MIS Quarterly, MISQ Executive,* and *IBM Systems Journal,* among others. She has coauthored two books: *IT Governance: How Top Performers Manage IT Decision Rights for Superior Results* and *Enterprise Architecture as Strategy: Creating a Foundation for Business Execution.* Her third book, *IT Savvy: What Top Executives Must Know to Go from Pain to Gain,* will be published soon. Jeanne is a founding senior editor of *MIS Quarterly Executive* and has served as its editor-in-chief. She is also a member of the SIM Executive Board and serves as its vice president for academic community affairs.

Brian Salmans, PhD, recently completed his doctorate at the University of North Texas and is an active-duty lieutenant colonel in the United States Air Force. He holds a master of military operational art and science from the Air Command and Staff College, an MBA from the University of Nebraska at Omaha, and a BBA in CIS from Baylor University. In his eighteen years as a communications-computer systems officer, he has served in a variety of positions with a focus on computer security and computer network defense. His last assignment was as director of technical integration and as adjunct professor for the Air and Space Power and Information Operations Courses. His research interests include enterprise architecture, information warfare, and enterprise computer security issues.

Anna Sidorova, PhD, is an assistant professor at the University of North Texas. Before joining UNT, she worked for PricewaterhouseCoopers in Moscow, Russia, and as an assistant professor at the State University of New York–Albany. She received her MBA and PhD in MIS from Washington State University. Her research and professional interests include IT-enabled organizational transformation, business process management, enterprise architecture, and open-source software development. She has published in such journals as *MIS Quarterly,* the *Journal of Management Information Systems,* and *Communications in Statistics,* as well as in numerous conference proceedings.

Gary F. Simons, PhD, currently holds the position of associate vice president for academic affairs with SIL International (Dallas, Texas). While serving in that role, he has participated in the development of cyberinfrastructure for the field of linguistics as cofounder of the Open Language Archives Community, codeveloper of the ISO 639-3 standard of three-letter identifiers for the known languages of the world, and executive editor of the *Ethnologue.* He has also served as enterprise architect within the senior leadership team at SIL International, which since 2000 has been guiding enterprise reengineering and the implementation of a web-based enterprise information system that supports interoperation among more than a hundred operating entities around the world. He is the author of over eighty publications.

Kathie Sowell is a recognized leader in EA, having been the principal author of DOD's original architecture framework and a principal developer of other frameworks for government and industry. Her expertise has been tapped by NATO Headquarters, the Australian Ministry of Defence, Canadian corporations, the Danish Embassy, the Swedish military, and state and local governments. For five years she served as a curriculum developer, technical director, and director of the

DOD division of the Federated Enterprise Architecture Certification Institute (FEAC). She now provides enterprise architect certification through her company and National-Louis University.

Tim Westbrock is a managing director of EAdirections, an EA research and advisory services firm. He has a BS in applied science for systems analysis from Miami University. He has worked with 300+ companies in various industries and the public sector to mentor them in their approach to enterprise architecture. He was the driving force behind META Group's EA research agenda and METAmethod—a best-practice transformation method for EA development. He has over eighteen years of experience in the IT industry as an analyst, consultant, and architect. He is a dynamic speaker and is a frequent lecturer at industry events and workshops. Before joining META Group, he was the chief architect for Anthem, Inc., responsible for driving its enterprise architecture strategy. He began his career with Andersen Consulting.

Nancy Wolff is the director of IT strategy and enterprise architecture at Aixis. She has more than eighteen years of experience in building and delivering reliable, powerful, and cost-effective IT services and solutions for a wide variety of commercial and government organizations. As a former CIO, Nancy has firsthand experience in strategic planning and organizational leadership, service-oriented architecture, large-scale project management and planning, ERP implementations, systems development life cycle, fiscal IT management, enterprise architecture, and IT portfolio management. As practice director of EA and IT strategic planning at SRA International, Nancy established and led SRA's Center of Excellence for Enterprise Architecture, which provided expert advice and counsel on information technology (IT) strategy, governance, and enterprise architecture to federal, state, and local government IT organizations. As corporate CIO at Lodgian, Nancy developed and managed the enterprise-wide IT strategy and architecture for one of the largest independently owned hotel organizations in the country. Nancy received her bachelor's of science degree in industrial and systems engineering from the Georgia Institute of Technology.

John Zachman is the originator of the "Framework for Enterprise Architecture," which has received broad acceptance throughout the world as an integrative framework for understanding enterprises and the systems, people, technologies, and processes that comprise and support them. The Zachman Framework is a model or ontology for understanding and managing change in enterprises. He is known not only for this work, but also for his early contributions to business systems planning, IBM's widely used information planning methodology in the 1970s, as well as intensive planning, the basis for IBM's executive team planning techniques. He is a member of the International Advisory Board of the Data Administration Management Association, DAMA International; a member of the International Information Resource Management Advisory Council of the Smithsonian Institution in Washington, DC; and a member of the board of directors of the Depository/Architecture/Development Users Group.

Foreword

Let me propose the following hypothesis:

Although EA was initially a function within the IT organization, we will soon find IT to be a function within EA.

This is actually not a wild theory; it's a trend. Companies like BT (formerly British Telecom), Cemex (exemplary Mexican cement company), and Southwest Airlines have vested enterprise architecture in a senior executive, responsible both for enterprise process design and for some or all of IT. This may sound like bad news for CIOs, but I suspect that it's actually really good news.

For years, both IT practitioners and IT academics have argued that IT should have a place at the management table. But in most industries, IT has long been an enabler of business strategy; not a force in setting strategy. Indeed, in most industries, it makes no sense to assign IT the responsibility to lead strategy. Meanwhile, in most industries, IT budgets are below 5 percent—in most manufacturing industries IT constitutes less than 3 percent of operating budgets. Think about it: how many management team members enable rather than lead and/or manage minuscule operating budgets? Thus, it is hard to argue that, except for media and perhaps financial services, the CIO should be an equal force on the senior management team.

Enterprise architecture comes to the rescue! In the global economy, most firms are looking for appropriate synergies among business units, functions, and geographies. They are also looking to extend their boundaries with joint ventures and strategic partnerships. This will demand visionary leadership in the design of business processes. More importantly, it will require leaders who can be held accountable for integrated and shared business processes—and a strong digitized platform to support those processes. This is a relatively new business requirement, made evident by the difficulties that many firms have experienced in driving value from their ERP, CRM, and other enterprise system implementations. Senior management teams have, over time, come to understand that integrated systems require senior management commitment to integrated processes. What they overlooked (and are starting to recognize) is that they can't manage integrated systems and processes by committee. Someone needs to provide the leadership to design the processes, implement new systems and processes, change behaviors, and drive value.

Because IT people are the people most likely to understand cross-functional, standardized, multi–business unit processes, they are the natural leaders to assume responsibility for architecting their companies' business operations. Savvy CIOs at firms like Dow Chemical Company, Procter & Gamble, and JM Family are already being promoted to business process leadership roles or to the head of all shared services. These are roles that slip technology into its rightful place in the firm—as support for enterprise business processes. They are also roles that offer enormous opportunities for firms to use IT strategically.

But not every CIO will naturally progress from head of IT to head of the enterprise's digitized processes. Business process management is important whether or not IT executives provide the vision and leadership to realize the potential value of a firm's digitized platform. If the CIO does not take the lead, someone else will emerge, and the CIO will have a new boss. This is the immediate challenge of IT executives. Enterprise architecture is still an immature science, but its importance in enabling global business should not be underestimated. Even as they are still trying to understand how to "do" architecture and to demonstrate its value, IT leaders need to work toward rational, valuable business processes. They cannot wait.

This book addresses some of the ongoing challenges of doing enterprise architecture well. It's a timely and important book. Since so few firms have mastered business process management, it is time for IT to step up and take the lead. I hope it will encourage more IT professionals to aggressively lead business process design and implementation in their firms.

Jeanne W. Ross
Director and Principal Research Scientist
Center for Information Systems Research
MIT Sloan School of Management

Preface

It is amusing that the first part of this book to be read is the last part to be written. It provides, however, an opportunity to share with you a little about how writing and editing this book has changed my thinking not just about enterprise architecture (EA), or about the role of information technology (IT) and IT professionals in organizations, or even about enterprises themselves; although, certainly, all those evolved too during this journey of discovery.

Writing about an emerging discipline like EA is kind of like writing about the life history of a person when he or she is only ten years old — so much hope and promise, but not much time yet for actualization. Perhaps that is a bit of hyperbole since it has been over 20 years since the first article was published proposing how the principles of architecture and engineering could and should be applied to managing organizations and their ITs. That's equivalent to about 1945 in the history of the quality movement, or about 40 years before "Quality is Job 1" became the advertising slogan for a major U.S. auto manufacturer. Or maybe 1800 in the history of the Industrial Age, when there were about 500 steam engines, pretty much all residing in England, and none of them working all that well.

Still, EA practices and tools progressed appreciably these past 20 years and we see significant advantages and improvements in those organizations investing their time, monies, and talents in EA-related activities. Yet these are the exceptions and largely invisible to the managers of most organizations, much like the IT-enabled strategic advantages that transformed companies and industries were invisible to most as they began to emerge in the late 1960s. So while working on this book, my appreciation grew for the intellectual revolutions that accompany technological ones, as did my patience, for it is one thing to invent or acquire a game-changing idea or technology, but quite another to discover the ways to use it well.

Writing about the Information Age organization, the enterprise of the future, is equally problematic. Maybe more so since the Information Age at its core is about communications and convergence enabling us to do more with less at an ever-increasing pace. But communications, and thus cooperation among converging business units, disciplines, or even specialties within disciplines, requires shared language. EA is about creating that shared language to communicate about and think about, create and manage the Information Age enterprise. The fact is, if the people in the enterprise cannot communicate well enough to synchronize their ideas about conceptual things like strategy, goals, and objectives, then they will not be very able to synchronize the physical things they manage, such as applications, data, projects, goods, services, and jobs.

The "enterprise" term in the moniker "EA" makes clear that EA is about the entire enterprise, as well as its parts. In order to be complete the architecture of an enterprise by definition requires collaboration and communication from all areas and levels of the enterprise. Yet, perhaps because of its relative infancy, communications about EA itself is fairly limited and would be furthered significantly by clarification and consensus on fundamental terms like architecture, framework, ontology, meta-model, methodology, method, and model. And that is just a starting point for enabling communication, convergence, synergy, and progress, since so much EA-related work today is done independent or unaware of EA. So my appreciation has grown for the connectedness of all things, along with my concurrence with Socrates' belief that "the beginning of wisdom is a definition of terms." So too has my acceptance that one thing does not seem to be changing at an ever-increasing pace—human nature.

Perhaps that is where the next great innovations are needed. Consider that data sharing is still the exception more than six years after the U.S. Department of Homeland Security (DHS) united 22 agencies on March 1, 2003. Not requiring significant technical prowess, this condition makes it clear that IT and EA are not just about building and running information systems and it is unfortunate that the U.S. federal government's Clinger–Cohen Act of 1996 (CCA) frames EA that way. Still, thanks to CCA, whether the U.S. government accrues significant direct benefits or not, its investments in EA will probably turn out to be as important to the Information Age as its investments in the first computers 65 plus years ago and the Internet some 40 years ago. As important perhaps as the investment initiated in 1792 by the Second U.S. Congress to create the internet of the early Industrial Age—the U.S. Postal Service. So if it is desired, important, and not technically difficult, why then so little progress with data sharing at DHS? Not to oversimplify, but since it is well known how critically important executive leadership is to IT project success, it should come as no surprise that it is the lack of leadership that stifles the sharing and is a major reason for most all of the IT problems in Washington, DC and just about everywhere else. It's just that the U.S. federal government is open enough to share most of its failures with the rest of us, while private organizations only do so reluctantly.

Since the architecture of an enterprise includes the strategic as well as the tactical, the long-term as well as the short, the logical as well as the physical, and the technical as well as the human, it is patently obvious that executive and senior management leadership and participation are absolutely essential to the success of EA activities and to the actions that are based on that architecture. It appears that the world is currently suffering from a significant leadership deficit that not only contributed to, some say even caused, our global economic difficulties. More importantly, this leadership shortfall hinders much-needed progress, change, candor, communication, convergence, and action at nearly all levels and locations of our globalizing world. My appreciation for the importance of leadership has grown on this creative journey, as well as my awareness that everyone leads in one way or another.

Notwithstanding nearly four decades of research and experience with organizations, while writing and editing this book I learned much about enterprise architecture, the role of IT and IT professionals in organizations, and enterprises in general. First and foremost I have tried to share all that with you, dear reader, in the pages that follow. I also learned a great deal about the history of innovations, both physical and cerebral, and gained an appreciation for the importance of language, the connectedness of everything, and the often-lumbering pace of significant change. I believe all this has helped me better understand where we might be now in the history of this Information Age, the vast potentialities for where EA, IT, enterprises, and our global economy could go, and how long it might take for us to get there. But most notably of all, my knowledge and appreciation increased for the supreme importance of the people who will do the work, make the decisions, and create the capabilities to get us there. I now realize that even if we are able to acquire all the necessary resources and perfect all the technologies, techniques, terminologies, capabilities, and skills, we will likely arrive somewhere much less desirable without candid and courageous leaders able to balance long-term and short-term objectives for the whole as well as the parts—not just with their words, but especially with their deeds.

It appears that good progress is being made on all fronts save leadership. But such a vacuum cannot long endure and I am optimistic that a new era in leadership is near. This book is not about leadership per se, but about the vision, foundations, and enabling talents and technologies of the Information Age organization, the existence of which requires Information Age leaders who can inspire and guide an Information Age workforce in which everyone in some small or large way is part of the enterprise leadership team. That which we today call "enterprise architecture" is an essential part of this transformation. And EA is the subject of this book. But the real purpose of this book is to inform, inspire, and invigorate the people who will take us there. This book is dedicated to you. I hope it serves you as well as creating it has served me.

Leon A. Kappelman
Dallas, Texas

WHAT IS EA? WHY DOES IT MATTER?

1

It is not the strongest of the species that survives, nor the most intelligent, but the one that is most responsive to change.

—**Charles Darwin**

Introduction

Enterprise Architecture (EA) has been in SIM's peripheral vision for many years. SIM's IT Complexity Reduction Working Group wrote a report in 1999 titled *Enterprise Architecture Requirements for Information Technology Vendors*.[1] Professor and former SIM board member Jerry Luftman's assessment of "IT-business strategic alignment maturity" included the degree to which "the enterprise architecture is integrated."[2] Professor Kate Kaiser, who led a "SIM study of 104 CIOs to determine their skill needs through 2008," found that "there is much more emphasis on the business domain," and went on to rank "enterprise architecture" at the top of the "business domain" skills.[3] An article titled "Enterprise Architecture Maturity: The Story of the Veterans Health Administration" was published in 2007 in the SIM-affiliated research journal, *MIS Quarterly Executive (MISQE)*.[4]

Yet despite the awareness among IT professionals of the EA concept and its importance, there is not a standard or even a generally accepted definition within the IT community of the terms "enterprise architecture," "enterprise," or "architecture." Thus, there exists a high potential for ambiguity. *CIO Magazine* opined that "enterprise architecture has long been the concept that dared not speak its name. Some CIOs go to great lengths to avoid using the term with their business peers for fear of scaring, alienating or simply boring them to death. But companies … that have stuck with it are beginning to reap the savings, flexibility and business alignment that its proponents have been promising for nearly 20 years."[5]

The SIM Enterprise Architecture Working Group (SIMEAWG) views EA (in ten words or less) as "the holistic set of descriptions about the enterprise over time."[6] However, for further illumination we offer as a working definition the more comprehensive one used by the IT and EA auditors in the General Accountability Office (GAO) of the U.S. federal government: "An enterprise architecture is a blueprint for organizational change defined in models [using words, graphics, and other depictions] that describe (in both business and technology terms) how the entity operates today and how it intends to operate in the future; it also includes a plan for transitioning to this future state."[7] EAs "provide a clear and comprehensive picture of an entity, whether an organization (e.g., federal department, agency, or bureau) or a functional or mission area that cuts across more than one organization (e.g., financial management)."[8]

The difficulty many of us seem to have in getting our minds around the concept of EA is in part a function of the subject matter, perhaps what is one of humankind's most complicated creations, the enterprise or organization. Our professional biases and historically stovepiped world exacerbate the situation. Interestingly, the definitions of EA offered earlier say nothing specifically about IT or building and implementing systems. In fact, they don't explicitly mention any of those things. John Zachman, ostensibly the "godfather" of EA, describes his journey of understanding EA this way: "I began by trying to discover what Information Systems Architecture was and actually discovered that it was not Information Systems Architecture that I was looking for at all … it was Architecture in general and ENTERPRISE Architecture in particular. The end object IS NOT to build and run information systems. The end object is to engineer and manufacture THE ENTERPRISE."[9]

What You Have Here …

This publication from the SIMEAWG aims to provide information and intelligence that will help you and your organization better understand and manage EA activities, and thereby all of the organization's activities and resources. This first chapter provides context for the rest of the publication, and a model to help the reader see one way the pieces can fit together. Besides the general introduction to EA that follows, there is only one other article in this chapter.

It's not exactly an article though, but rather a transcript of a once-in-a-lifetime panel discussion with five of the "pioneers of EA" that was held in November 2008 at SIM's annual SIMposium conference. So as we wander into the second generation in the ongoing EA revolution (more about that in Chapter 2), which is only part of our larger evolution into the Information Age, we spend an hour with five of those who laid the foundations in the first generation, for us to build upon, by defining EA and the metaphysics of the enterprise, conducting the first research to show EA's value, providing guidance for doing EA, creating maturity models and metrics to assess EA progress, and helping public and private organizations get started and succeed with their EA programs. Sharing their lessons learned and visions of the future, these EA pioneers provide the rest of us with unique and fascinating perspectives.

Part of the mission of the SIMEAWG is to determine the current state of EA practices. The case studies, practical anecdotes, theory, guidelines, and prescriptives we offer in Chapters 2 and 3 provide these. Our primary state-of-the-art metrics are survey based, and the results of our survey are reported in Chapter 4. These results can provide SIM members and other professionals with benchmarks that they can use to determine how their organizations compare with others. EA-related references and resources can be found in Chapter 5, including a reading list, Internet sites, a glossary, as well as information about SIM and the SIMEAWG.

Reinventing the Wheel?

One approach to conceptualizing EA and its potential importance to the organization is to view the relationship using a hub-and-spoke analogy. Such a model often assumes that IT is the hub from which the organization's various business activities, functions, and processes radiate outward, forming the spokes of a wheel. This is not to advocate a stovepiped view of the organization; but rather recognition that different parts of the organization have differing IT needs and that IT is central to supporting all the activities of the enterprise. At the end of these spokes, an outer ring representing the strategic goals of the organization provides for the integration of the individual spokes into the overall strategy of the enterprise. Thus, implies this model, IT aligns itself with strategic goals through its support of the various activities of the enterprise.

However, information technology in and of itself holds only the potential to be a force for alignment. Just as IT can be used to foster either a centralized or decentralized management style, the use of IT can result in alignment, misalignment, or any other objective or its converse. Moreover, experience suggests that an IT-focused core (hub) may not be the best way to conceptualize the role of IT within the organization or to foster business-IT alignment. This makes sense since integration and alignment, independent of the means or mechanisms used, must first begin with an integrated and aligned conceptualization of the enterprise shared by the people who manage and work in it.

In other words, true alignment begins with the alignment of the concepts and ideas of the people, and then with the alignment of resources, activities, and technologies—from thought to action, from the logical to the physical. Author Napoleon Hill more generally captured this idea when he said, "Cherish your visions and your dreams ... as they are the blueprints of your ultimate achievements" and "What the mind can conceive and believe, the mind can achieve."[10] Actor Bruce Lee simply said, "As you think, so shall you become."[11] In organizations, enterprise architecture holds the potential to be the mechanism for this alignment of concepts and ideas so that the people can align themselves and the organization's things.

Thus, it makes more sense to recognize IT as not only one of the fundamental activities of the enterprise (i.e., a spoke), but also an integral part of just about every other activity of the enterprise. Or as John Zachman often says, "The system is the enterprise."[12] In other words, properly managed IT is an inseparable part of the enterprise much like the human nervous system is inseparable from the human body.

Enterprise architecture holds the potential to align the intangible concepts and ideas about the enterprise so that the enterprise's tangible things can be aligned, synchronized, made one. This is the view we have depicted in our version of the hub-and-spoke model shown here as Figure 1.1. We use this model in this publication to help provide context to the various theories, case studies, prescriptions, opinions, research findings, articles, and other resources we offer you in this publication. This particular depiction of the "Enterprise Wheel," as we call the model in Figure 1.1, identifies eight spokes; however, any number of business activities, processes, or functions can be represented using this conceptualization. Strategic planning, purchasing, and treasury are examples of critical activities that are not represented as spokes in the Figure 1.1 version of the Enterprise Wheel.

This publication from the SIMEAWG is focused predominantly on the EA hub and the EA activity spoke, and to some degree on the IT activity spoke. As we

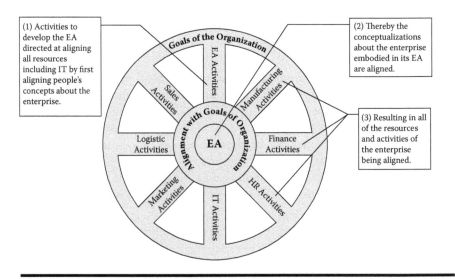

FIGURE 1.1 The Enterprise Wheel.

introduce the articles at the beginning of each of the chapters that follow, we utilize the Enterprise Wheel to provide a contextual reference point.

IT Starts between Your Ears

As the Enterprise Wheel suggests, strategic and comprehensive alignment can best be achieved through the organization's overall enterprise architecture. Moreover, in order for the ideas about the enterprise captured in its EA to be aligned, the processes and activities for creating that EA must first be directed at achieving such an alignment of the organization's people and their ideas about the enterprise, and thereafter of the things managed by those people. Mitch Kapor, founder of Lotus Development, architect and creator of the Lotus 1-2-3 spreadsheet application, cofounder of the Electronic Frontier Foundation, and a board member of the Mozilla Foundation and Linden Research (originator Second Life), succinctly recognized this when he said, "Architecture is politics."

EA done right provides the capability and the road map for alignment of everything one wants aligned in the enterprise, including the alignment of its IT infrastructure and other subsystems that provide the requisite support for all of the activities in the enterprise. Sure EA is about modeling a "comprehensive picture" of the enterprise that captures all of the knowledge about the enterprise. But much of the value of EA comes through the processes and interactions of its creation, and value realized through its use. The architecture of the enterprise, properly created and properly captured, is not only a thinking, conceptualization, and design tool, but a management tool as well—perhaps the most critically needed management tool for this Information Age we are living and working in, and at the present time a tool that is largely unavailable.

In other words, doing EA is key to the culture change needed to become the "Information Age Enterprise" described by the likes of Peter Drucker,[13] Peter Senge,[14] and Alvin Toffler,[15] to name but a few. Senge describes his vision of the enterprise of the future as a "learning organization" "where people continually expand their capacity to create the results they truly desire, where new and expansive patterns of thinking are nurtured, where collective aspiration is set free, and where people are continually learning to see the whole together."[16] He goes on to explain that such learning organizations are characterized by the mastery of five basic disciplines or "component technologies"; specifically these are: personal mastery, systems thinking, mental models, building shared vision, and team learning. All five of these are fundamental EA disciplines or capabilities, although arguably to a lesser extent personal mastery.

Nearly sixty years of experience gathering and meeting business requirements makes IT professionals particularly well positioned to lead this enterprise evolution by building their EA capabilities upon the foundations of their up until now stovepiped system requirements capabilities. After all, specifying system requirements (more generally called "systems analysis and design") is presumably all about applying systems thinking to enterprises while building shared vision with shared models, all the while working in teams to bring about said shared vision (more generally called "systems development"). Sure the end object up until now has been to build and run information systems. But if, as Zachman opines, the end object is to reengineer and remanufacture the enterprise (typically described as making it more aligned, agile, lean, nimble, effective, efficient, competitive, or whatever the design objectives may be), then it would seem that no other group is better prepared to facilitate this evolution of the enterprise into the future than IT professionals.

But IT Doesn't Stop There

But just how capable are IT professionals when it comes to determining and communicating business requirements? Is the IT profession's ongoing fixation on alignment a sign of their strength or weakness, success or failure? After more than three decades, one would think that misalignment or a lack of alignment of IT with the business would be all but a fading memory. Is the annual reminder that alignment remains paramount on IT's collective mind a sign of the inherent difficulty or of deeper problems with how IT approaches the goal of determining and meeting the organization's requirements? It's probably some of both, but there is little doubt that the IT profession's ongoing obsession about alignment is not unlike an obese person obsessing about his or her weight—standing on the scale will not solve the problem, but a change in attitude and behavior will. Likewise, a change in attitude and behavior is needed to achieve alignment (or any other objective) within the enterprise. We believe that EA represents a major part of that change.

Moreover, EA as we see it includes many things IT and the business are already doing, such as IT strategic planning, requirements analysis, network design, and standard setting. *But,* we recognize that EA is much, much more than that. EA is about a different way of seeing, communicating about, and managing the enterprise and all of its assets, including its technologies. We believe that EA is the key to achieving business-IT alignment and a seat at the strategic table. We believe that EA gets to the essence of IT success. We believe that EA gets to the essence of enterprise success. Paraphrasing Hill, first conceive, then achieve—EA holds the potential to be the tool for creating and communicating that shared conception and for managing the execution of its achievement.

In her 2003 article "Creating a Strategic IT Architecture Competency: Learning in Stages," Jeanne Ross summed it up this way: "The payback for enterprise IT architecture efforts is strategic alignment between IT and the business. ... Ultimately, enterprise architecture leads to "happy surprises."[17]

We, the members of the SIMEAWG, hope our efforts help lead you to many "happy surprises" too.

Notes

1. SIM IT Complexity Reduction Working Group, October 1999, *Enterprise Architecture Requirements for Information Technology Vendors,* http://www.simnet.org/Content/NavigationMenu/Resources/Download_Page32/ICRWhitepaper.pdf.
2. Luftman, Jerry. 2003. *IT-Business Strategic Alignment Maturity Assessment,* October 7, http://www.simnet.org/Content/NavigationMenu/Resources/Library/Download_Page3res/ITBusinessAlignment.pdf.
3. Collett, Stacy. July 17, 2006, "Hot Skills, Cold Skills," *Computerworld,* http://computerworld.com/action/article.do?command=viewArticleBasic&articleId=112360.
4. Venkatesh, Viswanath., Hillol Bala, Srinivasan Venkatraman, and Jack Bates. 2007 MISQ *Executive,* Volume 6, Issue 2 pp. 79–90.
5. Koch, Christopher. March 1, 2005, "A New Blueprint for the Enterprise," *CIO Magazine,* http://www.cio.com/archive/030105/blueprint.html.
6. SIM Enterprise Architecture Working Group. 2008. January 9, 2008, meeting at the University of North Texas, Denton TX.
7. GAO. 2006 *Enterprise Architecture: Leadership Remains Key to Establishing and Leveraging Architectures for Organizational Transformation,* GAO-06-831, August 2006, http://www.gao.gov/new.items/d06831.pdf.
8. GAO. 2002 *Information Technology: Enterprise Architecture Use Across the Federal Government Can Be Improved,* GAO-02-6, February 2002, http://www.gao.gov/new.items/d026.pdf.
9. Zachman, John A. 2009, "Architecture Is Architecture Again," monograph, Zachman International.
10. Cited from http://www.finestquotes.com/author_quotes-author-Napoleon%20Hill-page-0.htm (5 January 2008).
11. Cited from http://www.people.ubr.com/celebrities/by-first-name/b/bruce-lee/bruce-lee-quotes.aspx and http://www.ok312.com/e2j/a.htm (5 January 2008).
12. For example, "The system IS the Enterprise. Manual systems employ pencils, paper, file cabinets. Automated systems employ stored programming devices and electronic media" (Cited from http://www.damauk.org/John%20Zachman%20-%20Straight%20from%20the%20Shoulder.pdf, p. 11, 5 January 2008). Also see video at http://www.theanalyst.com/_Media_AV/Film%20Zachman_system_is_the_enterprise.wmv (5 January 2008).
13. Drucker, Peter F. 1999. *Management Challenges for the 21st Century,* Harper Business, New York; Drucker, Peter F. (1998). "The Next Information Revolution," Forbes ASAP, August 24.
14. Senge, Peter M. 1990. *The Fifth Discipline: The Art and Practice of the Learning Organization.* New York, Doubleday.
15. Toffler, Alvin. 1990. *Powershift.* New York. Bantam; Toffler, A. (1970). *Future Shock.* New York. Bantam.
16. Senge, Peter M. 1990, p. 7.
17. Ross, Jeanne. 2003, "Creating a Strategic IT Architecture Competency: Learning in Stages," *MISQ Executive,* Volume 2, Issue 1, p 43.

The Pioneers of Enterprise Architecture: A Panel Discussion

Leon A. Kappelman

November 12, 2008, was a beautiful Wednesday morning in Orlando, Florida, at the Contemporary Resort inside Disney World. At 8:00 a.m., folks were still meandering into the meeting room; but with only one hour for this once-in-a-lifetime opportunity to hear from five of the pioneers of enterprise architecture, the moderator got started. It was the final morning of SIM's annual SIMposium conference. Ten months earlier, Edwin Nassiff, the program chair of the conference, SIMEAWG member, and director of technical excellence and enterprise business services at Lockheed Martin, set out to organize this panel of EA pioneers. He couldn't have done better. Alphabetically the panelists were:

- Larry R. DeBoever, Managing Director, EAdirections
- Randolph C. Hite, Director, IT Architecture and Systems Issues, U.S. Government Accountability Office
- Dr. Jeanne W. Ross, Director and Principal Research Scientist, Center for Information Systems (CISR), MIT Sloan School of Management
- Kathie Sowell, President, Custom Enterprise Solutions, LLC
- John A. Zachman, CEO, Zachman International

The panelists were introduced by the moderator, Leon Kappelman, SIMEAWG founder and professor of IS at University of North Texas, and the session began with his description of their seminal contributions to EA:

Kappelman: I'm really honored to be the moderator of this panel today, so let's get going. It's almost like spending an hour with the guys and gals who first said the world was round while everybody else said it was flat. That's kind of who we're going to hear from this morning—the first people who said the world was round [laughter in audience]. Let me introduce our esteemed panel of enterprise architecture pioneers, and we'll get right into some questions for them.

John Zachman laid out the metaphysics of enterprise architecture. His first article about architecture was published in 1982 in the *IBM Systems Journal.* He was actually writing about BSP, IBM's full life cycle systems planning and systems development methodology, but five or six times in that article he talks about architecture and the strategic importance of it, and the importance it has for whatever you're building or changing so that you can do it within the context of the whole. In a 1987 *IBM Systems Journal* article, he published his enterprise ontology, commonly know as the Zachman Framework, which basically lays out the data model of all there is to know about the enterprise. Over the years he's refined the labels in his framework, although the logical construct has stayed consistent since the beginning. The labels are more precise now thanks to his work with linguists. I sometimes think of John as Socrates for organizations—the Greek philosopher advised people to "know thyself" by living the "examined life" while Zachman advises organizations to know themselves through their architectures because "someday you're going to really wish you had all those models."

Two of our panelists, Jeanne Ross and Randolph Hite, didn't start out to study enterprise architecture. They independently wanted to find out what was working in organizations. Randy, in the context of trying to do something within the federal government, went out in 1994 and studied best practices in industry. Randy's research led to what became the Clinger–Cohen Act in 1996, which requires all federal agencies to have a CIO and to do architecture. Jeanne's work started around 1995, and she didn't have enterprise architecture on her mind either. She just wanted to find out what worked, what was going on out there. Both of them ended up discovering that enterprise architecture was key to successful deployment and utilization of IT. Jeanne's 2006 book, *Enterprise Architecture as Strategy,* really raised the visibility of EA in a widespread way. Randy was doing the same thing in the federal government, raising awareness, guiding EA practices in 2001 with *The Practical Guide to Enterprise Architecture.* Interestingly, both Jeanne and Randy, independently, through their research, developed maturity models on how EA practices evolve. So both have laid groundbreaking foundations regarding how we think about the evolution of EA practices, and also have developed metrics to help us measure our progress.

Our next two panelists, Larry DeBoever and Kathie Sowell, both were focused more on actual EA implementation, helping people actually do the real work of EA. Obviously, everyone was interested in that, but Larry founded the first, on the private sector side, consulting practice focused on EA in 1990. He published a methodology in 1992 and founded the first research practice, which was later sold to the Meta Group and is now Gardner's enterprise architecture practice. Kathie was doing the same kind of thing, working at not-for-profit MITRE helping the U.S.

Department of Defense (DOD) do architecture, going back to the early 1980s. Not always calling it architecture, but working on architectural things and architectural concepts and helping DOD and other federal agencies learn how to do EA: developing methodologies, developing approaches, developing models.

So these five people have laid the foundations, in both the private and public sectors, as to how we think about EA, how in fact we do it, and how we measure our EA maturity. But the fact is that it's early; it's real early in the EA game. EA represents a change of thinking, and "paradigm shifts" of these kinds don't happen quickly.

Enterprise architecture is about seeing the enterprise in new ways. It's about seeing the discipline and the practices of IT in new ways, and for that matter management in general, too. The term "enterprise architecture" is a meager label for what is probably one of those very significant, once-in-a-lifetime, maybe once-in-a-millennium, changes in how we see the world—particularly how we think about and manage enterprises. It's about the organization of the future; it's about the Information Age enterprise, which is being defined by us and thousands of others who are trying to figure out how an enterprise can best take advantage of the remarkable capabilities of information technologies—capabilities that we've probably barely tapped at this point.

But the practice of EA is very, very young; we're twenty or twenty-five years into this. If EA had begun in 1945 when computing did, then maybe it's 1965. The first article about productivity was published in 1875, except it was called "scientific management" then. So for EA in the context of the productivity moment, which we're still a part of today, maybe it's 1895 or 1900. The concept of the steam engine was first written down in 200 BC; we didn't have a working model until 1665. It didn't work very well but it did run a few fountains. By 1708, things improved, and we had one that didn't work that well but dominated the scene for about fifty years. In 1769, John Watts got his patent, which is the one our grade school history books tell us marked the beginnings of industrial revolution; but thirty years later, in 1800, we still had only five hundred steam engines on the whole planet and they weren't very good, but they were a lot better than what we had fifty years before. We're kind of at that kind of point—we're in the very early stages of the Information Age and the very beginnings of this EA revolution.

So, I am very honored to be able to ask these EA pioneers some questions about how we've gotten here, what we've learned, and where we're going. So, the first question I'd like to put to them is:

> We've been going at this for twenty years. There have been many failed EA initiatives, and EA practices haven't really become very widespread. How do you account for this, and what challenges do EA initiatives face?

DeBoever: I'll start at the 100,000-foot level and speak to just one challenge so everybody has their time. I think, when I look at the fundamental challenge, we don't teach holistic optimization; we don't teach architecture in any meaningful way outside of building architecture. We don't teach people general system theory anymore or how to do holistic optimization, how to look at the world holistically. The IT profession is about engineering, about eliminating variables, trying to define a point solution; and while we preach that we need to optimize the enterprise, very few people do it.

By the way, often when I'm brought in to assess an enterprise architecture effort that is failing, the first thing I do is ask: "What does the enterprise want to holistically optimize? Are executive bonuses consistent across the entire enterprise? Do you have global processes? Do you have corporate strategic planning?" Because if you are counting on enterprise architecture to do holistic optimization across your organization, and executive management has voted through its bonus structure and its approach to processes and other things that show they don't want holistic optimization, such efforts are going to fail.

So in the beginning, we have to teach people how to do higher order abstraction in order to solve problems. Aerospace is a great example, and of course one of John's favorites, because when designing an airship you're always trading off a wing against the engine, load, capacity, distance, performance, and you have to holistically optimize. We do exactly the opposite in our enterprises—"You go build the engine, I'll build the wings, you build a fuel tank, we'll glue it together, and gee whiz this thing crashes." So, I'll start with that challenge. I really want to hear what the other panelists have to say.

Sowell: I have a couple of things that I would like to say about the question. First, I'm not sure that we have as many failures as we think we have. That's related to the expectation problem. Sometimes people go in with no problem in mind that they want to solve. So we come in and they say, "I want you to help us do enterprise architecture for this system." We'll ask, "What do you want the system to do?" "Oh, the system's already built. We just want you to do the architecture for it." Well, it's too late. But sometimes you do get value out of an architecture that was not the thing you went into it for.

Sometimes, organizations build an architecture, and they have these great expectations, which is the other problem, uncontrolled expectations. They think that the effort failed because they didn't get that one quantitative answer they were after. What they don't realize is that under the radar, people have been doing these architectures, building these models, talking to one another around the table; human communication happens because you're speaking the same language, looking at the same models. Your people then have a better common understanding of your organization and of the problem area so that the next time everything works better. But it's not always the problem that you went into it for that gets solved. So, I think there is more success out there than we think there is.

Ross: Actually I would disagree. I think there isn't a high level of success because there's too much architecture for the sake of architecture. I was actually asked to go into a nonprofit and give a speech on architecture, but "please don't use the word *architecture*. It's a bad word here." I think what we're looking for is some understanding on how organizations become more effective, and it may involve us not using the word because it's tainted by the number of failures out there. Going back to Larry's point, I think the risk that he's describing is that we will try to boil the ocean; let's just optimize everything. I think what we have is some people trying to boil the ocean; other people using architecture for the sake of architecture—it's already built but I think that now I should have its architecture. I think we have to get discussions [started] in organizations that ask the fundamental question: how does this company want to operate? To go back to your point, Larry, are we going to be standardized across this entire organization? Are we going to integrate across the entire organization or not? Let's just answer that question; and once we've answered it, then we can ask the question "How are we going to do that?" Instead of architecting everything, go after the most important things to make that happen. I think that when we see success in architecture it is because it is very targeted. The company knows how it wants to operate; it knows why it can't operate that way; and the architecture is about defining the gaps and how they are going to fill them so they can fundamentally act and run the organization the way they want to.

Hite: It's not fair to say that we've had failures and we haven't been successful. I do believe that there are pockets of successful architecture, particularly in the federal space. Part of the challenge there, and I'm going to add to some of the comments made so far, is that when I look at architecture across literally one hundred federal agencies, very rarely do you see a clear definition of the purpose of the architecture. What are you trying to accomplish with the architecture? Is it about business progress optimization at one end of the continuum, or is it simply about infrastructure consolidation? So, I don't think a lot of the organizations go into it understanding what they expect to get out of it. Now having said that, in the federal space we've also studied what's keeping architecture from being successful. What are the core challenges? The top four answers on the board: number one, I wouldn't think it would take anyone by surprise, is parochialism and cultural resistance—to change and giving up your space in the enterprise, perhaps for the benefits of others, and simply not willing to optimize the whole instead of just optimizing your part. Literally over 90 percent of a hundred federal agencies identified that as a significant challenge. The less significant challenges, but still identified incredibly by as many as 80 percent of federal agencies, deal with resources and in particular with regards to having the people with the knowledge, skills, and the abilities to do this successfully. Also, top-management understanding. They literally don't understand it so they're not backing it. So you're trying to wag the dog by the tail. One of the things we found, and interestingly it's been a theme at this conference, is this notion of leadership. If you have leadership, you're going to be able to overcome every one of these challenges. The challenge, which faces each of you in this audience who is trying to promote enterprise architecture, is to convince those above you that it's worthwhile and has value.

Zachman: In terms of why don't we see more successes, I think Leon in the introduction kind of outlined what the issue is. We're very early on here. The whole thesis is only twenty-five to thirty years old and I probably spent thirty to forty years of my life focused on this area. But we don't know everything. The body of knowledge is very big, and the bigger the body of knowledge gets, the more you know, the more you don't know. So, we're increasing all the questions that we have. I'm pretty careful to usually say I don't know all the answers. I'm getting better on the questions, but I don't know all the answers. I think that we're dealing with that kind of a phenomenon.

In terms of the challenges, I think there are two challenges. One, I don't think the general management community in general understands the issue or knows what the issue is. I think that from a management standpoint, it boils down to a classic short-term/long-term trade-off. If they want the short term, that is, if they want implementations, to get the implementations as quickly as possible, then we keep on doing what we have been doing—building and running systems. That's the short-term option. On the other hand, if they want enterprise integration, flexibility, interoperability, reusability, alignment, those kinds of things, those are engineering-derived characteristics. You have to do engineering to get those characteristics. So, then you're going to have to do architecture; that's the long-term option.

So the question is, do you want the short-term option to get the implementations as soon as possible? Well that's fine; then don't expect it to be integrated, flexible, interoperable, reusable, flawless, and seamless—don't expect it. On the other hand, if you want those engineering-derived kinds of characteristics, then you have to architecture. So, it's a classic long-term/short-term trade-off; and right now, they don't really understand the issue. IT people don't understand the issue very well for that matter either. So we're not helping them in this regard, and by default we tend to get the short-term option. It's a classic; by default, you get the short-term option. So, if you want the long-term option, it's a classic asset-based approach to life rather than an expense-based approach. So it's a classic long-term/short-term trade-off, in my opinion.

Then the second challenge is we have a cultural challenge. Those of us who come from IS, we tend to do implementation work. We actually have been manufacturing for the last fifty years. Fred Brooks is the one who said, "Programming is manufacturing; it is not engineering." So, we don't do engineering, we do manufacturing; we do implementation work. We're not doing engineering work; that is a different paradigm. The whole concept is different; the end object is different. We have this cultural problem; we have all this inertia to implementation. Very technology-dominant, you see it all over the place. I think Nicholas Carr is right. If we keep thinking that the end object is building and running systems, very technology-dominant work, then it is going to go outboard, basically. On the other hand, if you see the whole end object as the engineering and manufacturing of the enterprise, that is a different issue. In that case, engineering and manufacturing the enterprise will be a major role in the context of the enterprise of the future.

In summary, the challenges I think are that the general management folks don't understand the concept, which is the classic long-term/short-term trade-off; and the second problem is those of us that come from IS tend to gravitate toward the short-term option, building and running systems, and not the long-term option, engineering and manufacturing the enterprise.

Kappelman: And it takes time to change these kinds of professional practices. The first conclusive research was done in 1845 to indicate that if doctors washed their hands before they did surgery, there was significantly less infection and thereby death. The doctor who did the research was fired. Pasteur and Lister's work came along about twenty years later, and at that point people had no doubt bacteria spread disease. But if you look at photos of doctors doing surgery at U.S. medical schools in 1900, fifty-five years later, they have their street clothes on, they're not wearing gloves, they have long white jackets on but their street clothes are under them, and their shoes, shirt sleeves, and pants are exposed. Sure they were spraying carboxylic acid to kill the airborne bacteria, but the professional practices didn't change much over that fifty-five years despite the enormous advances in knowledge. They've got people's skulls open in those photos, and they're wearing their street clothes.

DeBoever: Leon, whenever I start to architect, I always wash my hands [laughter].

Kappelman: And that's why he's a pioneer. I'm glad you clarified that, Larry. The second question is:

> What is your vision of the future? What role will EA play in it? Where will we be in five, ten, twenty, fifty years from now, and how will EA help us get there? What is the future of the organization, and what role will EA play in that?

DeBoever: At the end of the day, I think that—I'll speak first and everyone can tell me I'm wrong—IT basically goes away and it is replaced with some form of information management and information leverage because the boxes go away. I think the deconstruction of systems is accelerating. We'll soon see the deconstruction of MRI [magnetic resonance imaging] so that all we need is the MRI machine because it's way more economic to do the rendering and presentation functions over the web than it is to have a data storage unit and all the rendering processes locally. I think what happens to EA in that context is that EA goes away.

I never tell anyone that I do enterprise architecture work. It's not one of the words for an executive suite, because I have to explain what it is. I think it gets replaced with or evolves; just like every MBA student for the past thirty years has had to have a basic knowledge of accounting, now they have to have a basic understanding of information systems, too. I think we evolve into a holistic enterprise optimization discipline. When I talk to other people, to the organizational dynamics folks, we're all looking at the same can of Diet Coke, we're just looking at it differently. I have my IT lens on, my EA lens on; I've got my human capital lens on; I've got my capital management lens on—but we're all still trying to optimize the can of Coke. I think that something emerges out of this; with heavy understanding of technology as an underpinning, but it is a discipline of optimizing the enterprise. I think it's a combination of business and where we're coming from and those kinds of things. But the good news is I'll be retired. So I have lots of consulting to do before then. Jeanne?

Ross: OK, I'll disagree with that then. I think the world is going to revolve around enterprise architecture. That the CIO will report to the chief enterprise architect, that, in fact, I'm not actually sure I'm disagreeing with you. I think we'll be about shaping the organization, and I think what you just said is like builders saying, "So eventually we won't need the architects anymore. We'll just go out and build." But I don't think you really meant that [laughter]. So I think we're going to design organizations, and the first thing we're going to do is architect them. And that will be the role of the chief enterprise architect. The CIO, who I think will eventually go away, but probably not in our lifetime, will report to the chief enterprise architect and that will be one of the most important building blocks in the organization.

Sowell: I would say that my vision is a little more modest. It's somewhere in between there. I'm just hoping that we can have enterprise architecture, the discipline of it, if not the name, and probably not the name, embedded in the thought processes of folks. This goes back to one of the challenges I forgot to mention, the return on investment. People always ask me, "Well, how much bang for the buck am I going to be getting if I paid you X dollars to do enterprise architecture? How many dollars is that going to save me?" You can't always attribute the success of a project to the enterprise architecture. If you had not done enterprise architecture or something like it, you would have even more failure. So, I'm hoping that the thought processes of enterprise architecture, although it may have another name, get more embedded in the daily management and thought processes of everyone and be taught in business school and high schools.

Hite: Gee, where will it be in thirty to fifty years from now? I guess I'll stay in my enterprise architecture box and say I think it'll be in the boardroom. I think the chief architect will be sitting at the board of directors' table, and I think when they talk about changes to the organization, then they're going to say, "Let's pull up the architecture. Let's have a real-time, decision support tool here if we're going to talk about changing this product or introducing this manufacturing capability or that new location, so we can see what it means for the organization." And you'll be able to put together very quickly in that scenario what it's going to cost and what the value proposition is that's coming out of that scenario. That's where I hope it'll be thirty to fifty years from now.

Zachman: I think we're all in violent agreement, even with Larry, the conscientious objector, or what did you call yourself yesterday?

Kappelman: The loyal opposition.

Zachman: Loyal opposition, that's it. I don't think anyone is in total disagreement. I wrote an article in 1999, "Enterprise Architecture: The Issue of the Century," and I actually believe it is the issue of the century. It's the enterprise that can accommodate these kinds of concepts that gets to stay in the game. And the enterprise that can't accommodate these kinds of concepts is not going to be in the game. And the logic on this is really strong. So, without digressing into what all that logic is, the fact is, it's going to be the heart of whether you're going to be viable or not, and I don't think we're talking about in the sweet by and by sometime. I think everybody in this room is going to see the players and the nonplayers, in the next maybe not five years, that may be a bit premature, the next ten years or so, ten years isn't a long time anymore; twenty years or so, you're going to find out the people who are in the game and the people who are not going to be in the game, and I think it's going to center around the whole issue of architecture. So, in that ten to fifteen years time frame, it's going to separate out the players from the nonplayers.

Now here's what the problem is; the problem is that the learning curve on enterprise architecture is pretty flat. You don't learn how to engineer an enterprise in a day. You don't send someone to two days of COBOL Programming School and expect them to come back and engineer an enterprise for you; it's not going to happen. To get a competent aeronautical engineer to engineer a Boeing 747, you're looking at twenty-five to thirty years. You're looking at the university level of education, graduate degrees; you're looking at apprenticeship; you're looking at thirty years of experience before you get someone that's competent to engineer something as complicated as a Boeing 747. Now, I'm going to suggest that enterprises are far more complex than Boeing 747s. You're just not going to learn to do that in a day. So people who expect this to be over by 3 o'clock this afternoon; it's not going to happen. It's going to take awhile to learn how to do this. We're talking about extreme complexity—the most complex object the human mind has conceived of and created thus far, an enterprise.

In fact, I think that in the Industrial Age, it was the industrial products that were increasing in complexity and the industrial products that were changing. It was only at the end of the Industrial Age that we got very sophisticated relative to architecture. One-hundred-story buildings appeared on the scene in the last seventy years or something like that.[18] The Boeing 747 appeared on the scene the forty years ago or something like that.[19] I think the key thing that allowed that to happen was architecture. The industry, whatever the industry might have been, stopped arguing about what architecture is, began to accept the common definition of what it is, and then they began to exploit that to create those complex objects. Well, in the Information Age, my assertion is that it is the enterprise that is increasing in complexity and it is the enterprise that is changing, and therefore, the key to the Information Age enterprise is going to be enterprise architecture. I think that's basically it. If I look out to where I think it will go in twenty-five, thirty, fifty years, the enterprise that makes it is going to be an enterprise that can dynamically restructure itself day by day to accommodate the demands being placed on it from the external environment. That is the whole idea, to accommodate change. The motivation for architecture has to do with complexity and change. I made that argument yesterday in the panel discussion. The enterprise of the future is going to be one that can dynamically reconstruct itself to accommodate the specific demands being placed upon it, whether private or public sector, it really doesn't matter. And the key to that is enterprise architecture.

Kappelman: So you think that we're still, within the enterprise community, still debating what architecture is?

Zachman: I've been more assertive about this issue recently. I'm going to make an assertion here and probably upset everybody in the room. I did not invent my framework; I did not invent that. It fell on my desk one day. My creative idea was to go ask somebody who knows what architecture is—someone who builds buildings, airplanes, locomotives, or something else—and asked them what architecture is. And all I did was put enterprise names on the same architectural artifacts that are used to build anything. So I never claimed that I invented it. However, it is architecture. The underlying logic says that this is architecture; and therefore I do not think that enterprise architecture is arbitrary, and it's not negotiable. I just don't think so. Architecture is architecture is architecture; I wrote an article by that name here recently, too. Architecture is architecture is architecture; we're arguing about the wrong thing. We ought to just say, "OK, here's what architecture is, historically, from the older disciplines. Let's start there and figure out how to do the work of architecture better." That's what we ought to be doing; in any case, we're arguing about the wrong thing; that's my opinion.

Kappelman: Our next question is one that many folks have come to me with at this conference:

> Where do you find a good architect? How do you train them? How do you identify people who are potentially good architects? If it is going to take some time to learn these skills, how do we find people now? Where do we train them? Where do we develop these skills? Where are these architects going to come from? I talk to people everywhere, and they're all in need of people who can do this.

DeBoever: I've given this speech to Leon's students and various other places. So, I'll just give you a few bullets that I look for. I look for extraordinary pattern recognition. Give me a musician any day of the week or someone that loves music. If you don't have pattern recognition, I don't even talk to you. You got to be an extraordinary communicator, and I mean that in the listening mode as well as the speaking and communication mode. I look for somebody that's not dogmatic at anything. If you've spent your life in networks, then you're probably not going to be a very good architect. I like someone who has ADD [attention deficit disorder] and finds a reason to think the Coke can is more interesting than the microphone. If you don't have ADD, then you're not going to ever work for me.

Now, having said those kinds of things, I'll give you my quick test because I really push this on people; I push this on my clients. After they pass all of that, and they're a good person, and I'd like to have a beer with them, and they put up with my lousy sports metaphors, my test for an architect is very simple. I bring them into a conference room, sit them on the other end of the conference table from me; their back is always to a pristine white board that I clean myself, no smudges, and a bunch of markers—and what I do is ask inane questions and wait to see how long it takes them to get up and start drawing pictures. I want somebody who dreams in pictures. They have to have extraordinary capability for spatial relationships. Do they abstract well and use their colors right? In fact, I often take a picture of it after they leave a room to really reflect on what they developed.

I got into this field through working at integrating heterogeneous systems in the mid-1970s at EPA [Environmental Protection Agency]. We had to string together Burrows, Univac, and IBM mainframes. So, we put in a DEC [Digital Equipment Corporation] layer to normalize the interfaces, basically across all the databases. So I made my career on integrating heterogeneity, and every time I tried to solve a problem, there was a higher order problem to be asked that eventually gets you to the boardroom saying, "What is it we're trying to do here?" So, when I'm looking for architects, I want to see them go through that process as I ask them more inane questions, "Well, why did you do that?" and I'll let them pick the problem. But trust me, the white board test works.

Sowell: May I shake your hand? That is exactly the speech that I have been hoping for from everyone. As a former and current musician, I want to thank you very much. It can be told now, I don't often reveal this, but my degrees are in music. I went to the New England Conservatory of Music and have a master's degree in flute. So, naturally …

DeBoever: That's why you have that styling thing going on? It's the whole concert thing.

Sowell: Yeah, it's the presentation, and I have found others like myself. There's some sort of secret handshake or something that we know, and there are a lot of musicians out there. When I was at MITRE, I was giving some classes in enterprise architecture and I let it slip that you don't have to be an engineer to do this—in fact, in my opinion, it's better if you're not—and people come out of the wood-work. "Oh yeah, I went to Oberlin and got a degree in percussion and now I'm here taking your class." "Oh yeah, I play the violin." There is a lot of that, and I think, looking back on it, the characteristics that helped me in music—well, they didn't help me make any money or I guess I wouldn't be here—but helped me be a successful musician are: logical thinking, ability to abstract, the ability to work all by yourself for a long amount of time and not expect results in hours, minutes, days, months, or sometimes even in years, and the ability to work with other people. You have to do all of those things, and you have to be able to do some things in real time—you can't always wait until the opportunity is correct; you have to jump in and do it. You have to be willing to uncover the problems and express them without being offensive. But I think that some of the worst architects I've seen have been the really narrow-focused engineers in a particular discipline who have been told all their lives, "This is what you do and don't bother to look at those other disciplines." So, I think that someone that has come up through a wide array of life experiences, is able to get along with other people, the language, the logic, and the ability to postpone gratification are all important.

Hite: Those are some excellent comments, and rather than repeat any of them I'll just offer you this analogy: When the FAA [Federal Aviation Administration] hires air traffic controllers, they're not looking for people with college degrees or particular types of backgrounds in certain disciplines. They're looking for people—and they have aptitude tests to determine this—that think spatially, who can think in three or four dimensions at a time, and who are good communicators. I would suggest to you that the same kinds of characteristics that apply to an air traffic controller probably apply to an architect.

DeBoever: My girlfriend, Kathy Taft, dumped me when I was a senior in high school in the spring of 1968. So, out of my wisdom, I went down to teach her a lesson. I went down to join the Marine Corps. Second week of boot camp in 1968, the Marine Corps gave me the choice of going to Vietnam as a forward artillery observer or becoming an IBM 360 systems programmer. Now, my mother was the head of "data processing" at the college; in fact, they were all women, they were all moms. That's what I thought moms did for a living; they were all computer programmers because in the 1960s, that's what my mom did on an RCA Spectra 70 [mainframe computer]. But I always wondered, even in grad school, why the Marine Corps picked me for those two things, and that's when I looked up the old IBM programmer aptitude test. Actually, the domain it tested was spatial relations [capabilities] and, it turns out, to be a forward artillery observer you have to think spatially, like your artillery's over here and the bad guys are over there, or your artillery probably won't hit the far side of the hill; or you can program mainframe computers. It's all spatial relations, and that's what I feel musicians have. You know, I'm an amateur musician and I love music. I think it's that dimension; you have to find those people, you really do. So I'm glad to hear that about the FAA, because they can fix their computer problem if they take all the controllers and put them on the FAA's computer problem.

Hite: Well, technology's not the problem there.

Ross: I'm going to take your word on the musician thing; I didn't know about that. I did talk to the CIOs at UPS and Conway because I've always been impressed on how focused they are in their architectural effort and how they get results. And I asked them where their architects came from, and they said, "Well, you look at your application developers and you realize that some of them, before they do anything, they'll step back and say 'I just want to understand this in a bigger context. So how does this fit with whatever else is going on in the organization?' If they ask that question, then we know that they have real promise as architects. If they just go, 'OK, I can get that done,' then we know they're more short-term driven. So we just identify those people who continually ask those questions." I was fascinated that both of these companies basically used that same method of identifying good architecture candidates.

Kappelman: Sounds like people who are system thinkers.

Zachman: I actually don't know how to define the characteristics of a good architect. But I learned a lot about myself just now. I'm a frustrated trumpet player; if I could have made money in the trumpet-playing business, I probably wouldn't be here talking about architecture; I'd be doing something else. The other thing is, Larry DeBoever talked about the Marine Corps. I spent quite some time in the navy and I worked with the original computer, which was a fire-controller computer and sat down in the combat information center. It was a steel box about this big and about that high, and it did one calculation—the elevation, the velocity of the shell, and the distance to the target. That was basically it. I tried to get to Vietnam and I couldn't get there; there were too many people on the waiting list. I wanted a riverboat command. That's what I really wanted.

DeBoever: You have to understand, John was an officer when I was enlisted. That's why he wanted to go. Enlisted people stayed away.

Zachman: Well, I called up my friend at BUPERS (Bureau of Personnel) and said, "Get me the riverboat command"; and he said, "You should have called me yesterday because there are so many guys on the list now, you'll never get there." So, forget it. I resigned from the navy to go back to a family business in the Midwest and then went to work for IBM because it kind of reminded me of the navy [laughter]. In any case, if I had gotten what I wanted, I probably wouldn't be sitting here today, either. So, how do you find architects? I don't know … but I really learned a lot about myself this morning.

Kappelman: I'd like to open this up to the floor for questions. We have time for a couple. Would anyone like to ask a question of our panelists?

Audience member #1: What do you find to be the best strategy for being able to communicate the need for architecture to senior management when they are desperate for near-term implementations?

DeBoever: I say this, "My goal is to reduce complexity and to enable rapid change in business." That's my elevator pitch, one sentence and they get that. They say, "If you can deliver that, I'll give you all your outrageous fees."

Ross: An alternative approach is to listen to what they say their problems are and offer to solve them. Don't talk about architecture.

Audience member #1: Do you say, "We'll give you what you really want right now but this is just an approximate version of what you're really going to need?"

DeBoever: Throwaway systems never get thrown away. How many people are still running Lotus Notes? I was with a client and they still had thirty-six hundred FoxPro databases on their network, but the database people weren't keeping track of any of it. All of them had copies of data off the mainframe. Nobody throws away throwaway systems. We can say that we will but we just don't do it. We find a reason to keep it around.

Zachman: In terms of how to communicate to the general management folks, I have two thoughts. One thought is, I think you have to communicate on the basis of a metaphor. That's the way I try to do it. Nobody has any trouble understanding the concept of a one-hundred-story building or a Boeing 747 or a battleship or a supercomputer. Those are the complex objects of the Industrial Age, and they're big and complicated, and people are not unrealistic about it. I say, "Hey, you can't engineer a one-hundred-story building in a day." I try to find whatever the issue is and explain that in the context of a metaphor. I think that's the only way to do it.

The second thing I would say is—I learned this from a friend, Carl Simcox, he was a CIO at Motorola Communications Sector for a while—Carl used to say, "I get my converts one at a time." The high probability is that you won't go back to your management meeting, make a fifteen-minute presentation with four bullets on a PowerPoint slide, and everybody leaps up in unison and yells, "Wow, that's brilliant! Here's a blank check. Do whatever you want." It's probably not going to happen that way. You are going to have to identify the people you will need to get on board and work on them however long it takes—a day, a month, a year; whatever, until you get them on board. Then Carl would say, once he gets them on board, "Go get me another convert."

Ross: Yes, and I think part of it is that sometimes we can see a very high value out of a big initiative. The other piece of this is going after the smaller things that can happen faster and show real benefits. Quite often, this is just IT getting its own house in order, building a lot of credibility, getting IT costs down, and generating trust so that they'll listen when you say "There's something bigger we have to do if we're going to solve the complexity issues. We're going to have to make some investments." Once that credibility is established, it's just a lot easier to make that argument. So I think sometimes we have to delay what we think would be of most value in order to provide a more immediate, visible, and tangible outcome.

Kappelman: So, in order to make the case for broad-based enterprise architecture efforts, sometimes IT must first eat its own EA cooking. I like that.

Audience member #2: Would you say that the enterprise architect has some kind of client or customer, and who would that be?

DeBoever: If I had to pick one, I would say it's the stakeholders in the organization; that is who we ultimately serve. At the end of the day, we're trying to optimize what is best for the enterprise. But to Jeanne's point, you have to ask the question, "What do you want to accomplish?" I absolutely believe in the importance of this whole issue around trust. Very often, when I see EA teams getting pushback from executive leadership, it's because they don't have trust or confidence in the IT organization or in IT's effectiveness. So, that really is the hidden objection, and they're just beating up on EA saying, "I don't get it, I don't understand." They push back, but the hidden objection is "I don't think you can do it, I don't trust you, and I don't trust the CIO; at least not with something that grandiose."

Audience member #3: So, I'm intrigued by your analogies in the building industry and I had the pleasure of working in the federal government for some time in the public building service. I would say the differences are mainly in the notions of liability. When a one-hundred-story skyscraper gets built, it's usually followed by a series of lawsuits where engineering companies would say to the architect, "You didn't get this right," and construction companies would say, "The engineers didn't get that right." It's not a pretty or particularly efficient process, but they do have pretty clear notions of who's liable for what. They may disagree with each other over that, but they can go to court and they can settle it; and one of the things I see absent from the information technologies industry is any resemblance of warranties of merchantability, warranties of consequential damages; and I think it's that business side that's lacking so you never do get a sense of who's responsible for what and what being responsible for it actually means.

DeBoever: I agree a thousand percent.

Ross: I had a fascinating experience at Gillette when Pat Zilvitis took over as CIO, and they bring him into the senior management team meeting his first day—he was a member of that team. And they said, "Oh we're so glad you're here because we have to get PeopleSoft in." He said, "Oh, OK. I can do that. So who's going to be responsible if it fails?" They're all looking around and going, "Well you. That's why we brought you in." He said, "No, no I understand, on the technology I'm going to do that, but I mean if it doesn't get adopted and used to drive value, then who is responsible?" He said they all thought he was crazy; they all thought that was his job. So, luckily he was in his first week and still on honeymoon, and because he said they really couldn't move forward on this, they broke up the meeting without a resolution. So, over time, one of the executive vice presidents, who had among his responsibilities HR, said, "Oh, wait a minute. I get what you're saying; I have to take responsibility for this." And it completely changed his behavior; he started going to every location and saying, "Here's what we're going to do. This is the behavior I expect from you." Once he said, "This is *my* job"; then Pat was able to put in PeopleSoft, slowly but surely. And I think that kind of accountability is often missing; so we're out there drawing pictures that we call "enterprise architecture" but nothing's happening because nobody says they're going to own some kind of outcome. That's exactly what you're talking about.

DeBoever: There's two tricks I use. One is, I videotape and have public design reviews. For example, I videotape every public design review under the guise that the next person to take over the project will have a history. It also causes people to behave well. The second thing I do is have everybody involved in the implementation sign a document that says this will achieve the requirements described herein. The act of signing a document with your name really causes people to think things through; and though it's a card trick, it has profound implications because by signing they're saying, "OK, this team, we're all signing off on a contract that this is going to work." And to do it in front of the CIO. You know how we used to talk about contract with our teenagers; same thing, because it works, most of the time.

Sowell: But there's another issue here with responsibility, and that is credit. You can assign blame and credit for the outcome of various parts of a project, but enterprise architecture is a discipline and it's hard to assign blame or credit for that. If PeopleSoft works, we would have put it in anyway, we wouldn't need to do this architecture analysis; or this satellite goes round and around and maybe it would have worked with or without enterprise architecture. Because it's so difficult to assign credit or blame to the discipline of enterprise architecture, I'm hoping that in our future, enterprise architecture becomes so embedded in the thought processes of people that we won't have to call it out separately for credit or blame.

Kappelman: Well, when it comes to IT, we do have a peculiar conceptualization of liability at this stage of the game. Take the same size or complexity piece of code, say two or three thousand function points, put it in a car, which we do, and we would never tolerate it if that car software crashed once a week and we had to reboot it. But you put that same code in a computer on our desktops, and we tolerate it all the time, without question. I think it's just what happens early in a new age like we're in. And it seems that industries tend to get regulated and more conscious of liability only after they kill a lot of people or cause lots of property damage. Think about it, buildings were regulated early because they burned; electricity was, plumbing was, because they caused lots of damage and destruction. Insurance companies don't want death or damages; people don't like deaths or damages. Cars were very late to be regulated for safety, perhaps because they only killed a few of us at a time. Maybe computing is like that.

Zachman: I learned this from Randy Hite. This is a really important idea because unfortunately, in our case, in the enterprise case, when we fail, we don't kill people. We don't build life-dependent systems, typically, so therefore, there's not a lot of visibility when the thing craters. Now, however, if enterprises start to fail because they can't accommodate change or can't accommodate extreme complexity, and people start to get unemployed and citizens start to get hurt, don't kid yourselves, the government is going to be in there with both feet, with regulatory action saying, before we allow you to operate in our geographic domain, we would like to see your architecture. Can you accommodate complexity and change? That was kind of where Randy came into this saying the Clinger–Cohen act came out of that. I don't know that Clinger or Cohen actually understood that in those days— it was a little early on—but that was fundamentally where it was going. They were saying that before we allow you operate and allocate money to you in the federal budget, we would like to see your architecture. It's pretty straightforward. So you may or may not like enterprise architecture, and you may not want to hear about enterprise architecture, but I'm here to tell you, sooner or later, it's not going to be an option. It's going to be a regulatory issue. In any case that's my view.

Audience member #4 (Ephraim McLean, Regents' Professor and George E. Smith Eminent Scholar's Chair in Information Systems at Georgia State University): Larry, your comment about sign-offs and in fact the discipline that it entails. The problem is that the after-action reports, the postimplementation audit, and whether there's actual follow-up. Napoleon said, "Victory has a hundred fathers, but defeat is an orphan." Who gets the credit if it does work and who gets the blame if it doesn't work? The problem that I see is many organizations have sign-offs or commitment documents, but there's no organizational backbone after the fact to reinforce them. I've seen it time and time again. So few organizations have a backbone to say, "You didn't live up to your commitments; the IT people didn't make the system they were supposed to, and the user didn't achieve the economic benefits they were supposed to." In the building context they may be suing each other, but we don't see people suing each other at the end of an IT project, and very, very few organizations have backbone, the intestinal fortitude, to enforce the kind of agreement Larry has people sign.

DeBoever: In the 1980s I did some projects with PepsiCo bottlers, and they did postimplementation audits, and those documents stayed in your personnel file for every project you did in IT and were to be counted for merit and promotions for the rest of your career. I don't know if they continued that practice but that was a great idea.

Audience member #4: I worked at Procter & Gamble, and they did, too. But my point is that maybe 5 percent or 10 percent of companies have that kind of discipline to make that kind of approach work, and that's my concern.

DeBoever: It goes back to the issue of leadership. IT organizations get—I'm trying to think of a polite word for "messed over"—by vendors all the time. The consultants fail to deliver, the software doesn't work, and we let people get away with just enormous, egregious acts of waste all the time. Man, how much waste have I seen!

Kappelman: Sadly, we are out of time. I'm going to ask each of our EA pioneer panelists to take thirty seconds or so to say whatever parting comments they would like to say to wrap up this discussion.

Hite: Just a quick thought to build on this notion of accountability and responsibility. If you view the optimized organization as a constellation, there are a number of stars that have to align for that constellation to be what it is. I don't want to leave you with the idea that I feel like enterprise architecture is the panacea, or that it's the end all be all, but EA is one variable in that equation that leads to a successful organization. If EA does its part and all the other parts are successful, then you can achieve an optimized organization.

Sowell: I think the most important thing to remember is that enterprise architecture is a human endeavor. It's all about human communication; the methods you use, the pictures you draw, all have to communicate to human beings, and it doesn't matter what automated tool you're using, at least that's not the most important thing. The most important thing is that you have a method for human beings to get together and understand each other first and then solve the problems together.

DeBoever: The challenge that I ask people to reflect on is the rate of change business demands—and I'm talking private sector—is inside our capacity to plan, our planning cycles. The effort we take to plan takes longer than the actual rate at which management wants that change to occur. Therefore, in enterprise architecture, we have to architect to enable rapid change without a discontinuity or disruption, and that's across the breadth of the entire enterprise. It's not a software issue, even though software is a popular manifestation; it is a much larger issue and it's only going to get worse. The rate of change is going to continue to accelerate.

Ross: I would add that we need to think of enterprise architecture as a learning journey. So, it's not about diagrams and concepts; it's about the organization getting smarter over time, about how to run itself and about how to use IT to do that. So, we should be constantly emphasizing how we can learn. The postimplementation assessments, the board meetings, the architecture acceptance processes, these are all learning opportunities and we should look for the learning opportunities in all of our management practices because then we can start to build on our experiences, and get smarter, and that's what the great organizations do.

Zachman: I think I'll kind of wrap up with a quote from Jay Forester, who managed a research project at MIT and in 1961 published a book called *Industrial Dynamics*. You can see the current version of it in Peter Senge's work, *The Fifth Discipline*, as he now manages that same research project. Anyway, Jay Forester in a speech entitled "Designing the Future" at a Spanish university on December 15, 1998, said, "Organizations built by committees and intuition perform no better than an airplane built by the same methods. As in bad airplane design, which no pilot can fly successfully, such badly designed corporations lie beyond the ability of real-life managers. Success of a pilot depends upon an aircraft designer who designed it to be a successful airplane. Who designs the corporations that a manager runs?"

Kappelman: How about these EA pioneers? [Applause from the audience.] We've probably not answered all of your questions. In fact, we've probably raised a whole new set of questions; but hopefully, we're asking questions at a higher level and about more important things. Thank you so much for your time this morning.

And so, with much applause, and a great deal of cavorting and talking in the hallway after the session, the Pioneers of Enterprise Architecture Panel came to an end. How about those EA pioneers!

Notes

18. Completed in 1931, the Empire State Building in New York City has 102 floors. (Ed.)
19. The first commercial flight of a Boeing 747 was in 1970. (Ed.)

ENTERPRISE ARCHITECTURE THEORY

2

> The act of discovery consists not in finding new lands but in seeing with new eyes.
>
> —**Marcel Proust**

Introduction

Doing enterprise architecture is not simple or easy, any more than managing an enterprise is simple or easy. Choosing among the various ideas, conceptualizations, theories, models, methods, and practices of EA is complex and demanding; and deciding how to best organize, staff, govern, or start an EA program in your enterprise is similarly difficult. This is particularly true since we are still "early in the game" and have little data by which to judge and evaluate different approaches. Chapters 2, 3, and 4 aim to help you with these decisions—the first addresses the theoretical and conceptual matters of EA, the second addresses the practice-oriented ones, and the third provides data on the current state of EA practices and perceptions.

There is a great deal of confusion and ambiguity about EA and thus a critical need for clarity before EA can realize its potential. Most think in terms of only the implementation-oriented and IT-specific aspects as EA, and thus very little about the larger concept of the architecture of enterprises—about two-thirds in a study of senior IT professionals we completed in 2008 (see responses to question 19a in the Detailed Survey Results in Chapter 4). It is likely the percentage is even higher among the junior ranks. Not only are we uncertain and unclear about the subject matter of the discipline of EA, there's even more confusion when it comes to the details. Distinctions like "SOA is an implementation strategy, TOGAF a methodology, and Zachman's Enterprise Framework an ontology" are almost never made, and thus we are often comparing apples and monkeys as if they are different varieties of oranges.

This situation is somewhat understandable given the newness of the EA concept itself, and the fact that many folks come to EA from IT backgrounds with all their IT biases (and as humans we all have biases of one kind or another). However, this is a potentially serious risk to EA and therefore enterprise success, given that IT people have been preoccupied with business-IT alignment for thirty years with only limited success. It appears that getting aligned is one thing but staying aligned in a timely manner, ideally in a real-time one, is quite another. Achieving *and* maintaining alignment requires EA because architecture is the best way humans have invented for managing complexity and change. And enterprises are very complicated and in a state of constant change.

The nine articles in this theory chapter address these challenges by helping us better understand the larger context by delving into the specifics of the EA hub and the EA and IT spokes in the Enterprise Wheel. This emphasis is depicted in Figure 2.1, a version of the Enterprise Wheel that we introduced in Figure 1.1 in Chapter 1. EA is a business activity, and the IT dimensions are only part of it. EA is a paradigm shift for IT and for business management—a different way of thinking about, communicating about, and managing the enterprise and all of its assets

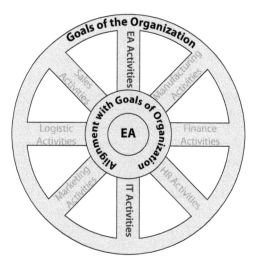

FIGURE 2.1   The Enterprise Wheel (with Chapter 2 emphasis).

including technological ones. EA is about reinventing the enterprise and inventing its future.

Professor Leon Kappelman's article titled "Bridging the Chasm" explains the historical context of EA by examining the delay innovations and transformations generally go through while they evolve and mature, eventually becoming standard practices. The potentials of "enterprise architecture," if they are to be realized, will evolve much like the examples of earlier intellectual innovations such as those once called "scientific management" and "statistical quality control." Eventually, Kappelman opines, EA's vision of comprehensive, centralized, accessible, and usable information about the enterprise—whether about its data, processes, jobs, objectives, timings, products, information technologies, or something else—will help us bridge the "chasm" between strategy and implementation, between business and IT, between thought and action. Enterprise architecture and general systems thinking will become standard, posits Dr. Kappelman, enabling managers to manage ubiquitous change and increasing complexity within the strategic and tactical environments their organizations operate. Enterprises that can successfully survive in the demanding business, social, and economic environments of the next few generations will have succeeded at managing all the organization's knowledge about itself through EA.

In beginning an EA practice within an organization, certain fundamental definitions and differentiations should be made, or at least discussions initiated, regarding basic questions like:

- What is architecture?
- What is the architecture of an enterprise?
- What is the purpose of an enterprise architecture?
- What schemas, ontologies, or data models are there for conceptualizing the architecture of an enterprise?
- What is an EA model?
- What architectural models or artifacts exist for doing EA?

EAWG member John Zachman, to many the "godfather" of EA, lays the foundations for helping us better understand these concepts and answer these and other questions about EA and EA practices in three closely related articles in this chapter. Here he elaborates and clarifies the general statements about architecture and enterprise architecture that he made in Chapter 1's EA pioneers panel discussion. In "Architecture Is Architecture Is Architecture," Zachman describes how his "framework" for EA is simply the application to enterprises of architectural fundamentals developed over thousands of years in creating physical objects like buildings and manufactured goods. Doing architecture about anything, according to Zachman, is about creating the total set of descriptive representations about the object of interest (be it a widget, building, computer chip, or an enterprise) by separately capturing and communicating the answers to six questions about the object—Who?

What? Where? Why? When? How?—from six specific points of view or perspectives (moving along a continuum from intangible to tangible, logical to physical, concept to instantiation).

Zachman also clarifies the distinction between architecture and implementation, or engineering and manufacturing, by pointing out the differences between architecture and instantiation and between primitive and composite models. Such distinctions are necessary and essential. Architecture is engineering and as such is about the creation of primitive models, but implementation is manufacturing and requires composite models based on those more fundamental, independent, and therefore more flexible primitives. Most all IT models tend to be composites because IT is largely implementation oriented. Eventually, composite implementation models are necessary for instantiation. The important question raised by Zachman is whether the composites are derived from primitives, and therefore easily changed when requirements change, or whether they are created in an ad hoc situation-specific manner without primitives. The result of beginning with composite models is a physical reality that is tightly coupled and difficult to change. This is the current state of IT, and just about everything else, in most every enterprise. Effectively practicing EA in an organization requires composite models that are derived from primitive models, not solely satisfying short-term needs by implementing from composites directly.

Zachman's distinctions raise a fundamental question about the future of the IT profession. If IT is only about implementation, then someone else will likely realize the importance and value of capturing all the knowledge about the enterprise through its EA. Thus IT will lose the opportunity it has been afforded as EA responsibility by default is often assigned to IT people. We will always need great IT mechanics and technicians, but the SIMEAWG believes IT people should also have a seat at the strategic management table—EA can be their ticket to that seat. As stated by Jeanne Ross in the Foreword: "Because IT people are the people most likely to understand cross-functional, standardized, multi–business unit processes, they are the natural leaders to assume responsibility for architecting their companies' business operations." And yet, as our survey indicates (see all of question 18 in Chapter 4's Detailed Survey Results), after more than sixty years—and over thirty years since Fred Brooks[1] pointed out that getting requirements right is the essence of IT—IT people rate their analysis and design capabilities and practices poorly. And analysis and design skills are the same basic fundamental skills required of architects and for doing EA. This is why we see problem solving, communication, collaboration and teams, and business analysis high on top of the IT skills list in the recent SIM member surveys.[2]

EAWG member Bruce Ballengee metaphorically enters the EA definition and theory waters in his article "Why Enterprise Architecture Matters: Surfing the Waves" by focusing on the widespread EA objective and long-lived key concern of IT management—enabling alignment. The difficulty of the business value chain, opines Ballengee, is the wobble created by IT, business, customers, and suppliers moving in various, uncoordinated directions. The IT, business, customer, and supplier waves sometime move in an integrated fashion and sometimes not, creating disruptive gaps. In Ballengee's view, EA is a method to conceptualize and facilitate alignment among suppliers, customers, the business, and IT. The enterprise architect surfs the waves by balancing between the wobbles using various tools to create value. Ballengee closes with a list of the benefits of practicing EA such as an increased knowledge of the business and its value creation processes, increased communication capabilities, and awareness of IT impacts. These benefits of EA as well as others are also among those that are included in the SIMEAWG's survey in ascertaining a respondent's view of potential EA benefits (beginning with question 20 in the Detailed Survey Results in Chapter 4).

In his article "To Be or Not to Be: Recognize EA as a True Profession?" EAWG member Mark Lane elaborates on the future importance of EA, as opined by other writers here, and makes the case for professionalization of EA practitioners. Implicit to Lane's position and his call to action is that given the critical importance of EA to the functioning and survival of the enterprise, and all the implications that this has to the economic and social viability of nations, it is imperative that EA be practiced only by those with the requisite skills, competencies, and ethical standards. In light of the fact that this position is unquestionably accepted when applied to medical doctors, accountants, lawyers, building architects, and many others, Lane's point is well taken given that fact that enterprises have profound implications for the health and welfare of individuals, societies, and nations. It appears that both EA and IT have a long way to go on the road to "profession," according to Professor Cem Kaner's view that "few or none" of the five "hallmarks of a profession" apply to computing, specifically: (1) extensive learning and training; (2) a code of ethics with standards above those of the market; (3) a disciplinary system for code breaches; (4) "a primary emphasis on social responsibility over strictly individual gain, and the corresponding duty of its members to behave as members of a disciplined and honorable profession"; and (5) a licensing prerequisite prior to admission into practice.[3,4] Lane's call to action is aimed at moving the EA profession forward.

The next two articles are also by John Zachman. In the first he provides a concise definition of his enterprise ontology. It is noteworthy that we found it helpful, even necessary, to include this little article. This was because of not only the early state of general EA awareness but also the very high degree of misconception about Zachman's "framework" almost everywhere we look. However, the SIMEAWG does not formally "endorse" Zachman's enterprise ontology. We simply find that it uniquely clarifies the EA object of interest, the enterprise. In "Framework Standards" Zachman opines why it is important, in fact essential, to have EA standards. This seems almost self-evident in light of the critical importance of enterprises to the viability of human society and the fact that we accept without question a high degree of standardization of terminology and concepts in the professions of medical doctors, lawyers, plumbers, electricians, and even barbers and manicurists.

The last three articles in this chapter have a more research-oriented theme, and all are written by university professors and doctoral students. The first delves into the highly political nature of doing EA by taking a particular theoretical perspective of enterprise politics. Building on her earlier work with actor-network theory, Anna Sidorova teams up with Leon Kappelman to examine the human aspects of doing EA. Brian Salmans, who also managed the EAWG's survey as it is reported in Chapter 4, then explains the state of the art and science of EA assessment by describing the various "EA maturity models" currently available. These models provide us with insights into how EA practices evolve in organizations and how one might monitor and assess their overall EA practices, activities, programs, and processes. Using the Enterprise Wheel hub-and-spoke metaphor, the maturity models discussed can be used to assess the overall health and value of the EA itself as well as the EA activities spoke as it evolves and matures. Among other things, the SIMEAWG's survey, described in Chapter 4, attempts to discover some of the similarities and differences among all of the different EA maturity models identified by Salmans in this article, and future research is planned to see to what extent they overlap and whether some higher order conceptualization of EA maturity is possible.

Chapter 2 ends with an article about "Charting the Territory for Academic Research" in EA. Here Kappelman, Salmans, and Sidorova team up with managing editor Tom McGinnis and EAWG member Alex Pettit, to provide researchers with a glimpse at some of the opportunities and needs for EA-related research. The EA research agenda they suggest is a work in progress aimed at academic and educator interests. As such, it would benefit from suggestions aimed at directly helping practitioners in terms of developing and especially assessing practices, methods, tools, models, and so on. The need for an unbiased central clearinghouse for EA-related information would be a valuable resource, too, and to whatever extent it can the SIMEAWG tries to serve that purpose.

EA success is critical to the successful creation of the Information Age enterprise and thus the realization of the true potential of the Information Age. If this were the Industrial Age, perhaps it's about 1835; enterprises and their technologies looked pretty good to the folks in 1835, but they look absurdly primitive to us today. The machines and building we were able to build in 1835 pale in comparison to those we were able to design and create in 1935, and those to today's buildings and products. In fact, the architectural capabilities of the Industrial Age gave us the technologies of the Information Age. Applying those architectural capabilities to the design, creation, and management of organizations will bring us the promise of the Information Age enterprise, the learning organization "where people continually expand their capacity to create the results they truly desire, where new and expansive patterns of thinking are nurtured, where collective aspiration is set free, and where people are continually learning to see the whole together."[5]

Notes

1. Brooks, F., 1995, *The Mythical Man-Month* (20th Anniversary Edition), Boston: Addison-Wesley Longman Publishing Co.

2. Luftman, Jerry. 2008 *SIM 2007 IT Trends Survey Findings*, http://simnet.org/Portals/0/ Content/Library/SIMposium/luftmanhandout.ppt; and *2008 SIM IT Trends Survey Results, 2008 SIM IT Trends Survey Results*, http://www.simnet.org/Portals/0/images/ SIMposium08Speakers/ITTrendsSurveySlidesReduced.pdf, available only to SIM members.

3. Kaner, Cem, 1997. *Computer Malpractice*, monograph at http://www.badsoftware. com/malprac.htm (last updated 10-Nov-97 and originally published in *Software QA*, v.3, n.4, (23-).

4. Although not formally required for all, IT professionals do have and aspire to extensive learning. There are also several good codes of ethics for IT professionals (e.g., ACM, IEEE, ISACA, and others). However, there is little development on Kaner's other three hallmarks of a profession. (Ed.)

5. Senge, Peter M. 1990. Fifth Discipline: *The Art and Practice of the Learning Organization*. New York, Doubleday, p. 7

Bridging the Chasm

Leon A. Kappelman

Those who study advances in health care and other fields find a "generation" lag of about twenty years before discoveries are adopted haphazardly into standard practice. And three or four generations before an innovation, be it technical or intellectual, becomes so common that we no longer think of it as an innovation at all. Thus it is said that "science proceeds by the death of scientists."

Management is no different, so it's not surprising that despite many strategic transformations via IT by the mid-1970s, most officers and directors were oblivious or indifferent to IT in 1990. Yet by the turn of the century almost all were aware of IT's promise and peril. But awareness is not mastery, or even competence.

EA represents a new way of thinking about the enterprise, and a new way of managing the enterprise, and its IT. Federal Reserve Chairman Ben Bernanke calls it "intangible capital." In his June 2006 MIT commencement speech, he said: "Important investments in intangible capital remain to be made, as much still remains to be learned about how to harness these technologies."

Enormous productivity gains occurred in the Industrial Age thanks to the intellectual or intangible capital of "scientific management" as described by Frederick Taylor. EA has the potential to contribute similarly to the Information Age.

Managing for productivity and quality is central to management practice today. But when we say "efficiency" or "productivity," most don't think of Taylor, his 1881 paper, 1911 book, or the words "scientific management" any more than we think of Joseph Juran, his 1928 pamphlet, his 1951 *Quality Control Handbook,* or the words "statistical quality control" when we say "quality" or "effectiveness."

I don't know what the "EA" of today will be called in a few generations. I do know we will achieve the EA vision of bridging the chasm between strategy and implementation, of capturing all the knowledge about the enterprise and making it available in real time for every imaginable management need, and of having a shared "language" of words, graphics, and other depictions to discuss, document, and manage every important aspect of the enterprise. I know this because the enterprises that survive those next few generations will be agile, adaptable, interoperable, integrated, lean, secure, responsive, efficient, effective, and thereby more able to succeed in a world that demands we do more with less, faster, while traditional boundaries blur, and the rules of engagement change.

Succeeding in such a world requires that the enterprise masters the management of all the knowledge about itself. We are in the early stages of developing such skills. EA is the name of this emerging discipline.

EA isn't the organization any more than a map is the highway, blueprints the building, or the idea the invention. But maps, blueprints, ideas, and EA are tools to help us efficiently and effectively get where we want to go. Without them, we're lost.

A version of this article also appeared as Leon A. Kappelman (2007), "Bridging the Chasm," *Architecture and Governance Magazine,* 3(2): 28.

Architecture Is Architecture Is Architecture

John A. Zachman

There appears to be a gross misunderstanding about Architecture, particularly in the information technology community. Many people seem to think that an implementation, an end result, is Architecture. To use an Architecture and Construction example, many people think that the Roman Coliseum is Architecture.

This is NOT Architecture!

This is the RESULT of Architecture.

The Roman Coliseum is NOT Architecture. The Roman Coliseum is the RESULT of Architecture. The RESULT of Architecture is an instance of Architecture, an implementation. In the end result, the implementation, you can see an instantiation of the Architect's Architecture. If an Architect had not created the descriptive representations (the Architecture) of the Roman Coliseum, they could not have built the Roman Coliseum. They couldn't have even ordered the stones they required in order to build the Coliseum without the Coliseum Architecture, which had to be created long before the Coliseum was constructed.

Architecture is the set of descriptive representations that are required in order to create an object. If you can't describe it, you can't create it. Also, if you ever want to change the object you created, Architecture constitutes the baseline for changing the object once it is created; that is, it is the baseline for changing the object IF you retain the descriptive representations used in its creation and IF you ensure that the descriptive representations are always maintained consistent with the instantiation.

If the object you are trying to create is so simple that you can see it in its entirety at a glance and remember how all of its components fit together at excruciating level of detail all at one time, you don't need Architecture. You can "wing it" and see if it works. It is only when the object you are trying to create is complex to the extent that you can't see and remember all the details of the implementation at once, and only when you want to accommodate ongoing change to the instantiated object, that Architecture is IMPERATIVE. Once again, without Architecture, you are not going to be able to create an object of any complexity and you won't be able to change it (that is, change it in minimum time, with minimum disruption and minimum cost).

So, the question is, what constitutes the set of descriptive representations relevant for describing an object such that you can create it and change it with minimum time, disruption, and cost?

The answer lies in several hundred years of empirical experience learning how to create and change complex industrial products.

There is a universal[6] set of descriptive representations for describing any or all industrial products. The sets of descriptions include:

Bills of Material	(What)
Functional Specs	(How)
Drawings	(Where)
Operating Instructions	(Who)
Timing Diagrams	(When)
Design Objectives	(Why)

I have labeled these sets of descriptions "Abstractions" in the sense that out of the total set of relevant descriptive characteristics of the object, we "abstract" one of them at a time for producing a formal, explicit description.[7] The Abstractions are universal in the sense that they are common to all industrial products as illustrated below:

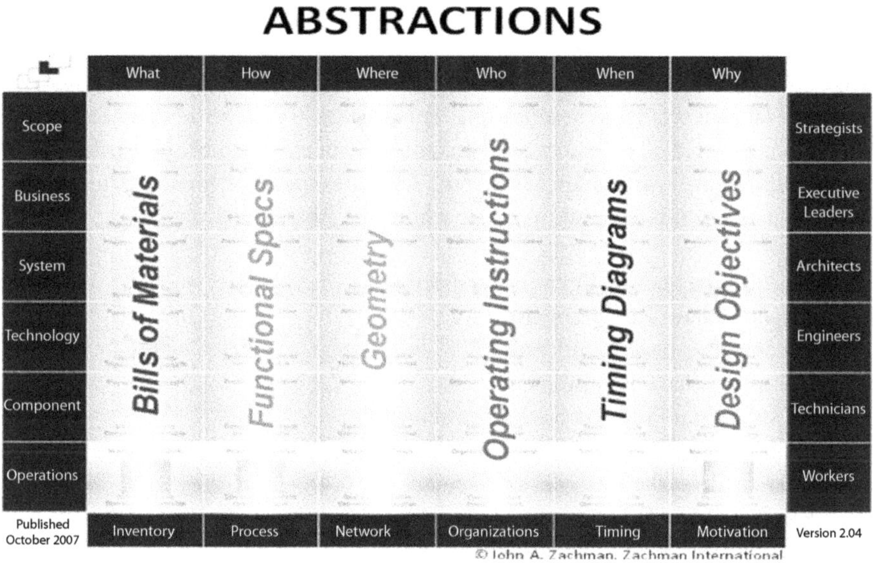

ABSTRACTIONS

FIGURE 2.2   Zachman Framework "Abstractions"

e.g., the Material Abstraction (What it's made of)
  Airplanes have Bills of Material.
  Locomotives have Bills of Material.
  Computers have Bills of Material.
  All Industrial Products have Bills of Material.

e.g., the Functionality Abstraction (How it works)
  Airplanes have Functional Specs.
  Locomotives have Functional Specs.
  Computers have Functional Specs.
  All Industrial Products have Functional Specs.

e.g., the Geometry Abstraction (Where the components are)
  Airplanes have drawings.
  And so on … and so on … and so on.

  By the same token, all industrial products have:

Scoping Boundaries	(Strategists)
Requirements (Concepts)	(Owners)
Schematics (Engineering descriptions)	(Designers)
Blueprints (Manufacturing Engineering descriptions)	(Builders)

Tooling Configurations   (Implementers)
Implementation Instances   (Operators)

I have labeled this set of descriptions "Perspectives" in the sense that each of the Abstractions is created uniquely for different audiences.[8] Each of the Abstractions has five different, I say again, "different" manifestations, depending upon the Perspective of the intended audience for whom the Abstraction is created.

e.g., Requirements (the Owner's Perspective)
    Airplanes have Requirements.
    Locomotives have Requirements.
    Computers have Requirements.
    All Industrial Products have Requirements.

e.g., Schematics (the Designer's Perspective)
    Airplanes have Schematics.
    Locomotives have Schematics.
    Computers have Schematics.
    All Industrial Products have Schematics.

e.g., Blueprints (the Builder's Perspective)
    Airplanes have Blueprints.
    And so on … and so on … and so on.

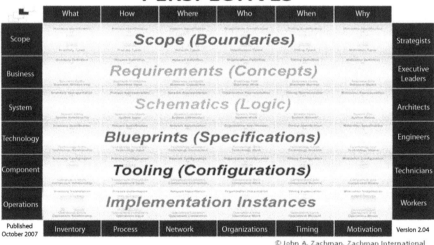

FIGURE 2.3   Zachman Framework "Perspectives"

Why would anyone think that the descriptive representations for enterprises are going to be any different from the descriptive representations of anything else that has ever been created?

In fact, we, the ENTERPRISE Engineering and Manufacturing community (of which I/S is a part), have been reinventing the same descriptive representations that have already been invented by the older disciplines of Engineering/Manufacturing and Architecture/Construction, only we are putting our own names on them.

Here are the Enterprise equivalent descriptive representations:

e.g., Enterprise Descriptive Equivalents of Abstractions
Semantic Structures equal Bills of Material (Semantic Models ARE Bills of Material) Process Models (or better, "Transformation" Models) equal Functional Specs Distribution Models (Geography) equal Geometry (Drawings) Work Flow models equal Operating Instructions Dynamics Models or "Control Structures" (or better, "Timing" Models) equal Timing Diagrams Design Objectives equal Design Objectives.

By the same token:

e.g., Enterprise Descriptive Equivalents of Perspectives
Scoping Models equal Scope Boundaries (CONOPS or Concepts Packages) Models of the Business (Concepts) equal Requirements Models of the Systems (Logic) equal Schematics (Engineering Descriptions) Technology Models (Technology Constrained Models) equal Blueprints.

(Manufacturing Engineering Descriptions) Tooling Configurations equal Tooling Configurations and the Enterprise implementation equals the Industrial Engineering Product instantiation.

Therefore, ENTERPRISE ARCHITECTURE[9] is the total set of intersections between the Abstractions and the Perspectives, which constitute the total set of descriptive representations relevant for describing an Enterprise.

This is the same total set of descriptive representations relevant for describing airplanes, locomotives, buildings, computers, all industrial products. I simply put the Enterprise names on the descriptive representations because I was interested in engineering and manufacturing Enterprises.

The Framework for Enterprise Architecture (the "Zachman Framework") is simply a schema, a classification scheme for descriptive representations of anything (I put Enterprise names on the descriptions and their contents—the metamodel) such that the schema is "normalized"; that is, no one (meta) fact can show up in more than one Cell.

The ENTERPRISE itself is the implementation, the instantiation, the End Result of doing Enterprise Architecture, assuming that any Enterprise Architecture

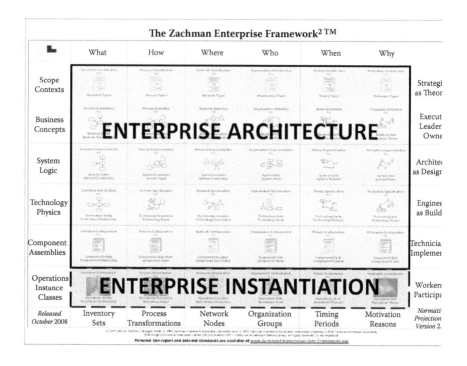

FIGURE 2.4 Architecture versus Instantiation.

has been done. I would observe that over the period of the Industrial Age until now, all airplanes, all locomotives, all buildings, all industrial products have been Architected. However few (if any) Enterprises have been Architected. Up until now, Enterprises have simply happened ... somehow. There may be many systems implementations, manual systems and/or automated systems, material-handling systems (blue-collar systems) and/or record-keeping systems (white-collar systems), a LOT of incoherence and discontinuity (ineffectiveness) and a LOT of compensation for that discontinuity (entropy, inefficiency). There is no Architecture. There are no "Primitive"[10] Models. There is no baseline for managing change. No Enterprise engineering has been done. Enterprise parts have been manufactured ... but the Enterprise parts are not fitting together.

I predict that over the period of the Information Age, the next one or maybe two hundred years, all Enterprises will be Architected. The same factors that drove the formalization of Architecture for industrial products in the Industrial Age will drive the formalization of Architecture for Enterprises in the Information Age: Complexity and Change. We are already beginning to see the trend.

My observation is, Architecture is Architecture is Architecture. What Architecture is, is not arbitrary and it is not negotiable. Architecture is the total set of intersections between the Abstractions and the Perspectives that constitute the set of relevant descriptive representations for any object to be created.

If you cannot show me the Bill of Materials quite independent from Functional Specs quite independent from Geometry quite independent from Operating Instructions … etc., etc. …

And if you cannot show me Requirements quite independent from Schematics quite independent from Blueprints quite independent from Tooling Configurations … etc. … etc. …

Then, I do not believe you are doing Architecture work (Engineering). A single variable model, that is, one Abstraction by one Perspective, a "Primitive" model, is the raw material for doing Engineering. If you have no "Primitive" models, you have no raw material for doing Engineering and therefore, you are not doing Engineering (that is, you are not doing "Architecture").

In contrast, implementations, that is Manufacturing, the creation of the end results, are the instantiation of composite, multivariable models, that is, models comprised of more than one Abstraction and/or more than one Perspective. A manufactured part (Material) has some Functionality in some Geometric location for some Operation at some Time for some Objective. An instantiation, by definition, is a "Composite."[11]

The question turns out to be, how did you create the composite, implementation instance? From Primitive models you have engineered from the perspective of the Enterprise? (Architected?) Or, did you simply create the Composite to produce an implementation ad hoc to whatever you were implementing (i.e., it was implemented, but NOT architected—i.e., NO Primitives)? And … is the Composite you created the whole complete object you are trying to create (the whole airplane or whole locomotive or whole Enterprise) or is the composite just a part of the whole thing (a wing or a boiler or a "system")?

Once again, if you cannot show me "Primitive" models, I know that you are not doing Architecture (Engineering). You are doing implementations (Manufacturing). And, if you are not creating "Enterprise-wide" Primitives, I know you are risking creating implementations that will not integrate into the Enterprise as a whole. You can manufacture parts of the whole iteratively and incrementally … however, they must be engineered to fit together or they are not likely to fit together (be integrated). You can even do the engineering, the Architecture, iteratively and incrementally, but in this case you must do something over and above building incremental, iterative primitives to mitigate the risk of misalignment and disintegration. Enterprise-wide integration and alignment do not happen by accident. They must be engineered (Architected).

If one thinks that an implementation, a result, a Composite model is Architecture (whether it is the whole thing or only a part of the whole thing), then this is probably contributing to the misconception that, for example, the Roman Coliseum is Architecture.

The whole finished product, the end result, is the total agglomerate instantiated Composite of all the Abstractions and all the Perspectives. If one's perception is that the end result is Architecture, there is little wonder why Enterprise Architecture, that is, ENTERPRISE ARCHITECTURE (as in Enterprise-WIDE Architecture), is perceived to be big, monolithic, static, inflexible, unrealistic, impossible, and generally unachievable, therefore creating a DIS-incentive for even attempting Enterprise Architecture.

NO!!!!! Implementations are not enterprise architecture!!! Implementations are the result of architecture … if any architecture has even been done!!!

If we ever want the Enterprise to be engineered so it is "lean and mean," so that it meets all the requirements of the "Owners," so that it is completely effective and efficient, so that it is integrated, so that it is dynamic, so that we can create new instances (implementations) on demand by assembling them to order from the Primitive constructs we already have in inventory, that is, so that we can "assemble the Enterprise to order" (in Manufacturing, "mass customization"), we have to start working on the raw material for doing Engineering, the single variable, "Primitive" models … ARCHITECTURE.

The manufactured RESULT (NOT the Architecture).

YES!! … we will have to continue to satisfy current demand for implementations by building Composite implementation constructs in the short term. BUT, as we get some Primitives engineered (Architected) and into inventory, we can stipulate that any Composite models to be constructed MUST be constructed from the components of the architected Primitives we already have in inventory. In that fashion, over some period of time, we could migrate (maybe "evolve") out of the disintegrated, discontinuous, inflexible legacy environment into an Architected, coherent, flexible, dynamic, optimized Enterprise.

We likely could achieve the quality and longevity ascribed to Boeing 747s or hundred-story buildings or other high-quality, long-lasting, superior-performing Industrial Age, complex engineering products that we have learned how to engineer over the last few hundred years.

Otherwise, nothing will have changed … we will just continue doing more of the same … building and running systems (legacy implementations, manual or automated, blue-collar or white-collar) and it doesn't make any difference what technologies we will be using. It is not a technical issue. It is an ENGINEERING issue, an ENTERPRISE engineering issue.

Are we going to start doing Enterprise engineering work (building Primitive models, i.e., Architecture) … or are we simply going to continue doing Enterprise manufacturing (building composite implementations, i.e., building and running systems)?

I would observe that it was Einstein who said something like, "Keeping on doing the same thing and expecting different results is one definition of insanity."

An earlier version of this article appeared as John Zachman (2007), "Architecture Is Architecture Is Architecture," *EIMInsight Magazine*, Volume 1, Issue 1—March, online at http://www.eiminstitute.org/library/eimi-archives/volume-1-issue-1-march-2007-edition/architecture-is-architecture-is-architecture, 5 January 2008.

Notes

6. The names of these descriptive representations may change slightly based on industry but the concepts represented are consistent. Furthermore, in some industries for some products, they may well be willing to assume the risks of not formalizing all of the relevant descriptive representations.

7. For an exhaustive discussion of "Abstractions," see "The Zachman Framework: A Primer for Enterprise Engineering and Manufacturing." www.ZachmanInternational.com. 2003.

8. For an exhaustive discussion of "Perspectives," see "The Zachman Framework: A Primer for Enterprise Engineering and Manufacturing." www.ZachmanInternational.com. 2003.

9. For an exhaustive discussion of "Enterprise Architecture," see "The Zachman Framework: A Primer for Enterprise Engineering and Manufacturing." www.ZachmanInternational.com. 2003.

10. For an exhaustive discussion of "Primitive Models," see "The Zachman Framework: A Primer for Enterprise Engineering and Manufacturing." www.ZachmanInternational.com. 2003. (Also see Glossary in Chapter 5, *Ed.*)

11. For an exhaustive discussion of "Composite Models," see "The Zachman Framework: A Primer for Enterprise Engineering and Manufacturing." www.ZachmanInternational.com. 2003.

Why Enterprise Architecture Matters: Surfing the Waves

Bruce V. Ballengee

Enterprise architecture has many meanings, depending upon one's perspective. However, its penultimate purpose converges around enabling alignment at several levels regardless of meaning.

Consider IT, the business, and its customers and suppliers, as they relate to each other within a value chain. Visualize them as nested waves moving through an economic sea (see Figure 2.5). The business is the enterprise itself. It has an architecture (people, structure, process, and technology) that attempts to deliver on a strategy to deliver value within its value chain. Customers and suppliers are the immediate links in the value chain that tie the business into their industry and the overall economy. The IT organization resides within the business and has its own value chain of customers (executives and organizations) and suppliers (technology products and services).

The business is part of the larger economy and its industry and integrated to them through its value chain. When the economy, industry, customers, and suppliers move, the business moves, typically with a lag effect. The business faces a highly unpredictable world where the most dramatic changes often come from the most unexpected places. It behaves like a wave within a sea of economic and technological change. The impact of economic forces is dramatic. Anita McGahan and Michael Porter showed that 68 percent of business performance was caused by forces outside the business or could not be explained.[12]

We have also seen technology tear apart existing value chains. In this decade of post–Internet bubble collapse, we have seen the music industry turned upside down by Internet download business models. We have also witnessed the emergence of

Customers & Suppliers – Industry & Economy

Business – Executives & Organizations

IT – People & Technologies

FIGURE 2.5 The waves of business.

new business models for movie delivery leveraging the Internet, in the ongoing battle between Netflix and Blockbuster. The potential future disruptive force of information technology on the global economy should not be underestimated. Ted Lewis of the Postgraduate Naval Institute projected Moore's Law, showing that only about 40 percent of computing hardware potential would be achieved by 2005.[13]

IT is part of the business. It forms its own wave and reacts primarily to changes in the business and secondarily to changes in the larger economy. While it may seem predictable on its surface (e.g., the IT plan as it supports the business plan), it is not. It is actually more opaque. It is harder for IT to track the movement of the larger wave because it is somewhat insulated inside that of the business.

The effect of all this motion is to send IT, business, and customers and suppliers off in different directions (see Figure 2.6).

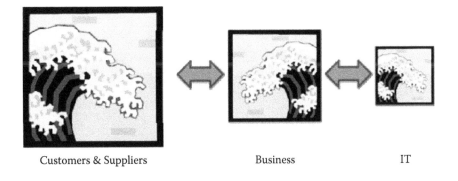

| Customers & Suppliers | Business | IT |

FIGURE 2.6 The waves decomposed as the wobble.

The business often moves counter to customers and suppliers. Implementing a new distribution channel, making a strategic acquisition, or introducing a new product or service can represent changes in direction. To the extent such changes align or integrate across the larger value chain, the business will be successful. If the gaps between customers or suppliers widen, then the odds of failure rise dramatically.

As the waves move in different directions, the desires of the business and its demands on IT also change. For example, the new customer that was going to require a higher level of service integration has just been acquired by one of its competitors that has an exclusive long-term relationship with the business's competitor, so IT no longer has Project X as priority one. In fact, IT needs to stop immediately and work on Project Z to catch up with the competitor that wound up winning the customer. This sort of event happens every moment in the business world. The cumulative effect of all these events causes the waves to move to and fro. They wobble. Often IT winds up engulfed by the tides of business.

In IT, this wobble is most often called the IT-business alignment problem (see Figure 2.7). The key to success of the business is to stay, relatively speaking, in competitive alignment within its value stream between its customers and suppliers. It is ever planning offensive and reactive moves to maintain balance. While never stable, it tends to wobble back and forth between equilibriums. At the lowest level of granularity, it is typically at its most stable. The higher up one moves, for example, at the enterprise level, the further apart the business will be between its customers and suppliers. Consider the following example. Product A has been the business's mainstay offering for years, has relatively modest growth, which tracks the industry cycle, and has become a cash cow. It is relatively closely aligned with customers' current needs. However, as customers' strategies change, this product will come under increasing risk of falling sales and decreasing relevance if the business does not adapt its strategy to that of its customers.

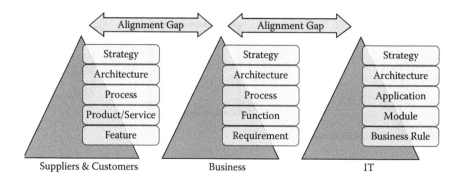

FIGURE 2.7 The wobble modeled as the alignment problem.

IT faces a similar challenge within the business itself. That legacy application has wonderfully rich business rules that support the current business function quite adequately, but as the business strategy moves forward, entirely new applications are needed that share much of the same information and business rules. This growing alignment gap eventually forces IT to play catch-up and replace applications and adopt entirely new architectures that work with newer technologies as well. The only point of stasis is if the business ceases to exist. Success or failure of IT is measured against how well it can maintain and close existing and emerging alignment gaps between itself and the business.

Enterprise architecture is a way of thinking about and addressing the problem of alignment and a set of people, structures, and processes along with sets of tools and techniques. Remember the waves of business and visualize the enterprise architect as a surfing among them (see Figure 2.8).

This is where enterprise architecture proves its value to IT and the business. Understanding it as a way of thinking illustrates how it delivers value. It is the enterprise architecture person's act of balancing (countering wobble with wobble) on the board (structure, process, tools, techniques, etc.) to ride the waves of change that creates value. There are two different kinds of values from successful enterprise architecture endeavors to consider, the outcomes, or deliverables, from the learning process itself and those from engaging in the activity as a continuous learning process for the business and IT.

FIGURE 2.8　The enterprise architect.

When most practitioners discuss enterprise architecture, they talk about its deliverables. Some examples include business systems plans, application portfolio assessments, IT principles and standards, system or application migration plans, business process analysis, etc. There is a potentially long list of outcomes depending upon which level of alignment gap the enterprise architect is focused on closing in a particular domain or problem space.

Of greatest value are the broad-ranging benefits of practicing enterprise architecture as a way of thinking throughout the enterprise, and not just in IT.

- *Knowledge of the business, its value chain, and how value is created.* By studying the business inside and outside the enterprise, IT increases its business acumen, its grasp of business jargon, and where the opportunities and problems truly lie. To the extent IT can bring a different perspective to these situations, the business can benefit from a fresh approach and improve its understanding through the process of educating IT in the nuances of the business.
- *Understanding of how information technologies can be applied throughout the value chain.* Taking the knowledge of opportunities and problems to the next level, IT can look for potential applications of information technology and the business can learn more readily about the limits and risks of applying information technology to a particular business problem.
- *Communication between IT and the business using a commonly understood language.* Through the aforementioned practices, IT and business converge on a common set of models, principles, frameworks, and jargon that facilitate clear and consistent communication between them. As a consequence, not only are interactions more effective, business-IT alignment gaps are narrower and less likely to drift wider.
- *Awareness of potentially disruptive information technologies impacting the business itself, its customers or suppliers.* Beyond the tactical application of established information technologies lies the unpredictable future of what information technologies may emerge in other parts of the business value chain. Ongoing business-IT dialogue, whether in formal scenario-planning sessions or one-on-one over lunch, coffee, or that "got a minute?" after-hours conversation before calling it a day, is perhaps the ultimate, priceless value enterprise architecture can offer.

As a result of the aforementioned, IT can establish a relationship with the business based on trust and respect beyond effective project delivery and keeping the lights on. Trusted relationships are the most direct means of maintaining the alignment wobble between IT and the business on a day-to-day basis. This is also the path to alignment between IT and business at the strategic level—when the business and IT organizations work in harmony on a broader basis. And to the extent information technology continues to advance and impact the business, also offers the business increased alignment with its customers and suppliers.

Between process and outcomes, the benefits of process offer the greatest long-term sustained strategic value over the entire enterprise. Implemented even on a small scale, they can begin to close the cultural and knowledge gaps between IT and the business quite quickly. However, both ultimately depend on the ability of IT to execute effectively to secure the respect and trust of the business.

Notes

12. McGahan, Anita, and Michael E. Porter, 1997. How Much Does Industry Matter Really?, *Strategic Management Journal* (18), 15–30.
13. Lewis, Ted, 1996. Surviving in the Software Economy, *Upside* (March 1996); 67–78.

To Be or Not to Be: Recognize Enterprise Architecture as a True Profession?

Mark Lane

This article explores the professionalization of enterprise architecture (EA), why it matters and what it means. We pinpoint the current state of affairs in EA and set a course for future work on its value proposition in society as well as its organizational role. The target audiences are academics, government agencies, practicing enterprise architects, professional societies, potential employers, and general consumers of EA capabilities. The paper is not intended as an in-depth comparison of professional organizations, and an examination of their professional education, training, and certification programs is beyond the scope of this article.

The Importance of Enterprise Architecture Professionalism

The Current State

There is much uncertainty today with regard to EA professionalization, making it very difficult for an individual architect to set and follow a career path across organizations in a way that other professions take for granted. The current state of the EA profession is progressing slowly. Some practitioners are disappointed to see EA in the state it's in—this is a call to arms for all stakeholders. Every organization has enterprise architecture activities (whether recognized as such or not), yet the enterprise architecture profession does not have a shared set of roles, skills, and functions.

What are the issues and what can we do to fix them?

The legitimacy and formalization of EA is not consistent across organizations. EA is many times constrained by political, cultural, and social elements instead of professional status. EA does not have professional autonomy as found in the medicine, law, engineering, or accounting professions. There is a lack of attention and focus paid to sustained legitimacy and a clear direction in pursuit of professionalism.

The current state of marketing EA is a debacle, notwithstanding the valiant attempts made by its proponents to position it within industry. Indeed, EA has an identity crisis. No consistent branding exists that is grounded in answers to the tough questions: Why do I need EA? Why should I care? What value does EA bring?

Branding issues are compounded by deficient industry convergence. There is no clear branding on a consistent set of architect capabilities or a clear differentiator. The critical importance of EA is not yet seen. Paul Preiss, president and founder of the International Association of Software Architects (IASA), opined that few other professions have the impact that IT architecture has on health and human safety, cultural issues and corporate fiscal interests.[14] And software architecture is only a small part of the architecture of an entire enterprise.

Roles, skills, and functions are not consistent across the industry or within organizations. Filling the gap between the "what is" and "does what" will go a long way toward branding and differentiation between groups of architects and other professions. It's time to ask yourself, "What can I do to contribute to the advancement of EA? How can I give back so that future generations will benefit from my experience and knowledge and wisdom?"

EA has done little to justify its value proposition. How the public perceives EA is a key. Answers must be developed to questions like: How do we clarify in the public eye as to what a professional does? How do we gain the public's trust as a profession? How do we assure the public they are dealing with a competent professional?

Without authoritative answers to these questions, EA cannot develop and progress across the continuum toward professionalization.

The Future Vision

The aspiring professional first undertakes education (the education that precedes the first day on the job, usually provided by a university). The quality of a professional degree program is assured by accreditation. To become a professional, the individual must develop skill in the application (through university co-op programs, on-the-job training, apprenticeships, internships, or other means). Certification and/or licensing assure the competence of the individual to enter professional practice. Throughout practice, there are periods of professional development, possibly resulting in recertification or relicensing. The profession assures that its practitioners behave in a responsible manner through a code of ethics. A professional society helps assure that all other components interact appropriately.[15]

EA professionalism must consider the following virtues and values as described by the International Federation for Information Processing:[16]

1. **Competences:** comprised of knowledge, technical and soft skills, capabilities, and experience in both technical and business domains; professional profiles should be based on a common competence standard and be recognizable by employers.
2. **Integrity:** including a commitment to an adopted code of conduct, including ethical standards.
3. **Responsibility and Accountability:** instilling the professional with responsibility for the consequences of their decisions and judgments, and with the duty to explain their reasoning.
4. **Public Obligation:** requiring that the professional works in the best interest of society and uses his or her knowledge, skills, ability, and experience to apply the practice for the public good.

Cultural differences across the globe impact jurisprudence and the approach to professions. These differences translate into more than one approach; for instance, some countries traditionally support the legal relevance of qualifications and set qualifying state exams as a requirement to access some professions, whereas other countries have a tradition based on the acquisition of knowledge through experience, on continuous professional development, or recognition by authoritative nongovernmental bodies.

Some practitioners do not see a need to professionalize EA as rigorously as medicine, law, engineering, or accounting. Other camps are in favor of professionalization to the fullest extent. The debate continues over the need to position EA as a legally recognized profession or generally accepted profession.

■ If EA is to be a legally recognized profession, it will be impacted by:
  – Government certification
  – Licensed by state or by "law"
  – State board and society group requirements
■ If EA is to be a generally accepted profession, it sets its own standards and governs itself at a minimum by the four E's:
  – Education
  – Examination
  – Ethics
  – Experience

Interactions between the preceding components are more complex than might be inferred. For example, the requirements for professional licensing can have a significant effect on the content of initial education. A professional society may manage the certification process or develop the code of ethics. Certification guidelines can influence the content of professional development.[17]

In either case (legally or generally accepted), there are common traits shared by both types of professional status:

- A body of knowledge rested on well-developed and widely accepted theoretical and practical base.
- A system for certifying that individuals posses such knowledge before practice.
- A system of certifying who possesses both knowledge and the experience to practice effectively.
- A commitment to use specialized knowledge for public good.
- A code of ethics, with provisions for monitoring individual compliance.

Certification and Accreditation: The future of EA is based on one significant belief: certification is more desirable than licensing. There will be growing demands for safety and security. If the profession does not provide effective mechanisms such as certification and accreditation to assure that its practitioners are doing everything possible to promote safety and security, then in the future government may perhaps eventually try to do it with licensing.[18]

The creation of profession, equivalent in prestige and structure to other established professions such as medicine, law, engineering, and accounting, will have at least these basic characteristics:

- Focused on improving the ability of business and other organizations to exploit the potential of EA effectively and consistently.
- Respected by its stakeholders—including employees, employers, customers, governments, and key bodies.
- A source of real pride and aspiration for practitioners.

Within a professional structure, there must be the creation of a professional certification and accreditation schema, recognized and trusted globally as representing the hallmark of a true professional practitioner of enterprise architecture. These certifications will be available to suitably qualified professionals and should be supported by development frameworks for both individuals and organizations. The key features of such a certification would be:[19]

- Vendor agnostic (independent of special interest).
- Operated by accredited professional member.
- Available and assessable to all individuals that meet professional requirements.
- Based on consistent globally recognized standards.

■ Built around a requirement for complete professional formation—including relevant knowledge, experience, competence, and commitment to a code of professional ethics.

■ Maintenance of a program of continuing professional education and development.

■ Supported by a disciplinary body with a process for public complaint and sanctions where appropriate.

While certifications provide valuable markers against capabilities and the path to full professionalism, it is equally important to provide the resources that support development of knowledge, skills, competence, and best professional practice for both individual practitioners and their employer organizations at all stages of that journey. The establishment of common certification guidelines for EA should follow sound recommendations such as:[20,21]

1. The profession should be founded on the essential elements of principles and values for the EA profession.

2. Assessment of competence should combine technical and nontechnical competences including communication and interpersonal skills, domain or business knowledge, and managerial culture.

3. The assessment of competences should take into account certificates, both vendor-neutral and as delivered by industry and the qualifications from formal education.

4. The purpose of the profession is equally to recognize professionalism itself and to support both individuals and organizations to develop that professionalism.

5. In structuring the profession, provision should be made for the recognition of an appropriate number of profiles at different levels, and there should be clear paths of entry and career progression to accommodate individuals from the widest possible academic and experience backgrounds.

Globalization and the Profession: Given recognition of a global profession, professionals must have clear standards that accommodate cultural differences in the regulation of professions, enhanced by strengthened competence requirements. Much can be learned from the International Federation for Information Processing and the American Medical Association. Given the ubiquitous role of EA, a wide range of individuals and organizations have a stake in the profession. Primary stakeholders are professionals and their employers. It is important to be recognized as an independent and individual-based profession where professionals are recognized universally without discrimination, an inclusive approach to the definition and measurement of competences. The practice and portability of professional skills are similar across diverse business environments, as well as cultural and geographical boundaries, and require a comprehensive vision along with a flexible approach. The model must be an inclusive one (e.g., of individual practitioners).[22]

Challenge: Delivering the Vision

As John Zachman recently said, "We need to get professional" (see Figure 2.9). The aim is to embrace and recognize existing capabilities, strengthening and augmenting existing certification schemes by giving them a broader professional context and coherence, and generally promoting the value of standards, certifications, and accreditations. The overriding aim is to develop, and to give recognition to individual practitioners and to employers who are ethical, experienced, and competent, and can be relied upon to form sound judgments and to make rational and principled decisions—qualities and capabilities that are especially important in our fast-moving business and rapidly changing world.

The profession reflected in the vision is one that has an extensive range of skills, encompassing not only the essential architectural practices but also the key business-focused skills that ensure real business benefit. This is depicted in

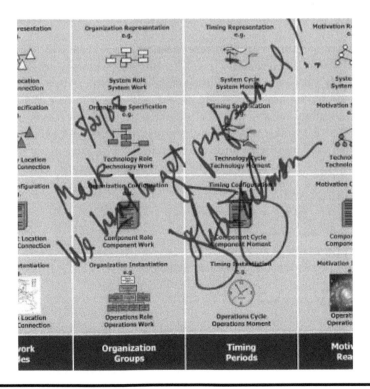

FIGURE 2.9   Zachman note to Lane (21 May 2008).

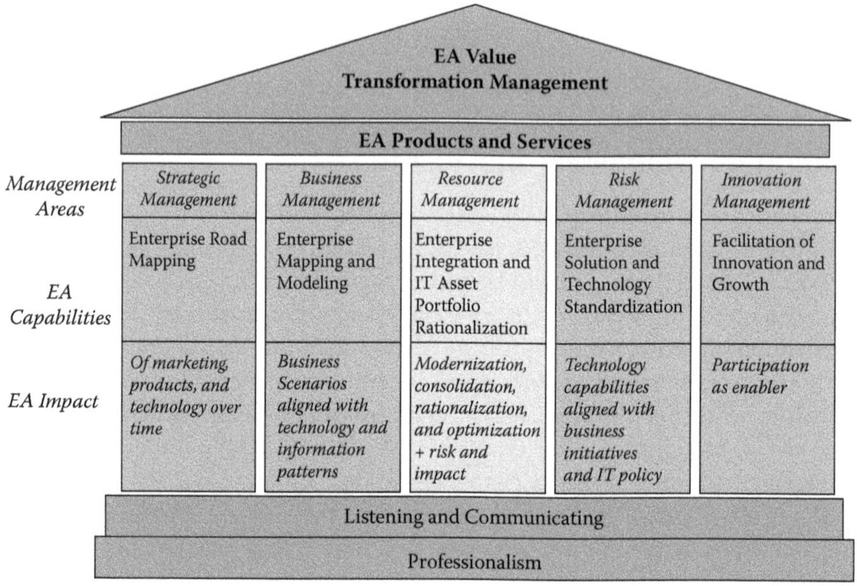
EA Value
Transformation Management
EA Products and Services
Management Areas
Strategic Management
Business Management
Resource Management
Risk Management
Innovation Management
EA Capabilities
Enterprise Road Mapping
Enterprise Mapping and Modeling
Enterprise Integration and IT Asset Portfolio Rationalization
Enterprise Solution and Technology Standardization
Facilitation of Innovation and Growth
EA Impact
Of marketing, products, and technology over time
Business Scenarios aligned with technology and information patterns
Modernization, consolidation, rationalization, and optimization + risk and impact
Technology capabilities aligned with business initiatives and IT policy
Participation as enabler
Listening and Communicating
Professionalism

FIGURE 2.10 EA management capabilities: The pillars of EA value creation.

Figure 2.10. In addition to architecture practices, a vital role will be played by broader skills such as in the area of business technology strategy, leadership, and the perennially important communication, collaboration, and coordination. A foundation of practices is today being defined and practiced by many business, information, application, and technical architects. It is only because of those base disciplines that EA is able to leverage the success of others and pave the way to a new frontier of enterprise architecture capabilities. It is particularly important that recognition be given to the growing importance of enterprise architects' primary capabilities and their relationship to the profession and to value creation for the enterprise:

- Enterprise road mapping
- Enterprise mapping and modeling
- Enterprise solution and technology standardization
- Enterprise integration and portfolio rationalization
- Facilitating innovation

Figure 2.10 indicates that that organizations that utilize professional enterprise architects can leverage EA capabilities as an enabler of continuous transformation and value creation, to lead change, manage complexity, and deliver organizational efficiency and effectiveness. Through the maturation and professionalization of EA and these EA management capabilities, organizations will realize EA not solely as a method for managing technology but as a management capability for strategic and tactical planning, control, operations, and transformation.

A Call to Action

The path forward requires the establishment of guiding principles for enterprise architecture professional practices such as:

1. An enterprise architecture is by definition about the whole enterprise.
2. An enterprise architecture exists in every enterprise whether explicit or implicit.
3. If explicit, it should contain a description for at least the current state "as is," a future state "to be," and a road map "transition plan."
4. The combination of these three encapsulates the description for the vision of the enterprise and is the plan of the enterprise.
5. The practice of enterprise architecture minimally follows a path of contextual-conceptual-logical-physical, with each being termed as views.
6. The enterprise architecture is constructed from different concerns that address interrogatives for domains called perspectives.
7. A minimal set of perspectives are the business, its technologies, knowledge, and capabilities.

Specific activities are also needed in areas such as:

■ Promote the art and science of EA by uniting like-minded individuals who support the legitimacy of the enterprise architecture profession.
■ Identify and establish a body of ethics, principles, and maturity measures that convey a consistent message about the enterprise architecture profession and its practice.
■ Develop and certify a body of knowledge that properly represents the enterprise architecture profession and its practice.
■ Improve the practice of enterprise architecture such that its practitioners are widely recognized as professionals.
■ Develop and evangelize EA professionalization maturity models.
  - The EA profession maturity model
  - The EA professionals (people) maturity model
  - The EA body of knowledge maturity model
  - The EA professional practice (activities) maturity model

■ Develop industry focus groups of relevant professionals and organizations to discuss maturity models and the potential:

- Cross-cutting plan for skills development and professional development from professional societies
■ Cross-cutting plan for professional education curricula and accreditation

Perhaps no human artifact is more important to the survival of the species than the organization or enterprise. Nearly everything humans do together is done in the context of some kind of enterprise—families, businesses, governments, social groups, educational institutions, military organizations, charities, and so on. Relatively small, static, or simple enterprises in general may not require an explicit enterprise architecture. But most enterprises of consequence are large, dynamic, complicated, and important. Random, organic, component-focused growth and management are no longer viable options for enterprise management. The current global economic situation is strong evidence of this. Enterprises must be architected and managed by that architecture if they are to remain viable in the Information Age. A viable EA profession is needed to make that happen.

Notes

14. "Architecture Journal Profile: Paul Preiss," 2008. *The Architecture Journal,* 15, 10–12.
15. Gary Ford, and Norman E. Gibbs, 1996. *A Mature Profession of Software Engineering,* Technical Report CMU/SEI-96-TR-004 ESC-TR-96-004, January 1996 http://www.sei.cmu.edu/pub/documents/96.reports/pdf/tr004.96.pdf.
16. International Federation for Information Processing (IFIP), *WCC 2008 Declaration on ICT Professionalism and Competences,* the 20th World Computer Congress (WCC 2008), September 2008, Milan, Italy.
17. Ford & Gibbs, 1996.
18. Ford & Gibbs, 1996.
19. IFIP, 2008.
20. IFIP, 2008.
21. The British Computer Society, 2007. *The International IT Professional Practice Programme,* http://www.bcs.org/.
22. IFIP, 2008.

John Zachman's Concise Definition of the Zachman Framework

John A. Zachman

The Zachman Framework is a schema—the intersection between two historical classifications that have been in use by humanity for literally thousands of years. The first is the fundamentals of communication found in the primitive interrogatives: what, how, where, who, when, and why. It is the integration of answers to these questions that enables the comprehensive, composite description of complex ideas. The second is derived from reification, the transformation of an abstract idea into an instantiation that was initially postulated by Aristotle and is labeled in the Zachman Framework: Identification, Definition, Representation, Specification, Configuration, and Instantiation.

Since the Zachman Framework classification was observed empirically in the structure of the descriptive representations (that is, "architecture") of buildings, airplanes, and other complex industrial products, there is substantial evidence to establish that the Framework *is* the fundamental structure for *Enterprise* Architecture and thereby yields the total set of descriptive representations relevant for describing an Enterprise.

The Zachman Framework typically is depicted as a bounded 6 × 6 "matrix" with the Communication Interrogatives as columns and the Reification Transformations as rows. The Framework classifications are represented by the cells, that is, the intersection between the Interrogatives and the Transformations. This would necessarily constitute the total set of descriptive representations that are relevant for describing something … anything, in particular, an enterprise.

The graphic depiction of the Framework for Enterprise Architecture can be downloaded from the website http://www.zachmaninternational.com with reference links to publications and the Zachman Framework[2] standards, terms, and graphics.

More specifically, the Zachman Framework is an ontology—a theory of the existence of a structured set of essential components of an object for which explicit expression is necessary, and perhaps even mandatory for creating, operating, and changing the object (the object being an enterprise, a department, a value chain, a "sliver," a solution, a project, an airplane, a building, a product, a profession, or whatever).

The Zachman Framework IS NOT a methodology for creating the implementation (an instantiation) of the object. The Zachman Framework IS the ontology for describing an enterprise.

The Framework (ontology) is a STRUCTURE. A methodology is a PROCESS. A Structure is NOT a Process. A Structure establishes definition. A Process provides Transformation. Processes based on ontological structure will be predictable and produce repeatable results (for example, Chemistry, based on the periodic table). Conversely, Processes without ontological structures are ad hoc, fixed, and dependent on practitioner skills (for example, Alchemy, based on trial and error).

The Zachman Framework is a metamodel and, unlike a methodology, does not imply anything about:

1. Whether you do Architecture or whether you simply build implementations; that is, whether you build Primitive Models, the ontological, single-variable intersections between the interrogatives and the Transformations, or whether you simply build ad hoc, multivariable, composite models made up of components of several Primitive Models.
2. How you do Architecture: top-down, bottom-up, left to right, right to left, where to start, etc., etc.
3. The long-term/short-term trade-off relative to instantiating the expression of the components of the object (i.e., what is formalized in the short term for implementation purposes versus what is engineered for long-term reuse).
4. How much flexibility you want for producing composite models (enterprise implementations) from your Enterprise Architecture (primitive models), that is, how constrained (little flexibility, e.g., 1:1) or unconstrained (much flexibility, e.g., m:n) you make the horizontal, integrative relationships between the cell components across the rows and the vertical, transformational relationships of the cell components down the columns.

Although these are significant, identifiable, methodological choices, they are not prescriptions implied or required by the Framework structure.

The Zachman Framework is the basis for Architecture. We know what architecture is for industrial products (buildings, airplanes, locomotives, computers, etc., etc.) because in the Industrial Age it was the industrial products that were increasing in complexity and the industrial products that were changing. If we had not gotten extremely sophisticated relative to architecture for industrial products, we would not likely be able to create and change complex industrial products, and we would likely still be in the Industrial Age learning about Product Architecture.

Now that we are entering into the Information Age, it is the enterprise that is increasing in complexity and the enterprise that is changing. It is my opinion that Enterprise Architecture is the determinant of survival in the Information Age. Therefore, the Framework for Enterprise Architecture, the "Zachman Framework," has some profound significance in putting definition around Enterprise Architecture, the survival issue of the century. We have yet a LOT to learn about Enterprise Architecture, but I submit that the "Zachman Framework" would be a good place to start (see Figure 2.11).

The Zachman Enterprise Framework² ™

	What	How	Where	Who	When	Why	
Scope Contents	Inventory Identification e.g. Inventory Types	Process Identification e.g. Process Types	Network Identification e.g. Network Types	Organization Identification e.g. Organization Types	Timing Identification e.g. Timing Types	Motivation Identification e.g. Motivation Types	*Strategists as Theorists*
Business Concepts	Inventory Definition e.g. Business Entity Business Relationship	Process Definition e.g. Business Transform Business Input	Network Definition e.g. Business Location Business Connection	Organization Definition e.g. Business Role Business Work	Timing Definition e.g. Business Cycle Business Moment	Motivation Definition e.g. Business End Business Means	*Executive Leaders as Owners*
System Logic	Inventory Representation e.g. System Entity System Relationship	Process Representation e.g. System Transform System Input	Network Representation e.g. System Location System Connection	Organization Representation e.g. System Role System Work	Timing Representation e.g. System Cycle System Moment	Motivation Representation e.g. System End System Means	*Architects as Designers*

	Inventory	Process	Network	Organization	Timing	Motivation	
Technology Physics	Inventory Specification e.g. Technology Entity Technology Relationship	Process Specification e.g. Technology Transform Technology Input	Network Specification e.g. Technology Location Technology Connection	Organization Specification e.g. Technology Role Technology Work	Timing Specification e.g. Technology Cycle Technology Moment	Motivation Specification e.g. Technology End Technology Means	*Engineers as Builders*
Component Assemblies	Inventory Configuration e.g. Component Entity Component Relationship	Process Configuration e.g. Component Transform Component Input	Network Configuration e.g. Component Location Component Connection	Organization Configuration e.g. Component Role Component Work	Timing Configuration e.g. Component Cycle Component Moment	Motivation Configuration e.g. Component End Component Means	*Technicians as Implementers*
Operations Instance Classes	Inventory Instantiation e.g. Operations Entity Operations Relationship	Process Instantiation e.g. Operations Transform Operations Input	Network Instantiation e.g. Operations Location Operations Connection	Organization Instantiation e.g. Operations Role Operations Work	Timing Instantiation e.g. Operations Cycle Operations Moment	Motivation Instantiation e.g. Operations End Operations Means	*Workers as Participants*
Released October 2008	*Inventory Sets*	*Process Transformations*	*Network Nodes*	*Organization Groups*	*Timing Periods*	*Motivation Reasons*	*Normative Projection on Version 2.01*

FIGURE 2.11 **The Zachman Enterprise Framework² ™.** ©1987 John A. Zachman; hexagon model ©1998 Zachman Framework Associates; derivative work ©2002 Zachman Framework Associates; MetaModel Projection ©2008 Zachman Framework Associates. 2009 Single Commercial Publication license 291354 issued to SIM EA Working Group for inclusion in the *SIM Guide to Enterprise Architecture*. All rights reserved. Do not independently reproduce this image.

Personal use copies and detailed standards are available at www.zachmanInternational.com/2/standards.asp.

Framework Standards: What's It All About?

John A. Zachman

Two years ago, some of my friends pressed me intensely to be more definitive about the Framework concepts. Even though, I had written "The Book," they were specifically asking me for definitions of the entities that comprise the meta-model of row 2 of the Enterprise Framework. It has taken me and a team of dedicated folks two years, however we have progressed far beyond the original requirement.

We have produced definitions, not only of the meta-entities of row 2 of the Enterprise Framework, but also we have dictionary definitions of the meta-entities of row 1, row 2, row 3, row 4, row 5, and row 6 of the Enterprise Framework plus dictionary definitions for the Product Framework (where I learned about the Framework classification in the first place), for the Profession Framework (which I used to call the I/S Framework, the "meta-Framework" relative to the Enterprise Framework), and for the Zachman Classification Framework (the Framework classification for all Frameworks).

Reasons for Framework Standards

This work is particularly significant at this point in time for several reasons.

Clarification

Although I first articulated the concepts of the Framework around 1980, almost thirty years ago, and although the concepts have never changed, and although I have written a book and thirty or more substantive articles about the Framework, there still is some confusion as to the specific contents of the models prescribed by the Framework classification. This is likely due to several reasons.

First, Enterprise Architecture constitutes a paradigm shift, and many people have not yet been inclined to make the mental, cultural, and behavioral adjustment to engineering and manufacturing the Enterprise. Second, in some cases we haven't chosen words, or there have not even been English words available, that accurately convey all of the Framework concepts. Third, we have not used common, universally agreed-upon (dictionary) definitions for the words used to express the concepts. Fourth, our understanding of the Framework has been enhanced and refined immeasurably over twenty-five years.

It is only appropriate to review the choice of words to ensure that the concepts are conveyed as accurately and clearly as possible.

Enterprise Orientation as Opposed to Information Systems Orientation

From its inception, the Framework has been a classification of descriptive representations of the Enterprise; that is, all of the descriptive representations embodied in the Framework are descriptive of the ENTERPRISE, not simply descriptive of a limited subset of the Enterprise that is related to Information Systems.

The Enterprise descriptions may or may not have anything to do with information systems technologies, depending upon whether such technologies are used as the "Builder's Constraints" in the row 4 models or not. Unfortunately, around 1980 when I first drew the Framework graphic, the only words I had at my disposal for the Framework concepts were words from my information systems vocabulary. Because of my choice of words and because many of the skills required to do the work of Enterprise Architecture are typically found in the Information Systems community, some people misconstrue the Framework intent as an Information Systems schema rather than its true intent as an ENTERPRISE schema.

In the new Framework Standards we have attempted to select words from an ENTERPRISE, general "business" vocabulary, not an information systems or technical vocabulary, to correctly convey the idea that Enterprise Architecture is an ENTERPRISE issue, not simply an information or technology issue.

The end object is to engineer and manufacture the ENTERPRISE, not simply to build and run systems.

Consistency

There are two dimensions to the consistency issue.

First, there is the universal consistency in the world at large. As global communication and collaboration expands, there is an increasing requirement for semantic coherence. If people's words do not mean the same thing, there is neither communication nor collaboration. It is imperative for any communication or collaboration within or among Enterprises to define Enterprise Architecture consistently. The instances of Architecture expression in different Enterprises may be different, however the underlying classification and components of Architecture must be consistent for any interoperability (internal or external) to be effected.[23]

A second dimension of consistency is that between the "meta" Frameworks of any given Enterprise. The instances of models of one Framework are determined by the Row 2 models of its meta-Framework.[24] Inconsistencies in the meta-structures within an Enterprise would render Enterprise Architecture unmanageable.

Differentiation

Enterprises are complex. Managing the knowledge base of the Enterprise that is required for Enterprise operation and change is complex. The key to managing complexity is classification. The Zachman Framework is a classification system for descriptive representations that constitute the knowledge base of Enterprises. However, each Enterprise potentially has four knowledge bases of importance to them: (a) knowledge about their Product (if a product is produced); (b) knowledge about the Enterprise itself; (c) knowledge about the Professional (likely "indirect," "Staff") community that is engineering (designing) their Enterprise; and (d) knowledge about the classification of knowledge itself.

Although the classification of knowledge (the Zachman Classification system) is the same, the knowledge bases within the Enterprise are different, but related in a deterministic fashion. The impact of inconsistencies between knowledge bases within an Enterprise is amplified (probably) exponentially.[25] The Framework Standards clearly differentiate the three knowledge bases, the Profession Framework, the Enterprise Framework, and the Product Framework, but maintain complete conceptual consistency with knowledge classification itself, the Zachman Classification Framework.

Certification

This may be the most pressing reason for publishing Framework Standards at the present time.

As the Information Age becomes more experientially real, the issues of complexity and change become more urgently confrontational for Enterprises, which intensifies the demand for Architecture. Humanity for seven thousand years has found no mechanism for accommodating complexity and change other than Architecture. Therefore, there presently is an increasing demand for "certified" Enterprise Architects.[26] In fact, if Enterprises are seen to fail because they cannot accommodate complexity and change, and people are forced out of work and pension funds cannot be sustained, there might even be regulatory action requiring certification of Enterprise Architecture in the process of licensing Enterprises to operate in any particular political jurisdiction, or to meet federal regulations.

If there are no published standards (criteria against which certification can be measured), certification is purely cosmetic. The concept of certification could be applied not only to Enterprise Architects or to work produced by Enterprise Architects but also to Enterprise Architecture methods and tools. Furthermore, there is also a requirement to establish a standard, "public access" basis for accommodating unique requirements through an elaboration of the base standards as the body of knowledge continues to explode.

Elaboration

The enormous complexity of Enterprises and the vast experience of those people who tend to focus on Enterprise Architecture mandate a capability to accumulate elaborations of the Framework Standards as practitioners' experience grows.

There has to be a single, authorized facility to publish certified elaborations as well as to publish certified compliance of methods, tools, skills, or models to the Zachman Framework Standards. Hopefully, this will protect the integrity of the Framework concepts from some of the misperceptions or even distortions of the Framework that derive from maybe well-intentioned, but misinterpreted or misguided self-proclamations of compliance, or even of misunderstanding of basic Framework concepts.

In Conclusion

The graphic and the metamodel standards overview for the most widely deployed Framework, the Enterprise Framework, will have "open access" through a free personal-use license at http://zachmaninternational.com. The graphics for the other three Frameworks with complete metamodel standards for all four Frameworks, along with associated elaborations and certifications, will be made available as they are completed on an "open access," personal-use, subscription basis.

I hope you will find the Zachman Framework Standards of great value to your Enterprise Architecture practice.

Notes

23. The instances of Architecture only have to be common in those specific areas of the Enterprise ("slivers" of Framework Cells) in which inter-operation is to be effected but the definition of Enterprise Architecture has to be common throughout.
24. See "The Zachman Framework: A Primer for Enterprise Engineering and Manufacturing" www.zachmaninternational.com.
25. See the comments on Consistency above.
26. Just as you would want certified engineers engineering your building, certified chemists designing your pharmaceuticals, certified accountants designing your chart of accounts, certified mechanics maintaining your Mercedes, etc., etc., etc. ... so should you probably want certified Enterprise Architects engineering (designing) your Enterprise.

Enterprise Architecture as Politics: An Actor-Network Theory Perspective

Anna Sidorova and Leon A. Kappelman

> Architecture is politics.
>
> —**Mitch Kapor**[27]

Introduction

The importance of enterprise architecture (EA), and its role in guiding managerial and technological decisions, has long been acknowledged by business and IT professionals from industry and governmental institutions. Architecture was fundamental to IBM's Business Systems Planning (BSP) systems development methodology from its beginnings in the early 1970s because "an enterprise-level architecture is required to constrain the design and development activity ... to serve as a context within which to make the trade-off decisions between the long-term and short-term options, ... [and] as a base line to manage the change activity which is inevitable ..." (Zachman, 1982, 32). Zachman's ontology of the enterprise and its architecture, used inside IBM in the early 1980s in conjunction with BSP, was first published externally in 1987 (Zachman, 1987), and to a large extent shapes the practitioners' view of EA.

The U.S. Defense Department (DOD) initiated its Technical Architecture Framework for Information Management (TAFIM) project in 1992 and developed the Command, Control, Communications, Computers, Intelligence, Surveillance, and Reconnaissance (C4ISR) Architecture Framework in the mid-1990s to promote interoperability across systems and services. The U.S. Congress passed the

Clinger–Cohen Act in 1996, which requires that every federal agency have a chief information officer (CIO) responsible for all IT spending, equipment, and personnel as well as the Information Technology Architecture for their agency. The DOD also developed the Joint Technical Architecture (JTA) in 1997 to facilitate the flow of information in support of warfare, and C4ISR evolved and is currently called the DODAF (DOD Architecture Framework). Steven Spewak published *Enterprise Architecture Planning* in 1995, providing guidance particularly for federal agencies to develop an EA consistent with Zachman's framework.

Responding to the need for guidance as federal agencies began to create their EAs, the CIO Council of the Office of Management and Budget (OMB) sponsored the development of the Federal Enterprise Architecture Framework (FEAF) in 1999 (CIO Council, 1999). OMB and the General Accountability Office (GAO) published *A Practical Guide to the Enterprise Architecture* in 2001 to provide guidance on setting up an EA program and for developing and maintaining an EA (CIO Council, 2001). Around that time GAO also developed an EA maturity model and an initial set of measures to assess EA progress and practices (GAO, 2003). Many groups offer various kinds and qualities of EA-related trainings and certifications, both Gartner and Forrester have EA research practices, and many vendors offer EA-related conferences, services, and products. A Society for Information Management (SIM) EA Working Group (SIMEAWG) was formed in October 2006. In the foreword to the SIMEAWG's forthcoming book *Getting Started with Enterprise Architecture,* Jeanne Ross presciently opines that "although EA was initially a function within the IT organization, we will soon find IT to be a function within EA" (Kappelman, 2008). Ross goes on to point out that "this is actually not a wild theory; it's a trend."

Yet, in spite of the practitioner interest and a number academic publications related to EA (Ross et al., 2006; Ross, 2003; Venkatesh et al., 2007), little theoretical understanding exists about what EA is and how it can be developed, managed, and used. Moreover, there is no one agreed-upon conceptualization of EA. For example, while some treat EA as a description of the status quo, others subscribe to the view of EA as a set of standards and blueprints for the future enterprise, and others still include both along with the transition plan between those present and future states. Similarly, some simply equate EA with IT or technology architecture, while others conceptualize EA as enterprise-wide requirements aimed at providing an all-encompassing model or approach for planning and running the business, capturing and providing management with all the knowledge about the enterprise, and serving as a shared "language" to align the ideas of strategy and with the reality of implementation (Kappelman, 2007). Furthermore, the focus among many practitioners and academics is on "doing EA," so they view EA as a process, confounding the product and process of EA, often with a focus on physical implementation while ignoring logical design objectives. The presence of such a multiplicity of views suggests that EA is a highly complex dynamic construct spanning the boundaries between the technical and social, the present and future, as well as the logical and physical dimensions of organizations.

Given this outwardly confusing and ambiguous situation, although not entirely an unexpected one given the infancy of the concept and practice of EA, we believe that our understanding of both the product and practice of EA can be significantly sharpened through the lens of a socio-technical process theory, which could encompass different definitions of EA as different process states and could also highlight social and political processes associated with EA. Such an approach may also be beneficial since at least to some significant extent EA is about requirements and that there are "complex patterns of interaction among users and analysts in defining requirements" (Davis, 1982, 5).

The purpose of this paper is to reexamine the meaning of enterprise architecture by viewing it though the lens of actor-network theory (ANT), a process theory concerned with creation of, and interaction among, socio-technical entities. Following such reexamination, *we propose a new definition of EA, which highlights its political and strategic importance, and also illuminates key challenges in EA implementation.*

In the next sections we briefly review existing research on EA as well as key principles and concepts of ANT that are most instrumental in understanding the nature of EA. We then analyze the architectural process and the enterprise from the actor-network creation point of view, and based on this analysis we develop a definition of EA. Finally, we discuss the potential directions for dealing with EA challenges, limitations of this paper, and directions for future research.

Review of Related Literature

Overview of EA Research

The concept of EA evolved from academic and practitioner, as well as federal, state, and local government efforts. The data-modeling techniques and system analysis, design, and development methods developed and promulgated in the 1970s and 1980s by ideas like Ed Yourdon's structured analysis and design methods (Yourdon, 1975; DeMarco, 1978), Peter Chen's (1976) entity-relationship diagrams, and Clive Finkelstein's information engineering (Finkelstein and Martin, 1981) laid some of the foundations. In 1987, John Zachman used concepts from classical architecture in the development of his framework for information architecture, which provided the integrating ontology of an enterprise. Throughout the 1990s, the term "enterprise architecture" appeared in a number of academic publications; however, such studies either adopted a black-box approach to EA (e.g., El Sawy et al., 1999), or treated EA as a close synonym to information architecture (e.g., Miller, 1997).

Academic interest in EA was renewed in the 2000s, with EA being proposed as a solution to alignment and IT integration challenges. In her 2003 article "Creating a Strategic IT Architecture Competency: Learning in Stages," MIT's Jeanne Ross concluded that "the payback for enterprise IT architecture efforts is strategic alignment between IT and the business" (43). Jerry Luftman's (2003) assessment of "IT-business strategic alignment maturity" included the degree to which "the enterprise architecture is integrated." Under the leadership of Syracuse University's Scott Bernard, the Association for Enterprise Architects began publishing the *Journal of Enterprise Architecture* (http://www.aeajournal.org/) in 2005. Kate Kaiser led a "study of 104 CIOs to determine their skill needs through 2008" and found that "there is much more emphasis on the business domain" and ranked "enterprise architecture" at the top of the "business domain" skills (Collet, 2006). An article titled "Enterprise Architecture Maturity: The Story of the Veterans Health Administration" was recently published in *MISQ Executive* (Venkatesh et al., 2007). Ross, with her MIT colleagues Peter Weill and David Robertson, released the book *Enterprise Architecture as Strategy* in 2006. Yet, most of the aforementioned academic contributions are either very technical in nature, failing to take into account broader organizational and social issues, or empirically based focusing of specific EA practices. In the next section, we review some key concepts from the actor-network theory, which we believe can be helpful in the development of a theory-driven view of EA that goes beyond a narrow IT architecture definition of EA.

Overview of ANT

Actor-network theory was originally developed by Bruno Latour and Michael Callon in the early 1980s (Callon and Latour, 1981) to describe the creation and evolution of socio-technical networks, and was later extended to focus on the dynamics of relationships among such actors and actor-networks (e.g., Law, 2000). ANT was also recently further formalized and elaborated upon in the book *Reassembling the Social: An Introduction to Actor-Network-Theory* (Latour, 2005). In its original conceptualization, the theory focused on "actors" defined as "any element which bends space around itself, makes other elements dependent upon itself and translates their will into the language of its own" (Callon and Latour, 1981, 286).

This translation of interests leads to the creation of networks of aligned interests, or actor-networks. The term actor-network reflects the fact that such actor-networks are often perceived by external observers as individual actors, and their coherency (the internal alignment of interests) is taken for granted, a phenomenon referred to as *punctualization* (Monteiro, 2000). When examined more carefully, such an actor is in fact a finely aligned network of individual actors, which, too, can be decomposed into networks. Modern organizations represent an obvious example of actor-networks. While most organizations are commonly viewed by outsiders as distinct legal entities with strategies, legal representations, even identity, members of those organizations view them as constantly changing collections of people, objects, rules, ideas, politics, and so on (Law, 2003). Such disaggregation can be applied not only to social entities, but also to technical artifacts.

The creation of actor-networks by a focal actor through the process of translation is detailed in the study of scallops and fishermen (Callon, 1986). The translation process is defined from the point of view of a focal actor, and its goal is to align the interests of other actors and actor-networks with the interests of the focal actor. The translation processes is described as a multistep process involving *problematization, interessement,* and *enrollment* stages[28] (Callon, 1986). Once the alignment of interests is achieved, it is often inscribed into technical artifacts (e.g., a computer application) or other elements that are difficult to change, such as legal contracts, or even such "mundane artifacts" as a car seat belt (Latour, 1992). Such inscription process may, in turn, require recruitment of yet additional actors (such as programmers or lawyers), and consequently may lead to the need to consider their interests. The actor-network theory takes a "radically relational" approach to defining actors, where "entities … achieve their significance by being in relation to other entities" (Law, 2000, 4). For example, the student registration system can be defined as such only when placed within a larger network of an educational institution. ANT does not make an a priori distinction between human and nonhuman actors, thereby making it appropriate for examining entities that are comprised of social and technical elements, such as information systems or organizations.

The flexibility of ANT with regard to the level of analysis and its ability to treat technical and social alike made it attractive for studying problems related to the development and use of information systems (Walsham, 1997). Among the early applications of ANT in IS research, Walsham and Sahay (1999) used ANT concepts for analyzing the case of GIS implementation in India. Recently ANT was used to examine a variety of IS-related phenomena. For example, ANT was used to examine causes of failure of a large business process change initiative (Sarker et al., 2006), to examine issues related to standardization in IS (Hanseth et al., 2006), and so on. ANT was also used for exploring a variety of organizational and business issues (e.g., Newton, 2002). In the next section, we apply concepts of ANT to describe EA and its related processes.

Actor-Network View of EA

Architecture as an Actor-Network

Architecture is about actors and negotiations. To demonstrate this, let us revisit the hypothetical example of creating architectural representations for a house used by John Zachman in his seminal article "A Framework for Information Systems Architecture" (1987). The example follows the evolution of a house from an owner's idea through a variety of architectural representations to the house itself. Because the example is aimed at defining and differentiating among various architectural representations, it focuses on the nature of such representations. Yet, to set the stage Zachman (1987) describes the process of creation of such representations through negotiations among several actors, the owner, the architect, the contractor, and the subcontractors, where the presence of various diverse interests and elements of negotiations is apparent. Let us examine the same process of creating architectural representations from the actor-network theory perspective by following one of the actors, the owner, through the negotiation steps. The owner has some land, some money, and some ideas. He also has two children. So, in fact, he represents an actor-network with a number of interests, which may include the achievement of financial and social goals. Likewise, the architect represents another actor-network, which may be even more complex, as it includes the architect himself with his career and financial goals, as well all the past architectural designs that the architect has been involved in. Such past designs are likely to significantly influence the architect's drawings. As a result of the hypothetical negotiations described by Zachman, architect's drawings are created (see Figure 2.12).

Although the next step (Stage 2 in Figure 2.12), the creation of the architect's plans, do not necessarily include negotiations among multiple human actors, they do involve negotiations with such socio-technical actor-networks as standards, regulations, technical specifications, past designs, and so on. Depending on the relative power the owner (the key actor in the Architect's Drawing AN) has vis-à-vis the architect, the architectural plans may or may not be faithful (i.e., aligned) to the architectural drawings. For example, after a careful elaboration, the architect may decide that it is technically nonfeasible to have French windows where originally planned. If the owner has sufficient power, he may convince the architect to reconsider materials, technologies, etc. Otherwise, the owner may be merely notified of the changes. Moreover, the parties involved may neglect updating the original architect's drawings (considering it to be a non-value-added step).

Similar negotiations occur when the architect's plans are translated into contractor's plans (in Stage 4 of Figure 2.12). Again, depending on their relative power, the owner and architect may be able to convince the contractor to change its common business practices or modify its subcontractor network to accommodate the architectural plans. Alternatively, the architectural plans may need to be changed to accommodate the interests of the contractor. Skipping through the subcontractor and shop plans, the last point of negotiations in Stage 5 is between the subcontractors in the Contractors' actor-networks and the physical materials, such as wood, concrete, cables, and so on, so that all those unrelated materials are translated into a house. Once again, this final translation does not always lead to a faithful instantiation of even the most technical and detailed of plans, the shop plans: though it is highly unlikely that any of such plans explicitly suggest crooked walls or uneven ceilings, those occur with a remarkable frequency.

A very similar process occurs as a part of IS development and implementation activities. Among the key actors are project sponsors, users, legacy systems, analysts, consultants, vendors, IT solutions, server farms, networks, and so on. Each step of the traditional SDLC could be represented as a negotiation, or translation, process, in which actors try to align their interests. Each stage of such a negotiation process can be detailed as *problematization, interessment,* and *enrollment.* Similar to the architectural drawings and contractor plans, various *immutable mobiles* are

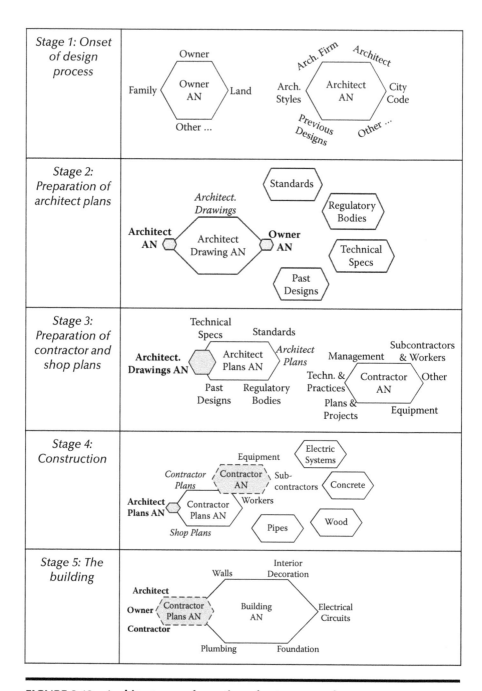

FIGURE 2.12 Architecture as formation of actor-networks.

created to inscribe the agreement achieved among various actor-networks. These include artifacts such as conceptual, logical, and physical design diagrams, budgets, plans, user requirements, as well as contracts, purchase agreements, system code, user documentation, and so on. Similar to Zachman's (1987) classical architecture example, the sponsor and user interests are often compromised in favor of the interests of more technical actors, which are often less flexible and cannot, in the words of Callon (1980), "bend themselves." These may include legacy systems, existing IT infrastructure, packaged solutions, an off-the-shelf ERP, and other possibilities. These result in unfulfilled customer expectations and the disappointment of business users with IT, something commonly referred to as the lack of business-IT alignment. In extreme cases, a failure to achieve an acceptable compromise among all requisite actors results in failed IS projects.

Implications of the Actor-Network View of the Architectural Process

Several interesting observations arise from such an ANT conceptualization of architecture, which may explain some of the difficulties in EA research and practice, as well as provide insights into how these difficulties could be overcome. First, different architectural representations are not just different representations of the same objective thing, but instead they *are inscriptions of different stages of architectural negotiations,* and they belong to different actor-networks. Because more conceptual representations correspond to earlier actor-networks when not all the interests were taken into consideration, they may be substantially different from the final architectural implementation (either the house or the system). In such a case, they pose a potential threat to the alignment within the existing actor-network, and the existing actor-networks will attempt to reduce the power of such representations by relegating them to, say, remote storage whereby those particular requirements never come into being. This may in part explain the lack of up-to-date high-level conceptual IS designs in many modern organizations. The attempts to reconstruct such representations may be perceived as a non-value-added activity or even a threat to the current actor-network and are therefore met with resistance, since such representations might increase transparency into the fact that the as-built is not consistent with the as-designed. It may also shed light on why the visible and consistent support of management plays a positive role in IT project success.

Second, the *role of specific architectural representations and the persistence of design characteristics inscribed in them will depend on the relative power of the actor-network that has created such representations.* For example, if the contractor has high relative power compared to the owner, the architect, and the builder, the final architectural representation is likely to be fairly faithful to the contractor's plans, and may be rather different from the architectural drawings and the owner's idea of the house. In the case of information systems development, the role of specific architectural representations is related to the organizational and IT governance processes and structures. If such governance mechanisms require that architectural representations at all levels should be aligned, then actual alignment is more likely.

The third observation is related to the relative power of different actor-networks and the effect of it on the translation processes. Following French and Raven (1959), social science researchers often distinguish among the following bases of power: legitimate (based on a position in an organization), referent (based on the ability to attract others and build loyalty), expert (derived from skills and expertise), information, coercive, and reward power. The power of a network is also related to the level of alignment of interests within the network. At the onset of building a house, the owner has significant power, mostly related to the ability to reward others (including the architect, the contractor, etc.). The architect, on the other hand, possesses the expert power (related to his or her extensive knowledge of previous designs) and referent power, related to his or her existing relationships with potential contractors. As the actor-network associated with constructing a house or building an information system grows, the power of the original owner diminishes; as new rounds of negotiations bring in the arguments that are not familiar to the owner, the owner's sunk costs rise, diminishing his or her reward power, and the relative expert power of the architect, the contractor, and the subcontractor rises. Similarly, at the onset of an IS project, the power of the project sponsor is high as the negotiation is in the domain that is familiar to him or her, and he or she has an ability to reward other actors. As system design progresses and additional actors, such as IT vendors and network administrators, are introduced, the expert power of the sponsor diminishes as does his or her reward capacity. All these implications are evident, for example, in situations when the architecture inherent in a purchased IT product, an ERP for example, is not consistent with management's vision and design objectives or incompatible with existing infrastructure and systems.

Enterprise as an Actor-Network

Architecting an enterprise is different from architecting a house or a stand-alone IS because each enterprise is a very complex and not always well-aligned actor-network. To better understand the nature of the enterprise, let us follow the formation of a hypothetical enterprise through multiple *translation* processes (see Figures 2.13, 2.14, and 2.15). Let us assume that at the start of an enterprise there are two important actors, the entrepreneur in possession of ideas and technology and an investor in possession of capital and other resources. The enterprise is created as a result of a translation process whereby interests of the entrepreneur and the investor become aligned and inscribed into a number of artifacts, such as a business plan, a charter, a loan agreement, articles of incorporation, etc. Such artifacts usually include references to the design of the enterprise, such as the legal and governance structure, the business model that implies the core business processes, as well as references to technology and personnel requirements. As the enterprise grows, the enterprise

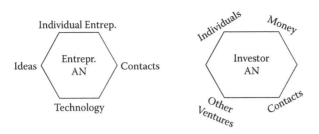

FIGURE 2.13   Creation of enterprise AN.

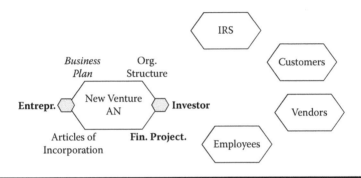

FIGURE 2.14   Growth of enterprise AN.

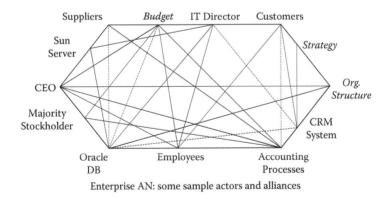

Enterprise AN: some sample actors and alliances

FIGURE 2.15   Illustration of interests and alignments in the enterprise AN.

actor-network grows to include vendors, customers, suppliers, employees, production technology, information technology, contracts, annual reports, SEC filings, and so on.

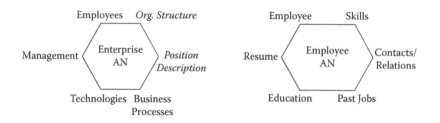

FIGURE 2.16   Enrollment of an employee AN.

The enrollment of each of these actors is usually associated with the creation of artifacts in which the interests of the newly created or expanded networks are inscribed. For example, hiring an employee usually involves creation of a contract and of a job description. As artifacts are created to ensure the stability of the network, they also serve as tools in protecting the interests of the actor-network in future negotiations with other actors. For example, the organizational structure chart (or description) may serve as a guide in making hiring and promotion decisions. However, in the case of some important hires, organizational structure may be modified (perhaps with the creation of a new department or a new position). It is important to recognize that enrollment of these actors in fact involves the enrollment of the entirety of associated actor-networks (see Figure 2.16). For example, a new CIO may bring together not only a new team of IT managers, but also his or her contacts, managerial experiences, vendor relations, technology preferences and biases, and so on.

It is important to remember that the architecture of the enterprise, as instantiated in the as-is or desired in the to-be vision of management, exists whether it is captured and represented in an architectural artifact or not. If not represented and therefore subject to assumptions, or even if represented and extant governance mechanisms do not ensure reconciliation and alignment, the conflict among the various actor-networks (i.e., product, management, infrastructure) at best creates problems and could easily result in failure.

IT Solution as an Actor-Network

It is especially interesting to explore the role of information technology (IT) in the enterprise actor-network. The ubiquitous nature of IT makes the enrollment of IT a required condition for the enrollment of other actors. IT is critical for accounting and bookkeeping; it may be a necessary condition for establishing a relationship with a vendor, a customer, or another stakeholder. IT solutions may be sought as a means to achieve realignment of interests within the enterprise actor-network, as in case of IT-enabled transformation initiatives. In order to enroll IT into the enterprise actor-network, its interests need to be translated into (aligned with) the interests of the enterprise actor-network, the process commonly referred to as system development and implementation (see Figure 2.17).

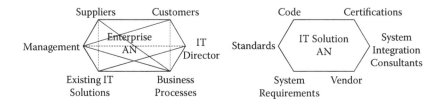

FIGURE 2.17   Enrollment of an IT solution AN.

Several aspects of such translation processes are of importance. As in the previous discussion of the IS development process, this translation process can be viewed as a series of negotiations among the enterprise actor-network, the IT, and a variety of other actors. Each IT can be viewed as an actor-network, which includes vendors, built-in business processes, protocols, standards, compatible technologies, consultants, administrators, and the like. If the interests of the enterprise actor-network are not well-aligned and strongly defined, one of two outcomes is likely: the translation fails or the interests of the enterprise actor-network are compromised in favor of the IT actor-network. In the former case, the renegotiation leads to the lengthy process of identifying the interests within the enterprise actor-network (requirements collection) with no agreement achieved. The latter case corresponds to the "successful implementation" but with the benefits of IT investments not being realized. The anecdotal evidence of both scenarios abounds in system implementation literature. Perhaps this explains in part the importance of requirements success to project success, and vice versa (Wallace, Keil, and Rai, 2004; Jones, 2000).

The fact is that larger projects are more likely to fail, since by their nature they are simply more prone to assumptions about EA, since there is simply more of it to represent, and thus more likely to result in misalignments and power conflicts. Rocket science seems relatively easy when compared to large IT implementations since enterprises are far more complicated than rockets, subject to not only the laws of physics and external weather conditions but also various government regulations, economic conditions at different macro and micro levels, the situations of their competitors, suppliers, and customers, including all of the jurisdictions and economies they operate within, and all this exacerbated by the conflicting interests of the various actor-networks directly affected by the project. Is it not surprising that business-IT alignment remains elusive given the infancy of actual EA practice at the present time.

EA as a Representation of Aligned Interests

While IT provides a good example of difficulties during an enrollment process, the logic is similar for other situations when interests of the enterprise network need to be aligned with those of another powerful actor-network, such as with mergers,

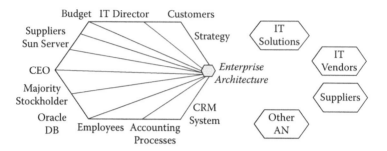

FIGURE 2.18   EA as a representation of aligned interests.

product line changes, business process outsourcing, and others. In order to enable an enterprise to successfully translate the interests of other actors into its own, it needs to have *an integrated and transparent representation of all interests and their current state of alignment.* We propose this as a working definition of enterprise architecture. We also propose that the role of EA is to serve as a negotiation interface between the enterprise actor-network and other actor-networks, customers and suppliers, IT solutions and their vendors, regulatory bodies, etc. (see Figure 2.18).

The definition of EA as an integrated and transparent representation of interests of the enterprise actor-network highlights several important qualities of EA. First, EA development is not so much a technical, but rather a strategic and political endeavor. Therefore, unless led by the most influential actors within the enterprise, any project aimed at the development of EA is bound to fail. Yet, the exclusion of technical actors is bound to result in underrepresentation of technical interests, and thus is also unlikely to succeed. Second, because the enterprise is a constantly evolving actor-network, the representation of its interests should also be constantly updated and reconciled, which relates to the notion shared by many EA practitioners that EA is a continuous and ongoing process.

The definition also illuminates key challenges associated with EA. "Integrated" implies that all the interests that are commonly inscribed in a myriad of artifacts need to be brought together and reconciled, which potentially leads to an impossibly large project given the current limited state of EA practices and tools as well as inadequate cultural capability of most enterprises to undertake such reconciliation. "Transparent" highlights two common challenges of EA. First, some interests currently aligned within the enterprise actor-network may be less than noble and at odds with explicitly stated enterprise interests; thus making them transparent may lead to an open misalignment. Second, transparency requires a common or shared language that can be understood by all somewhat influential actors within the enterprise actor-network, including the CEO, a salesperson, a programmer, a workshop application, and a router. The next challenge lies in the reference to "all aligned interests." As the enterprise actor-network is expanded, interests of certain actors within the network may become misaligned either as a result of changes in the interests of these actors or as a result of incomplete translations. Such misalignment is likely to be revealed during the EA process because it may pose a profound barrier to progress and success. Finally, the reference to all interests implies the need for identification of all actors, human and nonhuman. This is a challenge, because many of these actors are included inside seemingly *punctionalized* actor-networks (such as departments, vendor organizations), and also because it may feel unnatural to consider technical artifacts as having interests. Yet, the interests of such technical artifacts are becoming increasingly crucial as a variety of human interests get inscribed into IT products. These technical artifacts have some, but limited, adaptability, which may or may not preclude them from successfully being capable of alignment with the other interests in a particular enterprise. In the next section, we discuss the implications of the proposed definition of EA and directions for addressing the aforementioned challenges.

Implications of EA as a Representation of Aligned Interests

The proposed definition of EA as an integrated and transparent representation of all enterprise interests in their current state of alignment illuminates the political and strategic nature of EA and brings attention to integration, transparency, actor identification, and alignment challenges associated with EA. These challenges are discussed in the following.

The Integration Challenge

As discussed previously, the need for integration of the various interest-inscribing artifacts constitutes one of the key EA challenges. Broadly, this challenge can be decomposed into the identification of all interests and the reconciliation of these interests. While the issue of interest identification is related to the actor identification challenge discussed later, identification and reconciliation of all inscribed interests can be a significant advance toward the comprehensive EA. As the first step, a comprehensive *typology of all such inscriptions* needs to be developed. Zachman's enterprise ontology (1987, 2007) can also provide an insight into the types of inscriptions and interrelationships among them. In addition to identifying key classification principles, the typology should necessarily imply the hierarchical structure distinguishing among more or less influential inscriptions. The need for such hierarchy brings the typology development from the primarily data management and knowledge management domains, to the realm of strategy and policy. The presence of a typology will allow for easier identification of all important inscriptions, and will also serve as a guide for the resolution of conflicting interests.

Once all the inscriptions of interest are identified and classified, the integration and reconciliation of their content is required. Markup languages and text-mining technologies offer a promise for a possibility of comparing different inscriptions and thus pave a way for their reconciliation. Clearly, the need for different dialects and specialty vocabularies and models may be required to architect certain aspects of the enterprise, but alignment and integration can be optimized only if the ability to translate and reconcile exists. Thus the need for building an EA on a complete and comprehensive enterprise ontology, and having tools capable of supporting not only model creation but also translation and reconciliation. While some useful tools do exist, they are still just past the proof of concept and prototype stages (e.g., Simons, Kappelman, and Zachman, 2009), and complete capabilities do not exist commercially at this time.

The Transparency Challenge

As discussed earlier, in part the transparency challenge arises from the presence of covert interests. The need for elicitation of such covert interests calls for the development of new approaches as architectural and requirements-gathering approaches that assume candor may not be sufficient in such situations. Instead, mediation approaches from the conflict resolution literature may be more appropriate.

The other part of the transparency challenge is related to the need for the EA information during negotiations of the enterprise with other actor-networks. Addressing this challenge will require creating appropriate interfaces that would provide access to the EA repository. Such interfaces should ensure that only necessary and sufficient EA information is presented in an appropriate format each time it is requested by an actor, including human and nonhuman actors. In fact, in the ideal situation, such interface should assist in assessing how enrollment of other actors into the enterprise actor-network will affect the alignment of interests inside the enterprise. Here, extensive research on decision support and expert systems may offer useful theoretical foundations. Research is needed to examine the appropriate degree of accessibility to different parts of the EA repository from the security point of view.

The Actor Identification Challenge

The actor identification is related to stakeholder analysis, which has been extensively discussed in the strategic management literature (e.g., Savage et al., 1991; Mitchell et al., 1997; Turner et al., 2002). Yet the socio-technical and relational view of EA emphasized here highlights some important differences. First, attention needs to be devoted to the identification of important nonhuman actors and understanding their interests. Because such interests are often viewed as belonging to the engineering domain, they are often excluded at the strategic stage of enterprise planning, as C-level executives shy away from the dealing with such "low-level technical details." To overcome this, it is important that strategic planning and EA development methodologies explicitly require identification and evaluation of nonhuman actors. In addition, traditional stakeholder analysis techniques have a tendency to identify macro-actors as key stakeholders, such as employees in general, a supplier organization, etc. Such an approach works unless a misalignment occurs within such macro-actors. Therefore, for the purpose of EA development and maintenance, attention should be paid to early identification of misalignment within macro-actors. Additionally, therefore, research on agency problems may be useful for suggesting theoretical underpinnings for developing EA methodologies.

The Alignment Challenge

Even considering the aforementioned challenges, EA work would be significantly easier if complete alignment of all interests within the enterprise existed. Unfortunately, as the enterprise grows, the enrollment of numerous actors usually leads to the multiple misalignments. Such misalignments are often hidden due to low transparency of interests within the enterprise, and an attempt to create an integrated representation of all interests is bound to uncover such misalignments. As this situation is natural and expected, a certain level of misalignment may need to be tolerated within any enterprise; therefore EA methodologies and tools should be able to accommodate it. Again, research is needed to develop guidelines for the level of misalignment acceptable for different types of interests and actors within the enterprise. On the technical side, any reconciliation tools need to be developed with tolerance for misalignment.

Ethical Considerations in EA Development

The proposed view of EA as a representation of interests also draws attention to the ethical dilemmas in the development of EA. If some interests are underrepresented when the EA repository is created and the first artifacts entered, which is almost certain to be the case since representing the whole of an enterprise's architecture is a time-consuming activity, and if the EA repository is in fact used in negotiation with external or internal actors, the underrepresented interests will invariably be ignored. If such interests are not aligned with the rest of the enterprise interests, underplaying such interests may be a good thing. On the other hand, because of the potential power of EA in promoting certain interests, caution needs to be applied to ensure that acceptable rules of ethics are followed during the construction of EA repositories, artifacts, and interfaces. It is also important that processes are in place to dispute the interests represented in EA. The transparency of EA representations can be a key to enabling such processes.

Conclusion and Implications for Research and Practice

In this paper we have used concepts from the actor-network theory to reexamine the meaning of enterprise and of architecture through the lens of interest negotiations and network creation. Such reexamination led us to a definition of EA as an integrated and transparent representation of all interests within the enterprise and their current state of alignment. Thus, EA can serve as a negotiation interface between the enterprise and other actors. Such a view of EA opens several new directions for EA research.

First, research is needed to devise approaches for the identification of all significant interests and resolving potential misalignment. Because it is impractical that all interests within the enterprise are included in the EA, criteria for interest inclusion need to be developed, as well as guidelines of acceptable level of misalignment among such interests. Strategic-planning literature, as well as literature on negotiations, is likely to provide a source of relevant theoretical frameworks. Second, on a more technical note, research is necessary to develop appropriate interfaces to enable EA to serve as an important tool in the communication and negotiation of the enterprise with other actors. This would include the development of appropriate modeling and storage capabilities and the user and technology interfaces that would provide internal actors representing the enterprise AN (or any part of it) with access to the EA repository. Most importantly, tools need to be developed and tested that would allow checking the consistency of all interests inscribed within EA and identify potential misalignments. Yet another set of tools is necessary to check how the proposed alterations to the enterprise actor-network fit into the existing network of interests. Such validation would allow for a priori identification of sources of resistance to change initiatives and facilitate making appropriate managerial and strategic choices.

From the practitioner point of view, the proposed definition highlights the important and often overlooked political aspect of EA. On the positive side, such a definition should raise an interest in EA among C-level executives and strategists. The definition also highlights the important challenges of EA, which in the absence of necessary tools, including intellectual and conceptual ones, may discourage some business managers from embarking on EA initiatives. We hope, however, that the benefits of EA for representing the interests of the enterprise in negotiations with the fast-changing environment outweigh the perceived risks, and that this definition will inspire more organizations to EA development.

Notes

27. Mitchell Kapor, founder of Lotus Development Corp., designer of Lotus 1-2-3, and founding Chair of the Mozilla Foundation.
28. **Problematisation**: an actor analyses a situation, defines the problem and proposes a solution. **Interessment**: other actors become interested in the solution proposed. They change their affiliation...in favor of the new actor. **Enrolment**: the solution is accepted.... A new network of interests is generated." Gleirscher Norbert & Markus Schermer (2003), *The Use of Actor Network Theory to Analyse the Impact of Organic*

Marketing Initiatives on Regional Development, Centre for Mountain Agriculture, University of Innsbruck, http://www.iccr-international.org/regionet/docs/ws3-gleirscher.pdf.

References

Callon, M. 1986. Some elements of a sociology of translation: Domestication of the scallops and the fishermen. In *Power, action and belief: A new sociology of knowledge,* ed. J. Law, 197–225. London: Routledge and Kegan Paul.

Callon, M., and B. Latour. 1981. Unscrewing the big leviathan: How actors macro-structure reality and how sociologists help them to do so. In *Advances in social theory and methodology: Towards an integration of micro and macro-Sociologies,* ed. K. D. Knorr-Cetina and A. V. Cicourel, 277–303. London: Routledge and Kegan Paul.

Chen, P. P. 1976. The entity relationship model—toward a unified view of data. *ACM Transactions on Database Systems* 1, no. 1 (March): 9–36.

CIO Council. 1999. *Federal Enterprise Architecture Framework (FEAF).* Washington, DC: United States Office of Management and Budget (September).

CIO Council. 2001. *A practical guide to federal enterprise architecture,* version 1.0. Washington, DC: Chief Information Officer Council of OMB and the U.S. General Accountability Office, http://www.cio.gov/documents/bpeaguide.pdf (February).

Collett, S. 2006, Hot skills, cold skills. *Computerworld,* http://computerworld.com/action/article.do?command=viewArticleBasic&articleId=112360 (July 17).

Davis, G. B. 1982. Strategies for information requirements determination. *IBM Systems Journal* 21, no. 1: 4–30.

DeMarco, T. 1978. *Structured analysis and system specification.* New York: Yourdon Press.

El Sawy, O., A. Malhotra, S. Gosain, and K. Young. 1999. IT-intensive value innovation in the electronic economy: Insights from Marshall Industries. *MIS Quarterly* 23, no. 3: 305–35.

Finkelstein, C., and J. Martin. 1981. *Information engineering,* vols. 1 and 2. Englewood Cliffs, NJ: Prentice Hall.

Fletcher, A., J. Guthrie, P. Steane, G. Roos, and S. Pike. 2003. Mapping stakeholder perceptions for a third sector organization. *Journal of Intellectual Capital* 4, no. 4: 505–27.

GAO. 2003. *A framework for assessing and improving enterprise architecture management,* version 1.1, GAO-03-584G. Washington, DC: United States General Accountability Office, http://www.gao.gov/ (April).

Hanseth, O., E. Jacucci, M. Grisot, and M. Aanestad. 2006. Reflexive standardization: Side effects and complexity in standard making. Special Issue. *MIS Quarterly* 30 (August): 563–81.

Jones, C. 2000. Software assessments, benchmarks, and best practices. Boston: Addison Wesley Longman.

Kappelman, L. A. 2007. Bridging the chasm. *Architecture and Governance Magazine* 3, no. 2: 28.

Kappelman, L. A., ed. 2008. *Getting started with enterprise architecture.* Chicago: SIM International. http://eawg.simnet.org.

Latour, B. 1992. Where are the missing masses? The sociology of some mundane artifacts. In *Shaping technology/building society,* ed. W. E. Bijker and J. Law, 225–58. Cambridge, MA: MIT Press.

Latour, B. 2005. *Reassembling the social: An introduction to actor-network-theory.* New York: Oxford University Press.

Law, J. 2000. *Networks, relations, cyborgs: On the social study of technology.* http://www.lancs.ac.uk/fass/sociology/research/resalph.htm.

Law, J. 2003. Ordering and obduracy. http://www.lancs.ac.uk/fass/socioloty/papers/law-ordering-and-obduracy.pdf.

Luftman, J. 2003. *IT-business strategic alignment maturity assessment.* http://www.sim-net.org/Content/NavigationMenu/Resources/Library/Download_Page3res/ITBusinessAlignment.pdf (October 7).

Miller, D. 1997. Enterprise client/server planning. *Information Systems Management* 14, no. 2: 7–15.

Mitchell, R. K., B. R. Agle, and D. J. Wood. 1997. Toward a theory of stakeholder identification and salience: Defining the principle of who and what really counts. *Academy of Management Review* 22, no. 4: 853–88.

Monteiro, E. 2000. Monsters: From systems to actor-networks. In *Planet Internet,* ed. K. Braa, C. Sorenson, and B. Dahlbom, 239–49. Lund, Sweden: Studentlitteratur.

Newton, T. 2002. Creating the new ecological order? Elias and actor-network theory. *Academy of Management Review* 27, no. 4: 523–40.

Ross, J. W., P. Weill, and D. Robertson. 2006. *Enterprise architecture as strategy creating a foundation for business execution.* Boston: Harvard Business School Press.

Ross, Jeanne. 2003. Creating a strategic IT architecture competency: Learning in stages. *MISQ Executive* 2, no. 1: 31–43.

Sarker, S., S. Sarker, and A. Sidorova. 2003. Understanding business process change failure: An actor-network perspective. *Journal of Management Information Systems* 23, no. 1: 51–86.

Savage, G. T., T. W. Nix, C. J. Whitehead, and J. D. Blair. 1991. Strategies for assessing and managing organizational stakeholders. *Academy of Management Executive* 5, no. 2: 61–75.

Simons, G., L. Kappelman, and J. Zachman. 2009. Using language to gain control of enterprise architecture. In *The SIM Guide to Enterprise Architecture,* ed. Leon A. Kappelman. Boca Raton, FL: Taylor & Francis, pp. 127-146. (See article in Chapter 4, *Ed.*).

Spewak, S. H. 1993. *Enterprise architecture planning.* New York: Wiley.

Venkatesh, V., H. Bala, S. Venkatraman, and J. Bates. 2007. Enterprise architecture maturity: The story of the Veterans Health Administration. *MISQ Executive* 6, no. 2: 79–90.

Wallace, L., M. Keil, and A. Rai. 2004. How software project risk affects project performance. *Decision Sciences* 35, no. 2 (Spring): 289–321.

Walsham, G. 1997. Actor-network theory and IS research: Current status and future prospects. In *Information systems and qualitative research,* ed. A. S. Lee, J. Liebenau, and J. I. DeGross, 466–80. London: Chapman & Hall.

Walsham, G., and S. Sahay. 1999. GIS for district-level administration in India: Problems and opportunities. *MIS Quarterly* 23, no. 1: 39–66.

Yourdon, E. 1975. *Techniques of program structure and design.* Englewood Cliffs, NJ: Prentice Hall.

Zachman, J. A. 1982. Business systems planning and business information control study: A comparison. *IBM Systems Journal* 21, no. 1: 31–53.

Zachman, J. A. 1987. A framework for information systems architecture. *IBM Systems Journal* 26, no. 3: 276–292.

Zachman, J. A. 2007. *Enterprise architecture standards V2.01.* Available by free registration at http://www.zachmaninternational.com/2/Standards.asp (October).

EA Maturity Models

Brian Salmans

In his book *The Mythical Man-Month,* Frederick Brooks[29] discusses the essential importance of getting the requirements right in the software development process and the challenges the IS field has in getting those requirements right. Brooks states that "the hardest single part of building a software system is deciding precisely what to build. No other part of the conceptual work is as difficult as establishing the detailed technical requirements.... No other part of the work so cripples the system if done wrong. No other part is more difficult to rectify later."[30]

Not getting requirements right seems to be a continuing problem for the IS field. IS cannot get alignment right if we cannot get the requirements right, since the organizational goals we need to align with are part of those requirements. Brooks contends that architectural unity or conceptual integrity—that of a system consisting of one set of design ideas—is the most important consideration in system design. To attain conceptual integrity, Brooks maintains, the architectural process must be separate from that of implementation. This distinction between architecture and implementation is the same point that John Zachman made in his article earlier in this chapter.

Enterprise architecture facilitates the alignment between the business and IS domains, a possible answer to achieving conceptual integrity and getting the requirements right and dealing with the requirements challenges highlighted by Brooks. It ensures congruency between organizational strategies, process, and IS requirements, forming an inclusive IS strategy.[31] Thus, a central goal of enterprise architecture is the alignment of IS requirements to the goals and objectives of an organization.[32,33,34,35]

Quantifying the benefits of EA and the level of alignment is critical to understanding the impact of EA on organizations. This has been an area of interest with researchers. For example, Reich and Benbasat[36] conducted a study of life insurance companies in order to measure the characteristics and usefulness of alignment between the overall organization and the IS domain. They define alignment (they use the term "linkage") as "the degree to which the IT mission, objectives, and plans support and are supported by the business mission, objectives, and plans."[37] Alignment was measured by a survey assessing the understanding and congruence of IS and executive leadership. This is consistent with the view presented in Chapter 1 that "alignment begins with the alignment of the concepts and ideas of the people, and then with the alignment of resources, activities, and technologies."

The ability to achieve and maintain alignment leaves room for further research because it is neither well-documented nor understood.[38] Luftman presented a method to assess the maturity of the alignment of an organization and its information technology. In it, he defines five levels of strategic alignment maturity: (1) initial/ad hoc process, (2) committed process, (3) established focused process, (4) improved/managed process, and (5) optimized process. Each of these levels, in turn, contains a set of six criteria based on practices regarding: (1) communications maturity, (2) competency/value measurement maturity, (3) governance maturity, (4) partnership maturity, (5) scope and architecture maturity, and (6) skills maturity.[39] This alignment maturity model has been subsequently applied and validated.[40,41]

When considering alignment within an EA context, it is important to understand methods to assess alignment and EA, how to improve alignment and EA, and how to reach higher levels of maturity in alignment and EA.[42] More fundamentally, in the context of assessing the maturity of an organization's EA activities and processes, the quality and degree of alignment perhaps becomes a dependent or outcome variable to help us assess the quality and maturity of the EA activities. An effective tool to accomplish this is the use of maturity models. Maturity models are grounded in the notion of process improvement, which is based on work by Shewhart, Joseph Juran, and J. Edwards Deming.[43] Maturity models, derived from stage theories, are based on the belief that systems, processes, practices, activities, and even enterprises themselves, can and do go through distinct stages over time.[44] Implicit in these models is the basic biological principle that the systems are characterized by either growth or decay. An implicit assumption underlying the use of maturity models is that the processes of the organization possess an inherent capability that can be empirically assessed. This provides the basis to develop the predictability and repeatability of organizational processes.

Maturity models provide a basis for the control of IT as well as organizational processes and practices by identifying strengths, areas for improvement, and subsequent activities to effect improvement in the processes and practices. The standards defined by the maturity models establish levels of maturity and can be used in managing the IS or organizational improvements desired.[45] An assessment of maturity stages can help an organization understand where it has come from and where it wants to go (and help develop a plan to get there). It can also help develop proactive, reasonable plans rather than reactive ones. Maturity models include a set of specifically described stages, occurring in a given sequence, a list of aspects or conditions for changing or evolving from one stage to another, and a list of the aspects or conditions that must be present in order for the transition to another stage to have occurred and be identified as having occurred.[46] Maturity models have been categorized into three groups, depending on their use and contribution:

1. A descriptive tool such as providing an assessment of an EA program's current situation, helping to support process improvements (by describing the practices that an organization must perform in order to improve its EA processes), illustrating projected benefits, and supporting EA program management efforts by quantifying progress and as a tool for architects to manage their EA effort.
2. A prescriptive tool such as setting goals for the future based on a desired achievement level of a maturity model.
3. A comparative tool such as benchmarking the effectiveness of an EA practice by comparing with other EA programs using the same or similar maturity model and providing a yardstick against which to periodically measure improvement.[47]

An assessment of the maturity of the EA program in an organization not only can give leadership an indication of where and how their EA program stands, but also can indicate a proper path for where they want the EA program and their organization to go. Measuring the maturity of EA can allow leadership to make needed course corrections to their EA program and activities, helping to ensure the viability and success of their program.

In order to attempt to measure levels of EA maturity, important aspects of enterprise architecture can be characterized, such as: (1) a means of abstraction, (2) a means of communication, and (3) a management instrument.[48] Additionally, these authors identified the key architecture critical success factors as: (1) the need for acceptance of organizational change, (2) the availability of effective means (including skilled architects and effective tools), and (3) the proper use of architecture. These last critical success factors, then, should be accounted for in EA maturity models. Similarly, eight dimensions of EA maturity advanced by the Gartner Group are: (1) architecture scope and authority, (2) stakeholder involvement and support, (3) architecture definition process, (4) business context, (5) architecture content, (6) future state realization, (7) architecture team resources, and (8) architecture impact.[49]

In Van der Raadt et al.'s research,[50] their conceptualized model indicates that as an organization's EA matures, alignment becomes increasingly important.[51] In a similar manner, in their research of EA maturity at the Veterans Administration, Venkatesh, Bala, Venkatraman, and Bates looked at how a well-designed, mature EA program can benefit an organization. They found that moving to higher levels of EA maturity facilitated increasing levels of integration and standardization of processes, improving organizational performance at the Veterans Administration.[52]

The use of EA maturity models was integral to the formulation and structure of the SIM Information Management Practices survey, presented in detail in Chapter 4. Given the overall immaturity of EA as an organizational activity in general and the relative newness of all of the extant EA maturity models, there is very limited data available to assess EA activities or validate such models. In developing the SIMEAWG survey, all of the available EA maturity models were reviewed, with a core of four EA maturity models being used to develop and to which to map the survey's practices questions. Additionally, the key IT and business alignment enablers and inhibitors posited by Luftman and McLean[53] were integrated into the SIMEAWG's survey and the mapping to reflect the importance of alignment to EA, and vice-versa, and to reflect this persistent concern of top IT management.

The four maturity models chosen are widely recognized and used but differentiated enough to provide separate perspectives on aspects of enterprise architecture activities. Each of the EA maturity models is discussed in the following:

1. The Government Accountability Office (GAO) has a framework for assessing and improving EA management. EA practices have been mandated in the federal arena since the Information Technology Management Reform Act (also known as the Clinger–Cohen Act) of 1996 required agency CIOs to develop, maintain, and facilitate integrated systems architectures. This was formalized within the Federal EA Framework (FEAF) first published, and later updated, in 1999. The GAO maturity model uses five maturity stages (creating EA awareness, building the EA management foundation, developing the EA, completing the EA, and leveraging the EA to manage change), each with the same four critical success factors of: demonstrates commitment, provides capability to meet commitment, demonstrates satisfaction of commitment, and verifies satisfaction of commitment. These are further categorized into four groups of architecture-related activities, products, events, and structures: architecture governance, content, use, and measurement.

2. Carnegie Mellon's Software Engineering Institute's Capability Maturity Model (SEI CMM) is probably the best-known maturity model in the IT arena and is used as a foundation in developing many other maturity models in a variety of applications and approaches. The CMM is a staged concept, where all key process areas for a maturity stage (and all previous or lower stages) must be satisfied in order to mature or attain a certain stage. This capability maturity model is not EA directed per se, but rather focused on the maturity of system development maturity centering around project management and software engineering practices. It is based on five increasing levels of maturity (initial, repeatable, defined, managed, and Level 5 optimizing). Various more specific instances of the CMM (such as the Systems Engineering CMM, Software Acquisition CMM, People CMM, and CMM Integration) have been developed by the SEI.

3. The Federal Office of Management and Budget (OMB) is mandated by the Clinger–Cohen Act of 1996 to annually assess the maturity of EA in federal agencies. In response, the OMB has developed an EA assessment framework. The OMB EA Assessment Framework consists of five levels of maturity (initial, managed, utilized, results-oriented, and optimized), each with three capability assessment areas of completion, use, and results.

4. MIT's Center for Information Systems Research, based on a survey of 456 organizations, developed four stages of enterprise architecture, which are business silos architecture, standardized technology architecture, optimized core architecture, and business modularity architecture.[54]

Other maturity models, mny of which are based on the four just mentioned, were influential in developing the SIMEAWG survey (see Chapter 4 for description, report, and results of the survey). Some of these include the National Association for State CIOs (NASCIO) maturity model, which is based on the Carnegie Mellon SEI's CMM. It has six levels (no program, informal program, repeatable program, well-defined program, managed program, and continuously improving vital program), which also loosely align with the GAO's maturity model. The Institute for EA Developments has a six-stage maturity model including the following stages: no extended EA, initial, under development, defined, managed, and optimized.

Integrating EA maturity models into the SIM Information Management Practices survey reflects a belief in the importance and necessity of maturity concepts to the effective implementation and management of enterprise architecture and requirements processes throughout an organization. Using existing EA maturity models as a basis in the formulation of survey questions provides a rich foundation in established and rigorous assessment approaches that help to determine the current state of EA, requirements, and IS development practices, perceptions, and capabilities. Moreover, using these maturity models provides a foundation for future, longitudinal studies to assess the evolutionary progress of these practices, perceptions, and capabilities.

Complete results from the SIMEAWG's survey are provided in Chapter 4 on a question-by-question basis; further analyses of the data are anticipated to provide insights into the similarities and differences among these different maturity models, as well as the relationships that EA maturity may have with other IT activities, such as, for example, practices associated with developing systems or achieving alignment.

Notes

29. Brooks, F., 1995. *The Mythical Man-Month*, 20th Anniversary Edition, Boston: Addison-Wesley Longman Publishing Co.
30. Brooks, F., 1995. p. 199.

31. Young, C., 2001. The unexpected case for enterprise IT architectures. Gartner Research, No. SPA-12-7101, 1–5.
32. Henderson, J. C., & Venkatraman, N. 1993. Strategic alignment: Leveraging information technology for transforming organizations. *IBM Systems Journal*, 32(1), 4–23.
33. Vaidyanathan, S. 2005. Enterprise architecture in the context of organizational strategy. *BPTrends*, 11, 1–9.
34. Wieringa, R. J., Blanken, H. M., Fokkinga, M. M., and Grefen, P. W. P. J. 2003. Aligning application architecture to the business context. In *Proceedings of Advanced Information Systems Engineering: 15th International Conference*, Berlin: Springer-Verlag. 1028–1029.
35. van der Raadt, B., Hoorn, J. F., & van Vliet, H. 2005. Alignment and maturity are siblings in architecture assessment. In *Proceedings of Advanced Information Systems Engineering: 17th International Conference*, Berlin: Springer-Verlag. 357–371.
36. Reich, B. H., & Benbasat, I.1996. Measuring the linkage between business and information technology objectives. *MIS Quarterly*, 20(1), 55–71.
37. Reich & Benbasat, 1996. p. 56.
38. Luftman, J. 2000. Assessing business-IT alignment maturity. *Communications of the Association for Information Systems*, 4(14), 1–51.
39. Luftman, 2000. p. 10.
40. Sledgianowski, D., & Luftman, J. 2005. IT-business strategic alignment maturity. *Journal of Cases on Information Technology*, 7(2), 102–120.
41. Sledgianowski, D., Luftman, J. N., & Reilly, R. R. 2006. Development and validation of an instrument to measure maturity of IT business strategic alignment mechanisms. *Information Resources Management Journal*, 19, 3–18.
42. Luftman, 2000.
43. Chrissis, M. B., Konrad, M., & Shrum, S. 2003. *CMMI: Guidelines for Process Integration and Product Improvement*: Addison-Wesley Professional.
44. Nolan, R. L. 1979. Managing the crises in data processing, *Harvard Business Review*: Harvard Business School Publication Corp.
45. Steghuis, C., Daneva, M., & van Eck, P. 2005. Correlating Architecture Maturity and Enterprise Systems Usage Maturity to Improve Business/IT Alignment. *Proceedings of REBNITA 2005. First International Workshop on Requirements Engineering for Business Need and IT Alignment, Paris, France*, 64–73.
46. Wilson, D. W. 1997. *Maturity Models in IS Development in in Managing IT Resources and Applications in the World Economy*: Paper presented at the Proceedings of the 8th IRMA International Conference.
47. Rosemann, M., & de Bruin, T. 2005. Towards a business process management maturity model. *Proceedings of the 13th European Conference on Information Systems* (ECIS 2005). Regensburg, Germany, 26.
48. van der Raadt et al., 2005.
49. James, G. A., & Burke, B. 2005. *Understand the Maturity of Your Enterprise Architecture Program*, ID G00136105, Stamford, CT, Gartner Group.
50. van derRaadt et al., 2005.
51. van der Raadt et al., 2005.
52. Venkatesh, V., Bala, H., Venkatraman, S., and Bates, J. 2007. Enterprise architecture maturity: The story of the Veterans Health Administration. *MIS Quarterly Executive*, 6(2), 79–90.

53. Luftman, J., and McLean, E. R. 2004. Key issues for IT executives. *MIS Quarterly Executive*, 3(2), 89–104.
54. Ross, J. W., Weill, P., and Robertson, D. 2006. *Enterprise architecture as strategy.* Harvard Business School Press.

Enterprise Architecture: Charting the Territory for Academic Research[55,56]

Leon A. Kappelman, Thomas McGinnis,
Alex Pettit, Brian Salmans, and Anna Sidorova[57]

Introduction

Information systems (IS) have been credited with a variety of organizational benefits, including improved efficiency, automation of repetitive tasks, improvements in inter- and intraorganizational communications, and competitive advantages. The process of creating and implementing an IS is associated with "by-products," such as an assortment of representations of the enterprise and its various aspects, including business process maps, data models, decision trees, and other similar artifacts. Because such representations are often discarded (or at best relegated to storage) after the corresponding systems are implemented, they are considered an expense, and organizations strive to minimize the efforts involved in the creation of such artifacts. Was Fred Brooks (1986) wrong when he opined that getting the requirements right is the essence of being an IS professional?

By implementing prepackaged enterprise solutions, organizations adopt standard process and data configurations, thereby presumably reducing the need to understand their own businesses. Although often resulting in satisfactory outcomes at the subsystem level, this lack of attention to overall context and reusable requirements leads to wide-ranging enterprise degradation, since the knowledge about the enterprise needed to implement one system is often lost or otherwise not available for use when creating or modifying another. The result is the difficult-to-integrate-

and-change, often misaligned, amalgamation of information systems we call our "legacy" or "stovepipes."

Enterprise architecture has been suggested as the path to a comprehensive view of enterprise-wide requirements and thereby improved system interoperability and flexibility, as well as at least the on-ramps and signage on the highway to business-IT alignment. While the concept of EA has gained acceptance among IT professionals, it has been largely considered an "IT thing," resulting in difficulty obtaining broad support from business managers for EA activities. Although many IT and business professionals agree that EA offers significant benefits beyond the IT function, little research exists to support or refute such claims.

The purpose of this paper is to foster a dialogue about EA by examining how EA and its benefits are viewed by IT professionals and by suggesting directions for future research. Specifically, we set the stage by reviewing relevant academic research and the state of EA practice. We then present results of a survey of 376 IT professionals, members of SIM, detailing their views on the purposes and benefits of EA, and attempt to identify key underlying themes by means of factor analysis. Finally, we propose directions for future research on EA and its business value.

EA in Academic Research and Practice

Enterprise architecture has evolved from academic and practitioner, as well as federal, state, and local government efforts. The data-modeling techniques and system analysis and design methods developed and promulgated in the 1970s and 1980s by ideas like structured analysis and design methods (DeMarco, 1978; Yourdon, 1975), entity-relationship diagrams (Chen, 1976), and information engineering (Finkelstein and Martin, 1981) laid some of the foundations. The publication of John Zachman's framework for EA in 1987 provided the ontology to tie all the pieces together into the context of the whole enterprise. Yet until recently the construct of EA itself did not enjoy much attention by academics. Although in the late 1990s the term "enterprise architecture" appeared in several academic research publications, such studies either adopted a black-box approach to EA (El Sawy, Malhotra, Gosain, and Young, 1999) or treated EA as a close synonym to information architecture (e.g., Miller, 1997), a term commonly used in practice as a synonym for data architecture.

During the early and mid-2000s, EA gained visibility through a number of prominent academic publications (albeit mostly still appearing in practitioner-oriented academic journals). Ross (2003) suggested EA as a road map for IT-business alignment, an issue of uppermost importance for IT professionals (Luftman, 2003). A recent article by Venkatesh, Bala, Venkatraman, and Bates (2007) provided a review of EA maturity at the Veterans Health Administration. Boh and Yellin's (2007) research examined the effect of EA on information sharing and integration across disparate units in an enterprise. Other noteworthy developments included the development of the four-stage EA maturity model by MIT's Center for Information Systems Research (Ross, Weill, and Robertson, 2006) and the release of the book *Enterprise Architecture as Strategy* (Ross et al., 2006). Reflecting the perceived importance of EA research, the Association for Enterprise Architects began publishing the *Journal of Enterprise Architecture* in 2005.

The practitioner view of EA has been largely shaped by John Zachman's ontology of the enterprise and its architecture, which was used at IBM in the early 1980s, first published in 1987, additionally detailed in 1992 (Zachman, 1987; Zachman and Sowa, 1992), and further elucidated with the publication of the Enterprise Framework Standards (Zachman, 2005, 2007). Zachman was the first to contend that "the business strategy and its linkage to information systems strategy ... ultimately manifest themselves in architectural expression" (1987, 277). Interestingly, since Zachman's "Framework for EA" is about the whole enterprise and spans the logical-physical continuum as well as identifying the need to independently define the enterprise in terms of all six interrogatives (i.e., who, what, where, why, when, how), it can provide IS researchers a means for categorizing EA-related publications, models, tools, and so on.

The U.S. Congress passed several pieces of legislation in the 1990s in an effort to improve government management as well as IT investment. The Clinger–Cohen Act (CCA) required that every federal agency have a chief information officer (CIO) responsible for, among other things, an information technology architecture. Responding to the need for guidance as federal agencies began to create their EAs, the Office of Management and Budget (OMB) facilitated the creation of a federal CIO Council, which sponsored the development of the Federal Enterprise Architecture Framework (FEAF) in 1999 (OMB, 1999). OMB and the General Accountability Office (GAO) published *A Practical Guide to Federal Enterprise Architecture* in 2001 to provide guidance on setting up an EA program and for developing and maintaining an EA (OMB, 2001). Around that time, the GAO also developed an EA maturity model and a set of measures to assess EA progress and practices (GAO, 2003).

Despite all this, in 2002 the federal government still did not have a government-wide architecture or even a set of standards upon which to implement its e-government initiatives. Thus OMB began to promulgate architectural guidance and implementation standards through five reference models (business, performance, service component, data, and technical). Many private groups offer various EA-related trainings and certifications programs; both Gartner and Forrester have EA research practices, and many vendors offer EA-related conferences, services, and products. Yet, with little EA-related university-level education in place,[58] the EA practice world remains somewhat disjointed and stovepiped. The need for a more consistent conceptualization of EA led to the recent formation of the SIM EA Working Group (SIMEAWG), charged with the study and dissemination of successful EA practices. In the next section, we present the results of the SIMEAWG-sponsored survey that reflects the views of EA held by IT professionals.

EA Functions and Benefits: SIMEAWG Survey

In order to better understand the view of IT professionals regarding the value of EA, a survey was conducted under the auspices of the SIMEAWG. Preliminary definitions of EA functions and benefits were developed by the authors based on existing EA literature, including EA maturity models as well as EA and IT-business alignment research (e.g., Luftman and McLean, 2004; Luftman, 2007; Van der Raadt, Hoorn, and Van Vliet, 2005; Van der Raadt, Soetendal, Perdeck, and Van Vliet, 2004). Enterprise architecture maturity models were integrated as a foundational structure of many of the questions within the survey. This provided an opportunity to capture and assess the processes, capability, performance, maturity, and quality of EA activities conducted in industry. A variety of EA maturity models were reviewed, with a core of four EA maturity models used for instrument development. Additionally, the key IT and business alignment enablers and inhibitors posited by Luftman and McLean (2004) were integrated into the survey to reflect the importance of alignment to EA. The definitions of EA functions and benefits were further refined through a modified Delphi study approach with an expert group of EA professionals from industry and academia. The final survey included six statements related to the key purpose and functions of EA and twenty statements regarding potential benefits of EA. The respondents were asked to express their agreement or disagreement with the suggested statements on a 5-point Likert scale.

An invitation to participate in the survey with an embedded hyperlink to the web-based survey was sent out by e-mail to individuals on SIM's membership list. Measures were taken so that each participant could not participate in a survey more than once. Over the subsequent six weeks, three reminder e-mails were sent to individuals who had not completed the survey. A total of 376 quality responses were received, which represents a 13.13 percent response rate; this is consistent with other surveys of SIM members. Analysis of demographic data showed that 42.2 percent of respondents were C-level executives; directors represented 32.2 percent. "Other" roles accounted for 21 percent. Enterprise architects accounted for 4.3 percent of respondents (see Figure 2.19). Nearly two-thirds of respondents (63 percent)

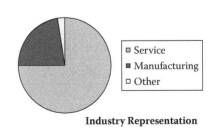

Respondent Job Title Details

	Frequency	Percent
Board Member	1	0.3
CEO	8	2.1
CIO	100	26.6
VP	38	10.1
CTO	13	3.5
Director	121	32.2
Enterprise Architect	16	4.3
Other	79	21.0
Total	**376**	**100.0**

Industry Representation

□ Service
■ Manufacturing
□ Other

FIGURE 2.19   Industry representation.

had enterprise-wide responsibilities, 16 percent had business unit responsibilities, while the remaining 21 percent had departmental or team responsibilities.

On average, respondents had been in their current position for 4.3 years; however, most (58 percent) had less than 3 years' job tenure. Seventy-five percent of respondents were from service industries, 22 percent from manufacturing (see Figure 2.19). The size of organizations represented in the survey varied greatly. Although some organizations had annual sales in excess of $50 billion, 50 percent of organizations had annual sales under $750 million. In terms of employees, most organizations (60 percent) have fewer than 2,500. The size of IT departments also varied. The median IT operating budget was approximately $5 million; 75 percent of organizations had fewer than three hundred IT employees.

For questions regarding the purpose and functions of EA, there was overwhelming agreement by respondents on five out of six suggested functions of EA. For example, 92 percent of respondents agreed or strongly agreed that EA provides a blueprint of an organization's data, applications, and technology; 89 percent of respondents agreed or strongly agreed that EA is also considered a tool for organizational planning (see Table 2.1 for more details).

For questions regarding the potential benefits of EA, we found that the majority of respondents agreed or strongly agreed to the suggested EA benefits (nineteen of the twenty items had Agree and Strongly Agree responses, accounting for more than 60 percent; the top five are shown in Table 2.2). For example, 87 percent of respondents agreed or strongly agreed that EA helps improve interoperability among IS. The only suggested EA benefit that did not support of the majority of respondents was related to improvement of organizational trust.

To examine the dimensionality of EA benefits and functions constructs, we performed principal component factor analysis with a varimax rotation. Factor loadings greater than 0.5 were considered adequate to identify practical significance.

TABLE 2.1   Purpose and Function of EA

	Mean	*Std. Dev.*
Provides a blueprint of organization's business, data, applications, and technology	4.397	0.682
A planning tool	4.249	0.676
Facilitates systematic change	4.016	0.739
A tool for decision making	4.134	0.709
An alignment tool	4.083	0.857
Communicating organizational objectives	3.667	0.903
A snapshot in time of an organization	2.872	1.096

TABLE 2.2   Benefits of EA

	Mean	Std. Dev
Improved interoperability among information systems	4.336	0.718
Improved utilization of IT	4.252	0.696
Aligning business objectives with IT	4.139	0.801
More effective use of IT resources	4.024	0.738
Better situational awareness	3.946	0.715

This was also the demarcation used for cross-loading (Hair, Black, Babin, Anderson, and Tatham, 2006). Two survey items failed this cross-loading criterion and were removed from the analysis. Bartlett's test of sphericity was found to be significant ($p < .000$, $\chi^2 = 3,741.111$, $df = 300$). However, this test is sensitive to large sample sizes; to complement the result, a Kaiser–Meyer–Olkin test was performed. The KMO measure of sampling adequacy was 0.908, meaning that the correlation matrix is suitable for factor analysis. The five factors (see Table 2.3) were retained based on a scree plot, explaining a total of 59 percent of the variance. Relatively low variance explained could be attributed to low variability in respondents' perspectives of the benefits, purpose, and function of EA. The factor solution confirmed the construct validity of the survey with all questions related to EA benefits loading high on factors one, two, and three, and questions related to functions of EA loading on factors four and five. The three factors representing EA benefits were interpreted as IT benefits, broad organizational benefits, and benefits for goal achievement.

IT benefits was representative of the first factor, with many of the survey questions associated within an IT-centric context (e.g., "More effective use of IT resources"; "Improved utilization of IT"; and "Faster development of information systems"). The second factor, broad organizational benefits, showed a definite difference in its component survey questions, with a transition to a broader, organization-wide view (e.g., "Standardizes organizational performance measures"; "Better collaboration within the organization"; and "Improves trust in the organization"). Finally, the third factor, benefits for goal achievement, seemed descriptive of its underlying survey questions with such goal-oriented questions as "Improved goal attainment," "Aligning business objectives with IT," and "Less wasted resources on projects."

The interpretation of the two factors related to EA functionality proved less straightforward. However, we believe these two factors represent the practitioner view of EA. First of all, the fourth factor can be seen within the context of EA as a planning tool, providing aspects useful for developing the "to be" architecture. The survey questions within this factor, "Provides a blueprint of an organization," "A planning tool," and "A tool for decision making," show this forward-looking characteristic of

TABLE 2.3 Factor Analysis—EA Benefits and Purpose

	1	2	3	4	5
Reduced IT complexity	**0.680**	0.140	-0.103	0.082	0.138
More effective use of IT resources	**0.674**	0.189	0.224	0.088	0.033
Improved ROI on IT spending	**0.669**	0.113	0.289	0.045	0.091
Improved utilization of IT	**0.652**	0.148	0.339	0.271	0.029
Faster development of information systems	**0.638**	0.280	-0.044	0.112	0.058
Improved interoperability among information systems	**0.607**	0.223	0.128	0.293	-0.153
More responsive to change	**0.568**	0.175	0.428	0.039	0.083
Improves information systems security	**0.563**	0.375	-0.062	0.300	-0.057
Standardizes organization's performance measures	0.169	**0.774**	-0.049	0.132	0.030
Better collaboration within organization	0.203	**0.773**	0.216	-0.002	0.094
Improves trust in the organization	0.356	**0.672**	0.227	-0.074	0.157
Improved communication within the organization	0.065	**0.647**	0.404	0.109	0.168
Assists with organizational governance	0.281	**0.592**	0.197	0.163	0.025
Reduced organizational stovepipes	0.266	**0.569**	0.215	0.033	0.187
Improved organizational communication and information sharing	0.185	**0.514**	0.459	0.042	0.182
Less wasted resource on projects	0.334	0.185	**0.684**	-0.004	0.054

Aligning business objectives with IT	0.071	0.194	**0.671**	0.339	0.002
An alignment tool	−0.061	0.192	**0.635**	0.331	0.139
Improved goal attainment	0.383	0.330	**0.575**	0.034	0.189
Provides a blueprint of organization	0.212	0.059	0.068	**0.758**	−0.104
A planning tool	0.180	−0.013	0.209	**0.753**	0.248
A tool for decision making	0.185	0.152	0.181	**0.690**	0.280
A snapshot in time of an organization	0.012	0.150	−0.089	0.006	**0.671**
Facilitates systematic change	0.270	0.033	0.233	0.241	**0.654**
Communicating organizational objectives	−0.081	0.219	0.344	0.114	**0.642**
Variance Explained (%)	16.2	14.85	11.75	9.04	6.79

EA. The final EA functionality factor, consisting of questions with language such as "A snapshot in time," "Facilitating systematic change," and "Communicating objectives," indicate a representation of the current state of EA, the "as is" view. By knowing this current state, an organization can facilitate change.

An analysis of variance was performed to determine if demographic factors measured in this study influenced the respondents' views regarding EA. None of the demographic variables such as position held, experience, education, organization size, or industry were found to have a significant effect on respondent perceptions of either EA's functions or benefits.

This finding seems to be counterintuitive on the surface: it was expected that demographic factors influence the perceived value of technology tools and constructs. In this case, there was a high degree of agreement with regard to most EA functions and benefits among the respondents. This may be a result of asking about hypothetical benefits, what EA should and can be, and not about the state of EA in a specific enterprise. Measurement of actual EA practices is a direction for future research to overcome this limitation, as might improvements to the job title selection.

Interpreting Survey Results

Respondents of this survey appear to have a consistent perspective on the function and benefits of EA. Equally interesting was the unexpected strength in agreement for the functions and the benefits. Six out of seven functions had agreement rates greater than 60 percent. The one exception ("EA as a snapshot in time of an organization") could be indicative of a more IT-centric view of EA's purpose or may be the result of the use of the terms "snapshot" or "in time" in the wording of the question. Although IT-related benefits received higher support among the respondents reflecting a traditionally IT-centric view of EA, many identified organizational benefits that received support of over 60 percent of respondents. This suggests that IT professionals see EA as a broader initiative expanding beyond the boundaries of the IT function. This is consistent with the Zachman EA framework and enterprise ontology (1987, 1999, 2007) as well as with the view that EA is likely to emerge as a broad organizational function encompassing IT as one of its elements (Ross, 2008).

Outlining Directions for Future Research

With relatively scarce EA-related academic research, and practitioners still struggling to harness the business value of EA, there is a unique opportunity for IS academics to produce research of high relevance by establishing theoretical underpinnings of EA and its business benefits. If the business value of EA is widely accepted, IS academics will claim "ownership" of an intellectual asset that is of interest to other business disciplines (Wade, Biehl, and Kim, 2006). In developing

EA theory, several key research directions can be identified. First, it is critical to gain a better understanding of what EA is. Second, it is important to define the nomological net of EA and thereby to better understand the position of EA in relation to other business and IT constructs. Finally, a theoretical understanding of business and IT benefits should be developed. Next, we elaborate on each of the aforementioned directions.

Establishing a Clear Academic Definition of EA

Examination of various definitions of EA, as well as of the common usage of the term in practitioner literature, suggests there is little agreement about the very nature of the EA construct. In many cases EA is treated as a black box, a tool that is useful in the achievement of a variety of goals. As such it is viewed as a planning tool, as a blueprint for organizational data, and so on. Among those who care to look inside the black box of EA, agreement lacks on two issues: the meaning of the word *enterprise* and the meaning of the word *architecture*. The "enterprise" portion of EA is understood by some as a synonym to "enterprise systems," yet by others as equivalent to "business" or "organization." For example, Miller (1997) adopted an IT-centric view of EA when he examined the benefits of EA planning for the implementation of client-server technology. Gregor, Hart, and Martin (2007), while examining the EA's role in enabling alignment, adopt a somewhat broader definition of EA by the International Organization for Standardization (ISO): "a descriptive representation of the basic arrangement and connectivity of parts of an enterprise (such as data, information, systems, technologies, designs, business processes)" (97). Ross's definition of EA (Ross, 2003; Ross and Beath, 2006), although somewhat IT-centric, expands the concept more into the organizational domain and sees EA as a tool to align IT with the enterprise through its processes, presumably themselves aligned with the strategic objectives of the organization.

Even less uniform is the understanding of the meaning of *architecture*. The most common understanding of the term is a collection of artifacts (models, descriptions, etc.) that define the standards of how the enterprise should function or provide an as-is model of the enterprise (Kaisler, Armour, and Valivullah, 2005; Khoury, Simoff, and Debenham, 2005). Yet others equate EA with the process of defining standards and creating as-is models and descriptions. More broadly, Bernard (2005) declares that "EA provides a holistic view of an enterprise" (23), and Kappelman (2007) opines that EA is about "creating and using a shared 'language' (of words, graphics, and other depictions) to discuss and document every important aspect of the enterprise" so stakeholders can align their thinking and thereby align the resources of the enterprise (25). The presence of such definitional multidimensionality suggests that perhaps there is a room for decomposing EA into a set of simpler, interrelated constructs. Knowledge management literature (Nonaka and Konno, 1998; Nonaka, Takeuchi, and

Umemoto, 1996; Polanyi, 1958) dealing with tacit and explicit knowledge provides one possible theoretical lens for defining such constructs. Actor-network theory (Callon and Latour, 1981; Sarker, Sarker, and Sidorova, 2003; Walsham, 1997) provides a tool for examining EA from the negotiation, power, and politics point of view.

Establishing Theoretical Foundations of EA Benefits

While the majority of the IT practitioners agree EA has a variety of potential benefits for IT and business in general, such claims are not consistently theoretically grounded. The role of IS research is to establish a theoretical foundation for examining such benefits. As a first step, a typology of EA benefits should be developed. The results of the SIM survey provide a first glimpse into types of EA benefits by distinguishing among IT-related, goal-related, and general organizational benefits of EA.

The next step involves developing and testing theoretical propositions for specific EA benefits. For example, EA has been often cited as an enabler of alignment between IT and business (Gregor, Hart, and Martin, 2007; Ross, 2003; Sauer and Willcocks, 2004; Van der Raadt et al., 2005). Further research is needed to solidify such claims, and to examine contextual and other factors that may influence such a relationship. Similarly, theoretical foundations should be developed for other types of benefits. For example, an information-processing view of the firm could be used to approach EA benefits for intraorganizational communication. With growing interest in organizational agility as a source of competitive advantage (Venkatesh et al., 2007), attention has been drawn to organizational modularity. The modularity theory (Shilling, 2000, 2001) could provide a link between EA and benefits related to organizational responsiveness to change. More broadly, research could examine the role of EA in achieving any enterprise design objective (e.g., aligned, agile, centralized, etc.).

Conclusions and Limitations

In this paper we examine how IT practitioners view EA and its benefits. While the results presented here are rather exploratory in nature, the main contribution of this study is to highlight the importance of EA and to inspire for future research on the topic. As evident from the results presented in this paper, both IS practitioners and academics believe EA has multiple benefits, not only for IT management, but for organizations as a whole. EA is seen by practitioners as both a planning tool and a representation of the current state of the enterprise. However, to ensure that the value of EA is realized, it is important to get a deeper understanding of how EA may lead to the desired organizational outcomes. Because there is often a lack of a common definition of EA, it is crucial to establish such a definition, as well as to relate it to other established IT and organizational constructs. Further research should focus on specific benefits of EA and how they can be best achieved.

It is important to mention some important limitations of this study. First, we focused on perceived *potential* benefits of EA, which partially explains the lack of variance among different types of organizations. Therefore, a natural extension of this study would be to measure the perceived organizational benefits of EA and to relate them to specific EA practices and organizational characteristics. In addition, the high degree of agreement on the benefits of EA could be partially explained by the selection bias: because survey participation was optional, it is likely that those who do not perceive the value of EA as high did not respond to the survey. Although we tried to avoid such selection bias by not putting the term "enterprise architecture" in the survey title, it is still a concern.

In conclusion, we believe EA presents immense challenges and opportunities. IT practitioners and academics have the first shot at taking advantage of the opportunity and challenge of EA. Thus there is a unique opportunity for IS researchers to leverage their knowledge and experience and to carve a new existential niche that would help foster and perhaps even ensure respect of the IS academic discipline by business practitioners and academics alike. Unless our vision for the future of the IT profession is only technical expertise related to our IT subsystems, IS academics and researchers should seek to encourage a vision of broader things for IS professionals. Perhaps it's time for something new, something different, something that helps us see past the IT stovepipe to the whole enterprise including its technologies. That something is enterprise architecture.

Notes

55. The survey portion of this project was sponsored by the Society for Information Management (SIM), the SIM Enterprise Architecture Working Group (http://eawg.simnet.org) and the Information Technology and Decision Sciences Department at the University of North Texas.
56. An earlier version of this article appeared in the Proceedings of the Fourteenth Americas Conference on Information Systems, Toronto, ON, Canada August 14th–17th 2008.
57. Author's names appear in alphabetical order.
58. No academic degrees, majors, or even minors in EA exist, and no college courses devoted to EA in the United States of which we are aware, aside from some college-affiliated programs directed at the federal government in Washington, DC.

References

Bernard, S. 2005. *An introduction to enterprise architecture*. Bloomington, IN: AuthorHouse.

Boh, W., and D. Yellin. 2007. Using enterprise architecture standards in managing information technology. *Journal of Management Information Systems* 23, no. 3: 163–207.

Brooks, F. 1986. No silver bullet—essence and accidents of software engineering. *Information Processing* 20, no. 4: 1069–76.

Brooks, F. 1995. *The mythical man-month* (20th anniversary ed.). Boston: Addison-Wesley Longman.

Callon, M., and B. Latour. 1981. Unscrewing the big leviathan: How actors macro-structure reality and how sociologists help them to do so. *Advances in Social Theory and Methodology: Towards an Integration of Micro and Macro-Sociologies* 1: 277–303.

Chen, P. 1976. The entity relationship model—toward a unified view of data. *ACM Transactions on Database Systems* 1, no. 1: 1–36.

Collett, S. 2006. Hot skills, cold skills. *Computerworld* (July): 1–5.

DeMarco, T. 1978. *Structured analysis and system specification.* New York: Yourdon Press.

El Sawy, O., A. Malhotra, S. Gosain, and K. Young. 1999. IT-intensive value innovation in the electronic economy: Insights from Marshall Industries. *MIS Quarterly* 23, no. 3: 305–35.

Finkelstein, C., and J. Martin. 1981. *Information engineering,* vols. 1 and 2. Englewood Cliffs, NJ: Prentice Hall.

GAO. 2003. *A framework for assessing and improving enterprise architecture management* (version 1.1). GAO-03-584G. Washington, DC: United States General Accountability Office. http://www.gao.gov (April).

Gregor, S., D. Hart, and N. Martin. 2007. Enterprise architectures: Enablers of business strategy and IS/IT alignment in government. *Information Technology and People* 20, no. 2: 96–120.

Hagan, P. 2004. *Guide to the (evolving) enterprise architecture body of knowledge (EABOK).* McLean, VA: The MITRE Corporation.

Hair, J., W. Black, B. Babin, R. Anderson, and R. Tatham. 2006. *Multivariate data analysis.* Englewood Cliffs, NJ: Pearson Prentice Hall.

Janssen, M., and K. Hjort-Madsen. 2007. Managing enterprise architecture in national governments: The cases of the Netherlands and Denmark. In *Proceedings of the 40th Hawaii International Conference on Systems Sciences,* 1–10. Washington, DC: IEEE Computer Society Press.

Kappelman, L. 2007. Enterprise architecture: Not just another management fad. *Align Journal* (March/April): 24–27.

Kappelman, L., ed. 2008. *Getting started with enterprise architecture.* Chicago: SIM International.

Luftman, J. 2000. Assessing business-IT alignment maturity. *Communications of the Association for Information Systems* 4, no. 14: 1–51.

Luftman, J. 2003. *IT-business strategic alignment maturity assessment.* http://www.simnet.org/Content/NavigationMenu/Resources/Library/Download_Page3res/ITBusinessAlignment.pdf.

Luftman, J., and E. McLean. 2004. Key issues for IT executives. *MIS Quarterly Executive* 3, no. 2: 89–104.

Miller, D. 1997. Enterprise client/server planning. *Information Systems Management* 14, no. 2: 7–15.

Nonaka, W., and N. Konno. 1998. The concept of "Ba": Building a foundation for knowledge creation. *California Management Review* 40, no. 3: 40–54.

Nonaka, W., W. Takeuchi, and K. Umemoto. 1996. A theory of organizational knowledge creation. *International Journal of Technology Management* 11, no. 7/8: 833–45.

OMB. 1999. *Federal Enterprise Architecture Framework (FEAF).* Washington, DC: Chief Information Officer Council, United States Office of Management and Budget.

OMB. 2001. *A practical guide to federal enterprise architecture,* version 1.0. Washington, DC: Chief Information Officer Council, United States Office of Management and Budget.

Polanyi, M. 1958. *Personal knowledge: Towards a post-critical philosophy.* Chicago: University of Chicago Press.

Peristeras, V., and K. Tarabanis. 2000. Towards an enterprise architecture for public administration using a top-down approach. *European Journal of Information Systems* 9, no. 4: 252–60.

Reich, B., and I. Benbasat. 1996. Measuring the linkage between business and information technology objectives. *MIS Quarterly* 20, no. 1: 55–72.

Rohloff, M. 2005. Enterprise architecture: Framework and methodology for the design of architectures in the large. In *European Conference on Information Systems Proceedings.* http://aisel.aisnet.org/ecis2005/113.

Ross, J. 2003. Creating a strategic IT architecture competency: Learning in stages. *MISQ Executive* 2, no. 1: 1–18.

Ross, J., P. Weill, and D. Robertson. 2006. *Enterprise architecture as strategy creating a foundation for business execution.* Boston: Harvard Business School Press.

Ross, J. 2008. Foreword to *Getting started with enterprise architecture.* L. A. Kappelman, ed. Chicago: SIM International.

Sarker, S., S. Sarker, and A. Sidorova. 2006. Understanding business process change failure: An actor-network perspective. *Journal of Management Information Systems* 23, no. 1: 51–86.

Sauer, C., and L. Willcocks. 2004. Strategic alignment revisited: Connecting organizational architecture and IT infrastructure. In *Proceedings of the 37th Annual Hawaii International Conference on Systems Software,* 232–41. Washington, DC: IEEE Computer Society Press.

Sledgianowski, D., J. Luftman, and R. Reilly. 2006. Development and validation of an instrument to measure maturity of IT business strategic alignment mechanisms. *Information Resources Management Journal* 19: 3–18.

Strano, C., and Q. Rehmani, 2007. The role of the enterprise architect. *Information Systems and E-Business Management* 5, no. 4: 379–96.

van der Raadt, B., J. Hoorn, and H. van Vliet. 2005. Alignment and maturity are siblings in architecture assessment. In *Proceedings of Advanced Information Systems Engineering: 17th International Conference, CAiSE 2005.* Berlin: Springer-Verlag: 357–371.

van der Raadt, B., J. Soetendal, M. Perdeck, and H. van Vliet. 2004. Polyphony in architecture. In *Proceedings of the 26th International Conference on Software Engineering,* 533–42. Washington, DC: IEEE Computer Society Press.

Venkatesh, V., H. Bala, S. Venkatraman, and J. Bates. 2007. Enterprise architecture maturity: The story of the Veterans Health Administration. *MISQ Executive* 6, no. 2: 79–90.

Wade, M., M. Biehl, and H. Kim. 2006. If the tree of IS knowledge falls in a forest, will anyone hear? A commentary on Grover et al. *Journal of the Association for Information Systems* 7, no. 5: 326–34.

Walsham, G. 1997. Actor-network theory and IS research: Current status and future prospects. In *Information Systems and Qualitative Research,* 466–80. London: Chapman & Hall.

Wieringa, R., H. Blanken, M. Fokkinga, and P. Grefen. 2003. Aligning application architecture to the business context. In *Proceedings of Advanced Information Systems Engineering: 15th International Conference,* 1028–1029. Berlin: Springer-Verlag.

Yourdon, E. 1975. *Techniques of program structure and design.* Englewood Cliffs, NJ: Prentice Hall.

Zachman, J. 1987. A framework for information systems architecture. *IBM Systems Journal* 26, no. 3: 276–92. IBM Publication G321-5298. http://www.research.ibm.com/journal/sj/382/zachman.pdf.

Zachman, J. 1999. Enterprise architecture: The past and the future. *DM Review Magazine* (December). http://www.dmreview.com/issues/19991201/1702-1.html.

Zachman, J. 2005. *Framework standards: What's it all about?* Monograph available at http://zachmaninternational.com/2/production/C4/pdfs/FrameworkStandards.pdf.

Zachman, J. 2007. *Enterprise architecture standards V2.01.* http://zachmaninternational.com/2/Standards.asp.

Zachman, J., and J. Sowa. 1992. Extending and formalizing the framework for information systems architecture. *IBM Systems Journal* 31, no. 3: 590–616.

ENTERPRISE ARCHITECTURE PRACTICE

3

We shape our buildings—thereafter they shape us.

—**Sir Winston Churchill**

Introduction

Doing enterprise architecture is not simple or easy, any more than managing an enterprise is simple or easy. This should come as no surprise in light of our journey in Chapter 2 through EA theory and concepts, and the fact that enterprises are "the most complex object the human mind has conceived of and created thus far," as John Zachman opines in the EA pioneer panel article in Chapter 1. The human element adds to the difficulty, complexity, and uncertainty of EA practice within an organization, as Anna Sidorova and Leon Kappelman remind us in their "Enterprise Architecture as Politics" article in Chapter 2.

Indeed, even if one has a perfect grasp of conceptual and practical aspects of EA, the nuances of individual organizations raise challenges to its successful initiation, diffusion, and institutionalization into the functioning enterprise. Such nuances include not only general matters like the state of the economy, industry, organization size, and public or private ownership, but also matters like organization culture and politics, geographical dispersion, product cycles, competitors, regulation, management style, and so on. Understanding EA is one thing; its proper utilization is another. In this chapter, five articles are provided to address the challenges of doing EA successfully.

"Enterprise Architecture: Not Just Another Management Fad," by Dr. Kappelman, begins the discourse from the theoretical to the practical. Regardless of the definition one prefers, one of EA's primary goals is to provide the vocabulary (of words and pictures) needed to identify, record, make available, and amend the architecture of the enterprise so that the vision and requirements of management can be created and managed. Just as the management of an enterprise is an ongoing process, not a finite project, so too is the management of its architecture. Nevertheless, EA activities should be integral to every project in the enterprise, IT or otherwise. Elaborating on the notion stated in Chapter 1 that successful EA practices "begin between the ears," Kappelman opines that "if the people in the enterprise can't adequately communicate to align their thinking, there's limited likelihood that the more tangible 'things' managed by those people … will be aligned with the more intangible things such as objectives."

Revisiting the Enterprise Wheel's hub-and-spoke model that we introduced in Figure 1.1 in Chapter 1, a straightforward approach is to demonstrate the practical value of EA by leveraging the fortuitous opportunity of an IT project, which typically is focused on the processes within a given spoke. Figure 3.1 depicts this kind of focus. Process leadership and other stakeholders may already be amenable to change, and EA can facilitate the technical, business, and human dimensions of it. These situations can provide the perfect opportunity to create value with EA and to win some "converts one at a time," as John Zachman described it during the panel discussion. Moreover, they must show that there is value in doing EA because EA helps improve the value-creating activities of the enterprise.

Properly executed, these first forays into EA start the development of the communications capabilities necessary to support the business objectives and the culture change needed to be an Information Age organization. Developing communications capabilities and shared language is not a trivial task—it must prove its worth from the beginning. Professor Kappelman also points to the importance of the IT organization being ready and willing to "eat its own cooking" when it comes to EA; IT, if it is to rise to the challenge and opportunity of EA, must not only talk the EA talk, but also walk the EA walk. Attitude is important too, and approaching EA as an enterprise-learning opportunity, in which answers are discovered and innovations born, will enable all involved to learn from their EA mistakes as well as their successes. "Don't underestimate the difficulty and complexity of architecting the enterprise," he proclaims, and "don't get discouraged … change of this magnitude takes time and perseverance."

Ed Cannon's article provides a focused perspective on the challenges of practicing EA within the marketing spoke as part of an IT-enabled e-commerce initiative. Thus the marketing and the IT activities are emphasized along with the EA spoke in the Enterprise Wheel shown in Figure 3.1. Cannon highlights how EA can

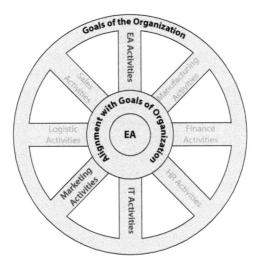

FIGURE 3.1   The Enterprise Wheel (with Chapter 3 emphasis).

help to align complex environments with the firm's overall goals, while rising not only to the challenges of EA but also to the challenges of e-commerce at the same time. Cannon explains how both the complexity of e-commerce (both technically and organizationally) and the fact that it can touch the entire supply chain (from raw materials to customer service) make enterprise architecture not only useful but critically necessary for e-commerce success.

In "Using Language to Gain Control of Enterprise Architecture," Dr. Gary Simons teams up with Leon Kappelman and John Zachman to provide an illustrative example of how an organization can incorporate EA theory into EA practice. This case study, covering nearly seven years of EA activity, is an example of what is probably the leading edge of EA work today. Perhaps unique in maturity of their EA activities at this time, senior management to the board level visibly supports EA and speaks the theoretical and applied language of EA. Furthermore, vice president–level managers own and validate the primitive EA models for their parts of the business. The lessons learned as they succeeded and stumbled in "eating their own cooking" to create value through EA point to the conclusion that assimilating EA into the organization can be done, but it requires a disciplined approach and an understanding that "one size does not fit all." Since every organization is unique, this rings true.

Simons's case study suggests that modeling the numerous subsystems aligned with specific business functions ("spokes" in the context of the Enterprise Wheel) is an effective approach to modeling, in other words "architecting," the entire organization. This was accomplished by leveraging their belief in EA theory into a shared language of their own invention to engage fully the various managerial aspects of the firm. Along the way they discovered that there was a dearth of digital EA modeling and storage tools available, and so they invented their own XML-based EA modeling language and repository. Perhaps the fact that this case study is about an enterprise of professional linguists enabled them to see that EA was fundamentally a language issue and that they had to invent a language to properly put theory into practice. Nevertheless, this is probably the most technical article in the book. Fortunately for the rest of us, their GEM EA modeling language is applicable to any enterprise, as are many of their lessons learned.

It is noteworthy that in Dr. Simons's article, he refers to the "Zachman Enterprise Framework" as the "Zachman Framework for Enterprise Architecture." This is consistent with the nomenclature as it was when the experiences described in his case study began. As it turns out, the collaboration of linguist turned enterprise architect Simons with Zachman and his colleague Stan Locke led to the evolution of the labels Zachman uses in his framework. Although the logic and theory of Zachman's ontology has remained unchanged since its inception, the more precise terminology has improved its usability for actual EA practice. Moreover, this collaboration also resulted in similar linguistic clarifications and improvements to the other three iterations of the logic—the Classification Framework, the Professional Framework, and the Product Framework.[1] This article also uses an earlier version of the graphical depiction of the Zachman enterprise ontology.

Bruce Ballengee, wave rider of Chapter 2 fame, returns here with "Enterprise Architecture: Time for IT to Break Out!" Though certain that EA "is unequivocally a good thing," Ballengee faces the current cost center reality of the IT organization in most enterprises, and concludes that "by thinking of itself as a business, IT can now serve the business with greater freedom of thought, and more often than not, freedom of action [... to solve] the age-old conundrum of IT-business alignment." However, strategic focus is required for success, opines Ballengee, and EA is key to being able to focus well while also providing basic IT services in order to maximize business value. Ballengee joins the "eat your own cooking" and "practice what you preach" chorus, and concludes that "once IT demonstrates to the business the power of using enterprise architecture to remake itself, the business will more likely accept the need of and value for enterprise architecture."

Maximizing value and the "one size does not fit all" sentiments are further illuminated in the closing article of this chapter, written by Larry DeBoever (EA pioneer panelist in Chapter 1), George Paras, and Tim Westbrock. Their focus is on the pragmatic approaches needed for an effective EA program. They stress that the assimilation of EA can be made more effective if it is presented to the organization as outcomes and activities rather than abstract definitions. They also opine that EA efforts create the most value when focused on reducing complexity of IT and business processes to optimal levels in order to cut costs and increase agility. Eighteen insights into EA assimilation are presented as well as insight into the challenges of restarting EA initiatives within an organization after initial stumbles. The "sale" of EA cannot be made by presenting the "hub" to upper management. The authors also examine the kinds of EA investments that create the most value, and those that do not; and close with a recap of some of the vast potentialities of EA despite the challenges.

It is the value that EA can generate (by optimizing and simplifying the enterprise, increasing its agility and productivity, and aligning business and technology within the spokes and across the whole enterprise) that have an impact on the goals of the organization (the outer ring in the Enterprise Wheel in Figure 3.1). Each success, in turn, will win a few converts and help garner further support. Continuing to create value through EA helps ensure that support for EA continues. It is a virtuous cycle. It is also a necessary one, given the characteristics of this Information Age that organizations must not only adapt to but master. These are:

1. doing more with less;
2. an increasing pace of everything, including change;
3. a blurring of boundaries, inside and outside the enterprise; and
4. the critical need to successfully manage information and knowledge.

EA success is critical to the successful creation of the Information Age enterprise and thus the realization of the true potential of the Information Age (at least from an economic perspective, which of course has implications across the fabric of society). If this were the Industrial Age—say, about 1835—enterprises and their technologies would look pretty good to folks, but they look absurdly primitive to us today. It took both technological and intellectual advances to bring about the IT products that led to the evolution of the Industrial Age into the Information Age. But we have barely begun to realize the potentials of those technologies because we are still seeing the world through Industrial Age eyes ("mental models" to be more precise).

Our Information Age technologies are largely utilized today in what are effectively still Industrial Age organizations, populated by Industrial Age ideas. Enterprise architecture is a key part of the intellectual advance, a paradigm shift if you please, that will enable us to bridge that chasm between strategy and implementation, and between vision and reality. But not only to create more widgets and services but to transform the workplace of today into a place "where people continually expand their capacity to create the results they truly desire, where new and expansive patterns of thinking are nurtured, where collective aspiration is set free, and where people are continually learning to see the whole together"[2] with EA.

Notes

1. See Zachman's "Framework Stadards: What's It All About?" article in Chapter 2 for more information about the four frameworks. A complete elaboration of these is beyond the scope of this book; however, see http://zachmaninternational.com for further details about framework standards.
2. Senge, Peter M. 1990. *The Fifth Discipline: The Art and Practice of the Learning Organization.* New York, Doubleday, p. 7.

Enterprise Architecture: Not Just Another Management Fad

Leon A. Kappelman

> And so these men of Indostan, Disputed loud and long, ... Though each was partly in the right, And all were in the wrong![3]

Despite awareness of the concept and its importance, there's no standard definition of enterprise architecture (EA) and considerable ambiguity in the use of the term. The difficulty is in part a function of the subject matter, what's probably one of humankind's most complicated creations: the enterprise itself. Our professional biases and historically stovepiped world exacerbate the situation.

Alignment, rapid introduction, complexity reduction, speed, and agility are design objectives that answer the question, "What do we want it to look like?" So EA is perhaps at least part of the answer to the question, "How do we accomplish it?" Federal Reserve Chairman Ben Bernanke calls it "intangible capital." In his June 2006 commencement speech at MIT,[4] he said:

> In the case of information and communication technologies, new economic research suggests that the investments in associated intangible capital—figuring out what to do with the computer once it's out of the box—are quite important indeed. In my view, important investments in intangible capital remain to be made, as much still remains to be learned about how to harness these technologies most effectively.

The fact is, "EA" is not the best name for the subject matter, but it is the best name we have today. Most current use of the term EA is focused primarily on what

117

might be called IT architecture, which is concerned with the logical and physical descriptions of data, applications, and hardware assets. Expanding on that, consider John Zachman's contention that "the business strategy and its linkage to information systems strategy ... ultimately manifest themselves in architectural expression."[5]

You can add the definition used by the U.S. General Accountability Office (GAO) that an EA provides "a clear and comprehensive picture of an entity, whether an organization ... or a functional or mission area that cuts across more than one organization."[6] The GAO adds that it "is a blueprint for organizational change defined in models that describe (in both business and technology terms) how the entity operates today and how it intends to operate in the future; it also includes a plan for transitioning to this future state."[7]

Before you concatenate all that into your EA definition, reflect on the notion that EA is all about creating and using a shared "language" (of words, graphics, and other depictions) to discuss and document every important aspect of the enterprise. Without such a communication capability, optimal alignment, agility, speed, and simplicity aren't possible, nor can we hope to realize the potentialities of strategic planning, performance measurement, or process reengineering, or ensure success with security, privacy, governance, project management, innovation, and managing transformation and change.

If the people in the enterprise can't adequately communicate to align their thinking, there's limited likelihood that the more tangible "things" managed by those people (such as software, data, products, people, channels, monies, and so on) will be aligned with the more intangible things such as objectives, motivations, or government regulations.

Carpe Diem (Seize the Day)

EA is a new way of thinking about the enterprise, and a new way of managing it. There's a parallel to the way scientific management, as described by Frederick Winslow Taylor,[8] was a key part of the intellectual or intangible capital that led to enormous productivity gains in the Industrial Age. EA has the potential to contribute similarly to the Information Age. The "productivity paradox" remains alive and well, and we still have much to learn about "what to do with the computer once it's out of the box." Who can afford not to seize the opportunity to better use all the knowledge about the enterprise?

EA is more a process than a project; more a journey than a task. EA is an ongoing innovation and transformation initiative. It's about change in processes, procedures, and language. But perhaps more important, it's about a change in the culture, as well as the hearts and minds in the enterprise. EA is about big-picture thinking, but it's also about the little picture (in the context of the whole). It's about achieving balance in optimizing the whole and the parts, and therefore about the alignment of the whole and the parts.

Too often, we optimize our subsystems to the detriment of the whole. Consider the U.S. health care system in which highly optimized and highly profitable subsystems of insurance, doctors, hospitals, pharmaceuticals, laboratories, and others, provide the most expensive, often the best, but by some measures the lowest quality patient care in the industrialized world. Support for this notion is abundantly available [e.g., 9, 10, 11]. Our enterprises are often just as dysfunctional.

Getting Started and Staying the Course

So how might you go about implementing an EA program in your enterprise? Start small and show early success. Try to identify EA initiatives of most value to the organization, and be opportunistic such as using EA to improve critical aspects of a new project or the outcome of a project currently in the pipeline. Find one that's already in the kind of trouble EA can help with. Before getting started, develop some understanding and agreement among key players about language, frameworks, models, and methods to be used. Remember, communication is key.

Engaged, clear, decisive, and continuing leadership from the highest executive levels of the enterprise is critical for fostering EA progress and paybacks. Determine the goals, focus, scope, and priorities, and aim for completeness and comprehensiveness, but accept that there will be trade-offs with the practicality and pragmatism of achieving daily business objectives.

And eat your own cooking. To the IT folks, that means use EA to continuously improve systems development, security, operations, and user support to better serve enterprise needs and to communicate with your customers and stakeholders. IT has already been doing EA to some extent under names such as analysis, design, and documentation. Don't just talk the talk; walk the walk. Whatever your job in the enterprise, do this and set an example.

Embrace change and learning. Remember that it's a journey and a process. Monitor, evaluate, and continuously improve. Quantify the benefits, and be able to show how EA helped make things better, and communicate that, too. Regularly take a hard look at cost and value, and keep making EA processes and products better, thereby improving the enterprise.

EA isn't easy or simple. It can't be outsourced any more than strategy can be outsourced. Although consultants and vendors can help, EA is about improving the ability of the people in your enterprise to communicate more quickly and effectively so they can manage and change the enterprise. EA is complicated and difficult work requiring courage, vision, and perseverance. Just like everything else, it's about properly planning and managing an enterprise.

EA is a new way of life. There's no quick fix; no silver bullet. It will take time and determination, as well as vision, courage, and commitment. Don't underestimate the difficulty and complexity of architecting the enterprise. Don't get discouraged; EA is a revolution in thinking, a discipline, and a process.

Change of this magnitude takes time and perseverance. Set realistic expectations. Don't assume anything. Make education and training a continuous process. Communicate and ensure you're communicating! Don't hesitate to ask, "What do you mean by that?" Use and reinforce new definitions, be they words or graphics, until they become part of the language and culture of the enterprise.

Accept that all this is subject to change, too, so keep learning. There's much that remains to be discovered and invented, and many opportunities to create advantage and value. Celebrate your progress and successes, and learn from your mistakes. Enjoy the journey; you're transforming the world, one enterprise at a time.

Take Aways

Business

- EA is about creating and using a shared "language" (of words, graphics, and other depictions) to discuss and document every important aspect of the enterprise.
- EA is about improving the ability of the people in your enterprise to communicate more quickly and effectively so they can manage and change the enterprise more quickly and effectively.

Technology

- With EA there is no quick fix, no silver bullet. It will take time and determination as well as vision, courage, and commitment.
- IT can use EA to continuously improve systems development, security, operations, and user support to better serve enterprise needs and to communicate with customers and stakeholders.

A version of this article appeared as Leon A. Kappelman (2007), "Enterprise Architecture: Not Just Another Management Fad," *Align Journal,* March/April, pp. 24–27.

Notes

3. Saxe, John Godfrey, 1869. "The Blind Men and the Elephant," in *The Poems of John Godfrey Saxe*, Boston: James Osgood and Co., 77–78. (Poem first appeared in 1863, New York: Whittlesey House.)
4. Commencement address by Ben S. Bernanke, June 9, 2006, http://web.mit.edu/new soffice/2006/comm-bernanke.html (6-January-2007).
5. Zackman, J. 1987. A framework for information systems architecture. *IBM Systems Journal.* 26(3): 454–470.

6. GAO 2002. *Enterprise Architecture Use across the Federal Government Can Be Improved.* GAO-02-6, February 2002, last retrieved on 1/2/2008 from www.gao.gov/new.items/ d026.pdf.

7. GAO 2006. *Enterprise Architecture: Leadership Remains Key to Establishing and Leveraging Architectures for Organizational Transformation,* GAO-06-831, August 2006, last retrieved on 1/2/2008 from http://www.gao.gov/new.items/d06831.pdf.

8. Taylor, F. W. 1911. *The Principles of Scientific Management.* Last retrieved on 1/2/2008 from http://melbecon.unimelb.edu.au/het/taylor/sciman.htm.

9. Banks, J., M. Marmot et al. 2006. "Disease and Disadvantage in the United States and in England," *Journal of the American Medical Association.* 295(17): 2037–2045.

10. Nordqvist, C. 2006. U.S. Infant Survival Rates Lower Than Most Developed Nations. *Medical News Today,* May 9. Last retrieved 1/2/2008 from www.medicalnewstoday. com/healthnews.php?newsid=4094

11. Bureau of Labor Education 2001. *The U.S. Health Care System: Best in the World or Just the Most Expensive.* University of Maine. Last retrieved on 1/2/2008 from http:// dll.umaine.edu/ble/U.S.%2v0HCweb.pdf#search=%22%22health%20care%22%20 USA%20compared%20countries%20industrialized%22.

Why Does E-Commerce Need Enterprise Architecture?

Ed Cannon

Benefit of Enterprise Architecture

Enterprise architecture is a way to plan, organize, and think about a complex "system" of interrelated elements including people, process, and technology, so that investment decisions are maximized. CIOs who view a "system" or enterprise architecture as a combination of people, process, systems, technology, and data, understand that it takes good planning to be successful in this complex environment. Using an enterprise architecture framework, CIOs communicate the vision of a new "system" from the computer room to the boardroom. In doing so, the CIO is using enterprise architecture to drive organization alignment to ensure that the right investment is being made and financial and organizational capital is maximized.

Enterprise Architecture History of Success

CIOs who successfully implemented ERP, Supply Chain, and CRM found that the enterprise architecture approach provided a framework to accelerate decision making and align the organization. Enterprise architecture strategy did this by providing a vision from a business perspective, identifying organizational requirements in people, place, technology, and data, and providing an expected time line or product road map based on the goals of the business.

The purpose of this article is to advocate that the same enterprise architecture approach be adopted for e-commerce due to improve the probability of success, while reducing the possibility of failure. Enterprise architecture incorporates strategic, tactical, and operational thinking required when considering the evolution of e-commerce over the next five years. The last thing you want to do is be in the position where you are trading out e-commerce platforms every two years and not leveraging existing assets. To optimize a company's investment in e-commerce, enterprise architecture should be adopted as a standard management decision "framework" to allow management to make more informed decisions.

Generally, enterprise architecture is viewed more as an IT back-office activity, not applicable to e-commerce. However, this author disagrees. Based on my experience with most of the major ERP packages and one of the first pure play supply chain implementations, e-commerce is more strategic than those systems. If ERP and Supply Chain were strategic in the 1990s, e-commerce is the strategic play in the twenty-first century. Opening new markets, servicing customers in new and rewarding ways, reducing inventory cost through real-time analytics—these are the promise and reality of e-commerce platforms.

Today's e-commerce platforms are comprehensive and provide the ability to add third-party software. They are technologically complex and require rethinking of existing business functions and processes in order to fully exploit the power of this unique business system.

Combined, e-commerce is strategically important and technologically complex. Enterprise architecture can help decompose this complexity and make it understandable so that it the organization can align around the vision and make better management decisions when investing in e-commerce.

E-Commerce Challenges

Maximizing e-commerce return on investment is difficult due to budget overruns, missed opportunities, and unmet expectations. New technologies are rapidly being developed and brought to market. What was best practice eighteen months ago has now been replaced by a new list of best practices and supporting technology. The more complex the technology, the higher the risk of failure. The belief of the author is that e-commerce from a technology point of view is more complex and more mission-critical than any of the previous technologies and therefore requires a disciplined way of thinking and making decisions.

Challenge #1

First, the myth that e-commerce is limited to the customer experience, is just that—a myth. E-commerce is about not just the customer experience, but the entire value chain, both e-commerce and traditional enterprise systems. Unlike ERP, Supply

Chain, or CRM, which each address a specific functional business process, e-commerce business processes include marketing, merchandising, order management, scheduling, inventory management, billing, cash collection and allocation, personalization, business intelligence, returns, and customer service. No other "enterprise system" does as much. So myth number one is that e-commerce is simple. It is not. E-commerce is complex from a transaction, business process, technology, and operations point of view, and requires that many policy, organization, and procedural issues be addressed before a company can maximize the use of e-commerce.

Challenge #2

Second, e-commerce, whether business to business (B2B) and business to consumer (B2C), is strategic and one of the fastest-growing segments of our economy. Structurally, e-commerce provides a highly cost-effective channel to market, sell, and service product, while simultaneously allowing customers global access to the entire inventory. E-commerce has radically altered industries such as travel, music, and real estate, and it will continue to do so. Due to its impact on the customer experience, the opportunity to change industry structures and redesign the way customers interact with your company, make e-commerce one of the most strategic technologies in any CIO's portfolio.

Challenge #3

Third, e-commerce is complex since it involves more systems and technology than are normally used in CRM, ERP, or SCM implementations. A state-of-the-art, robust e-commerce site could include many technologies. For example, you need different technologies for shopping cart, payment methods, credit checks, site search, search engine optimization, content management, gifting, bonus points, user recommendations, site analytics, single sign-on, personalization, online marketing and merchandising, wish lists, and the like. Without a structured way of thinking about these technologies and the impact they have on your organization, which enterprise architecture supports, return on investment in technology investments will not be maximized. Additionally, without a structured way of thinking about technology, designing organizational capabilities to deliver the technology will be lacking and will negatively impact your schedule or quality of your system.

Challenge #4

Most companies have organized their e-commerce department as a shared service that supports multiple lines of businesses or divisions. As a shard service, e-commerce departments are responsible for designing and implementing the various divisions' initiatives. Unfortunately, shared service operations are put in the uncomfortable position of managing demand, which eventually results in the elimination of some projects or initiatives: projects or initiatives that have a high probability of impacting that division's ability to deliver on their plan. Negotiating these competing priorities is an art rather than a science, but one that is helped by the use of enterprise architecture.

Using enterprise architecture as the framework, CIOs can have more meaningful conversations at the board level regarding demand for services, balanced against supply of talent or constraints such as tight budgets. By employing enterprise architecture to enable and facilitate such discussions, the CIO can enlist the help of the senior management team to prioritize, at an enterprise level, what is most important to the company's strategic vision.

Challenge #5

Technology change is one constant in the e-commerce space. Technologies that were just on the horizon three years ago, are now prime-time and considered standard. In fact many of the advances in technology over the past six years have been in the area of e-commerce. Compared to ERP or SCM, where the degree of change has slowed, e-commerce technology has exploded and will continue to do so in the foreseeable future. The challenge is not only picking the right technology, but managing technologies that are at various stages of their life cycles. Some e-commerce technologies such as shopping cart are well seasoned. Other technologies such as site search are newer and not as mature. Therefore different approaches must be taken to successfully manage various technologies to market. Enterprise architecture models help identify the key technologies to meet the business goals, and to plan for inevitable change. It is the responsibility of the technology department to recognize the maturity of the technology and take the appropriate steps to ensure successful implementation and ongoing operations.

The myth that e-commerce does not need as much structure or discipline compared to traditional IT initiatives is wrong. E-commerce is a strategic initiative that requires technology, one that touches every part of the business and has the potential to radically change the operations of a company. To align management, ensuring that the highest payback initiatives are being addressed, requires a framework in which to make those decisions. Enterprise architecture is that framework.

At the same time, e-commerce technology and the business processes it supports are rapidly changing. Tomorrow, a new technology could be introduced that improves customer conversion rates, or frequency of purchase, or increases the average order size. Having a framework that can help decision makers understand the people, process, data, and strategic implications of a new technology and how it fits into the overall plan for the site and the business is another useful application of enterprise architecture. It helps speed and potentially improve decision making in a rapidly changing world.

The bottom line is that enterprise architecture pays big dividends in highly complex environments, where there are many stakeholders and the technology/business investment is significant. As this article tries to highlight, due to its strategic nature and technological complexity, e-commerce should embrace enterprise architecture and adopt it as a standard management practice.

Using Language to Gain Control of Enterprise Architecture: On the Verge of Major Business Reengineering

Gary F. Simons, Leon A. Kappelman, and John A. Zachman

> Insanity is doing the same thing over and over again and expecting different results.
>
> **—Albert Einstein**

Seven years ago the senior leadership at SIL International (see Chart 3.1), a not-for-profit whose purpose is to facilitate language-based development among the peoples of the world, determined that it was time to build an integrated Enterprise Information System. There were three precipitating factors: mission-critical IT systems were almost twenty years old and on the verge of obsolescence, their landscape was dotted with dozens of silo systems, and commitments to new strategic directions demanded significant business reengineering.

John Zachman made a site visit to help launch an enterprise architecture initiative. SIL learned from him that architecture (see Chart 3.2) is the age-old discipline that makes it possible for humankind to construct complex systems. If an organization wants to build something that is highly complex in such a way that what the builder builds is aligned with what the owner actually has in mind (whether it be a skyscraper, an airplane, or an information system), then it needs a designer to create

127

CHART 3.1   WHAT IS SIL INTERNATIONAL?

- SIL is a not-for-profit, academic, faith-based organization committed to the empowerment of indigenous communities worldwide through language development efforts.
- SIL is focused on the role of language and culture in effective development.
- By facilitating language-based development, SIL International serves the peoples of the world through research, translation, and literacy.
- Since its founding in 1934, SIL has worked in eighteen hundred languages, in seventy countries, and grown to a team of five thousand from sixty countries.

CHART 3.2   WHAT IS ARCHITECTURE?[12,13,14]

Architecture is the set of descriptive representations that are required in order to create an object. Architecture is also the baseline for changing the object once it is created, IF you retain the descriptive representations used in its creation and IF you ensure that the descriptive representations are always maintained consistent with the created object (i.e., the instantiation). The Roman Coliseum is not architecture; it is the result of architecture, an implementation.

If the object you are trying to create is so simple that you can see it at a glance in its entirety and remember all at one time how all of its components fit together at excruciating levels of detail, you don't need architecture. You can "wing it" and see if it works. It is only when the object you are trying to create is complex to the extent that you can't see and remember all the details of the implementation at once, and only when you want to accommodate ongoing change to the instantiated object, that architecture is imperative.

---

a complete set of blueprints to which all the stakeholders agree and against which all will work.

Perhaps even more important in this age of increasingly rapid change is that architecture is the discipline that makes it possible for an organization to maintain a highly complex system once it is operational. Before the functioning building or airplane or information system can safely, efficiently, and effectively be changed, it is necessary for the owner, designer, and builder to first make the changes on the blueprints and come to agreement that the proposed changes will achieve what the owner wants and can be implemented by the builder.

Nothing So Practical as Good Theory

> In the case of information and communication technologies
> … investments in associated intangible capital … are quite
> important indeed.
>
> **—Federal Reserve Chairman Ben Bernanke**
> *(MIT commencement, June 2006)*

The Zachman Framework for Enterprise Architecture (see Figure 3.2 and Chart 3.3) seemed to offer a good theory for what the blueprints of an enterprise should look like: primitive models (see Chart 3.4) in each of the cells formed by the intersection of rows for stakeholder perspectives (e.g., owner, designer, builder) with columns for interrogative abstractions (i.e., what, how, where, who, when, why).

As the SIL leadership set out to reengineer the organization, they were inspired by Zachman's vision of an enterprise under control through a complete set of aligned blueprints. In an application of social psychologist Kurt Lewin's famous maxim, "There is nothing so practical as a good theory," they saw the practical value of the Zachman Framework and adopted it as their working theory. Conversely, there is nothing so good for the development of theory as good application in practice, and

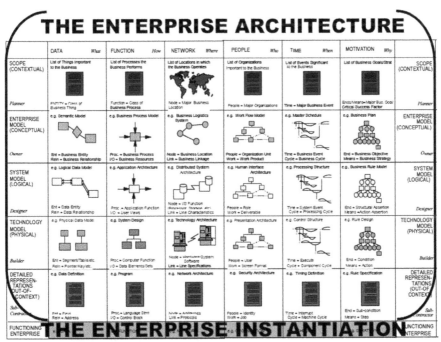

John A. Zachman, Zachman International

FIGURE 3.2   The Zachman Framework for Enterprise Architecture.

**CHART 3.3   WHAT IS THE FRAMEWORK FOR
ENTERPRISE ARCHITECTURE?[15,16,17,18]**

The Framework for Enterprise Architecture (the "Zachman Framework"; see Figure 3.2) is simply a schema, a classification scheme for descriptive representations of objects with enterprise names on the descriptions. It is represented in two dimensions as a table or matrix consisting of six columns and five rows. The schema is "normalized" so that no one fact can show up in more than one cell.

The columns (nicknamed "1" through "6" from left to right) answer the six interrogatives—what, how, where, who, when, and why, respectively—and correspond to the universal set of descriptive representations for describing any and all complex industrial products (industry-specific variations in terminology notwithstanding): Bills of Materials, Functional Specifications, Drawings, Operating Instructions, Timing Diagrams, and Design Objectives. These are termed "abstractions" in the sense that out of the total set of relevant descriptive characteristics of the object, we "abstract" one of them at a time for producing a formal, explicit description.

The rows (nicknamed from top to bottom "1" through "5") represent the set of descriptions labeled "perspectives" in the sense that each abstraction is created for different audiences: visionaries or planners, executives or owners, architects or designers, engineers or builders, and implementers or subcontractors respectively. Each of the six abstractions has five different manifestations depending upon the perspective of the intended audience for whom it is created. These are the industrial product equivalents of Scoping Boundaries ("Concepts Package"), Requirements, Schematics (Engineering descriptions), Blueprints (Manufacturing Engineering descriptions), and Tooling configurations; and these correspond to the enterprise equivalents of boundary or scope, business model, logical model, physical or technology model, and tooling configurations.

Enterprise Architecture is the total set of intersections between the abstractions and the perspectives that constitutes the total set of descriptive representations relevant for describing an enterprise: And the ENTERPRISE itself is the implementation, the instantiation, the end result of doing Enterprise Architecture, and is depicted in the framework as row 6.

Zachman with his associate Stan Locke entered into a relationship with SIL to help SIL put theory into practice, while SIL helped them refine theory through practice. Following Kotter's[19] eight-stage process for managing major change, SIL formed a VP-level guidance team chaired by the associate executive director for administration. Trained and advised by Locke, this team has met regularly since 2000 to guide the process of architecting a reengineered enterprise.

CHART 3.4   PRIMITIVE AND COMPOSITE MODELS: WHY THINGS GO BUMP IN THE NIGHT[20,21,22]

A "primitive" model is a model in one variable—the combination of one abstraction with one perspective—that is an artifact specific to one cell of the Zachman Framework. It is the raw material for doing engineering and architecture.

In contrast, a "composite" model is comprised of more than one abstraction and/or more than one perspective. Implementations are the instantiation of composite, multi-variable models. Implementations are manufacturing, the creation of the end result. An instantiation, by definition is a composite. An enterprise, an information system, and a computer program are instantiations and therefore composites.

The question turns out to be, how did you create the implementation instance? Was it engineered (architected) from primitive models or did you simply create the implementation ad hoc (i.e., it was implemented but NOT architected with primitives)? If you are not creating "enterprise-wide" primitives, you risk creating implementations that will not integrate into the enterprise as a whole. You can manufacture parts of the whole iteratively and incrementally; however, they must be engineered to fit together or they are not likely to fit together (be aligned or easily integrated). Enterprise-wide integration and alignment do not happen by accident. They must be engineered (architected).

Architecture Out of Control

> The problem with communication ... is the illusion that it
> has been accomplished.
>
> **—George Bernard Shaw**

SIL enjoyed excellent buy-in and participation by senior leadership and IT staff, and found that Zachman's framework was a powerful tool for helping conceptualize what they were doing. But SIL also found that they lacked the tools to deliver all the blueprints. Only in Zachman's leftmost column 1 of the framework (i.e., data) did they succeed in creating formal blueprints. The entity-relationship diagrams[23] commonly used by database designers are compatible with Zachman's notion of a primitive thing-relationship-thing model. Thus SIL was able to achieve alignment and control in column 1 by using a popular entity-relationship modeling tool. But SIL found nothing comparable for the other five columns (process, location, organization, timing, and motivation).

It turns out that existing modeling techniques, although useful for other purposes, were not well suited since they did not produce primitive models for the single normalized cells of Zachman's framework. Rather, they produced composite models combining elements from multiple rows or columns of the framework. An obvious alternative would be to use a general drawing program to simply draw the models. SIL tried this, but it did not work. Unlike the entity-relationship tool, which was inherently compatible with the Zachman metamodel for column 1 and thus could not generate anything but a compatible model no matter who used it, a general drawing program is unconstrained and cannot guarantee conformity with the framework or consistency between practitioners.

Another advantage of the entity-relationship tool was that it is based on a single underlying knowledge structure that keeps the owner, designer, and builder views of the blueprints in alignment. With the general drawing tool, however, once drawings were created, it was virtually impossible to keep them maintained and aligned. In order to give guidance to system builders, some models were described in documents and spreadsheets rather than diagrams, but these were similarly unconstrained and subject to all the same shortcomings. For the lack of tools to handle the models in columns 2 through 6, five-sixths of SIL's architecture was out of control.

Enterprise Architecture as a Language Problem

> In the beginning was the Word.
> —**John 1:1** *(King James Bible)*

Why didn't the drawing approach work? Modeling is about expressing ideas, not about drawing pictures. Thus the solution to the modeling problem is even older than architecture; the age-old discipline that makes it possible for humans to express ideas with precision is *language*. Language is the source of our ability to create, our power to wield ideas, and our freedom to build a better future. Ironically, language achieves this freedom by conventionalizing a strong set of constraints on how words and sentences can be formed. Paradoxically, language uses constraints to unleash freedom of expression. Consider that in any one language all the possible speech sounds are constrained to a relatively small subset that are actually used, syllable patterns constrain the combinations of sounds that could possibly be words, conventional associations of meaning constrain which of those sequences actually are words, and rules of grammar constrain the order in which words combine to express larger thoughts.

By analogy, in order to unleash the creativity, power, and freedom that are the promise of enterprise architecture, an enterprise needs to employ a constrained language for enterprise modeling. The metamodels of the Zachman Framework are too generic to support detailed engineering. This is by design since the framework is a classification system, not a methodology. In order to develop a methodology appropriate for its own use, an enterprise needs to adapt the framework to its specific context by adding both detail and constraint to Zachman's generic standard for enterprise architecture. The Enterprise Architecture Standards[24] define the notion of an elaboration of the framework. The allowed elaborations are:

- Alias a standard thing or relationship.
- Add named subtypes of standard things and relationships.
- Name the supported integrations between columns.
- Add named attributes to a type of thing or relationship or integration.

Such elaborations of the metamodels do not violate the standard framework as long as they follow a dumb-down rule that states, "When the elaborations are backed out of an elaborated model, the result must be a model that conforms to the standard metamodel."

GEM: A Language for Enterprise Modeling

> Obedience to a law which we prescribe to ourselves is liberty.
> —**Jean-Jacques Rousseau** *(The Social Contract, 1762)*

To gain control of their enterprise architecture, SIL created GEM—a system for Generic Enterprise Modeling. The complete system consists of a methodology, a repository, and a workbench, but at the center of all these is a language that is formally an elaboration of the Zachman Framework metamodel as defined in the Enterprise Architecture Standards.[25]

The GEM language is implemented as an application of XML. By analogy to a programming language, the architect writes XML source code to express the semantics (owner view) and logic (designer view) of a system—including things, relationships, integrations, transformations, added detail, and prose definitions. The system compiles the XML source into the graphic primitive models for each cell of the framework. The system also compiles the XML source into "textual models" for each cell—HTML documents that provide human-readable descriptions.

For example, Figure 3.3 shows a fragment from the owner-level process model (that is, the intersection of row 2 and column 2) for the subsystem that maintains and produces *Ethnologue: Languages of the World*.[26] The *Ethnologue* is a 1,272-page reference book published by SIL that catalogs all known languages of the present-day world. Now in its fifteenth edition, the *Ethnologue* identifies 6,912 living languages, both spoken and signed.

In the GEM language, each type of *thing* and *relationship* used in the primitive thing-relationship-thing models has its own XML element. For example, the fragment in Figure 3.3 illustrates two kinds of things in the owner-level process model: <inventory>, representing a process for maintaining an inventory of data entities,

```
<columnTwo>
  <businessProcesses>
    <inventory id="c2.WorldLang">
      <name>World Language Inventory</name>
      <description>The process that maintains the most up-to-
date information about the existence and status of every known
language.</description>
    </inventory>
    <publication id="c2.edition">
      <name>Ethnologue Edition</name>
      <description>The process that produces a particular,
published edition of the catalog of all known living languages
of the world.</description>
      <fedBy process="c2.WorldLang"/>
      <fedBy process="c2.LangMaps"/>
      <producedAt location="c3.HQ"/>
      <timing cycle="c5.Edition"/>
    </publication>
      .  .  .
  </businessProcesses>
    .  .  .
</columnTwo>
```

FIGURE 3.3   An example of GEM language source code.

and <publication>, representing a process for producing a publication. These are two kinds of processes that recur in SIL's enterprise, so Zachman's generic notion of a row 2 process has been elaborated by defining these two subtypes. Each thing element has an ID attribute, which provides a unique identifier that can be used as the target of relationships. Each thing element also contains a <name> and <description> element for human-readable documentation. The XML element for a relationship is embedded in the thing it originates from and contains an IDREF attribute that expresses the unique identifier of the thing that is the target of the relationship. In Figure 3.3, <fedBy> is an example of a relationship. The instance <fedBy process="c2.WorldLang"/> is embedded in the Ethnologue Edition process and points to the World Language Inventory process. It is therefore a formal statement of the fact, "The Ethnologue Edition publication process is fed by the output of the World Language Inventory process." Figure 3.4 shows the graphic representation of this model that is generated by GEM from the source fragment in Figure 3.3.

Relationships between things in different columns are called *integrations* and are expressed in the same way. In Figure 3.3, <producedAt> integrates the process to the thing in the column 3 model that represents the location where it is produced, and <timing> integrates the process to the thing in the column 5 model

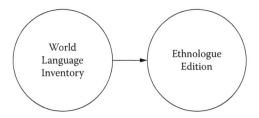

FIGURE 3.4   The graphic model generated from Figure 3.3.

that represents the timing cycle for the process. Figure 3.5 shows the textual model generated by GEM for the <publication> element in Figure 3.3. It is an HTML document in which the targets of the relationships and integrations are active links to the definition of the referenced thing. This example illustrates an important feature of the GEM language, namely, that the reverse relationships and integrations are never expressed explicitly in the XML source code, but always inferred by the compiler that generates the textual model, thus avoiding redundancy and the potential for update anomaly. For instance, in Figure 3.5, the "Produced by" and "Consumed by" integrations were actually expressed in the source code of the column 4 model, and the "Motivation" integration was actually expressed in the source code of the column 6 model.

Figure 3.6 summarizes the coverage of GEM for modeling the owner (row 2) perspective. This represents about one-third of the GEM language; the remainder is for modeling the things, relationships, and integrations of the designer perspective (row 3), plus further details like attributes of data entities and states of timing cycles that are needed to fully specify the logical design of a subsystem. The rows of

Ethnologue Edition

A publication process. The process that produces a particular published edition of the catalog of all known living languages of the world.

Relationships

Fed by:	Language Map Inventory
Fed by:	World Language Inventory

Integrations

Produced at:	International Headquarters
Consumed by:	Public
Produced by:	VP Academic Affairs Office
Timing:	Ethnologue Edition Cycle
Motivation:	Publish Ethnologue

FIGURE 3.5   The textual model generated from Figure 3.3.

	Things	*Relationships*	*Integrations*
C1	object association	hasAssociations associatedWith hasMembers hasStructure	Tracked in C2 *Model for C4* *Motivation is C6*
C2	inventory publication	fedBy	tracks C1 producedAt C3 hasTiming C5 *Produced by C4* *Consumed by C4* *Motivation is C6*
C3	site	linkedTo	*Produced here C2* *Located here C4* *Motivation is C6*
C4	orgUnit	AdministeredBy	modeledAs C1 produces C2 consumes C2 locatedAt C3 *Monitors C5* *Motivation is C6*
C5	businessCycle	spawns m intersects	monitoredBy C4 *Timing for C2* *Motivation is C5*
C6	goal objctive	meansFor	reasonFor C1, C2, C3, C4, C5

FIGURE 3.6   GEM vocabulary for Row Two models.

the table in Figure 3.6 correspond to the six columns of the Zachman Framework (labeled C1 through C6). The contents of the table cells list the XML elements for expressing things, relationships, and integrations in the given framework column. The latter entries also identify the column that is the target for the integration. The entries in the integration column that are in italics are for the implicit reverse integrations that are generated by the compiler.

The XML elements listed in Figure 3.6 can be likened to the vocabulary of the GEM language. From these "words" it is possible to construct sentences like,

"Object X associatedWith Object Y" and "Inventory Z tracks Object X." An XML DTD (Document Type Definition) along with a Schematron schema defines the grammar of the language (that is, the constraints on how the possible words can be combined to create valid sentences). For instance, the schema prevents a sentence like "Inventory Z tracks Site W" since the object of *tracks* must be a column 1 thing.

The Repository of Enterprise Models

> Any fool can make things bigger, more complex, and more violent. It takes a touch of genius—and a lot of courage—to move in the opposite direction.
>
> **—Albert Einstein**

Modeling an entire enterprise and then managing how its models change over time is a huge task. GEM supports enterprise-wide modeling in two critical ways. First, the complete enterprise (which is too big to handle in one model) is divided into numerous subsystems (each of which is of a manageable size). A subsystem represents a focused set of business functions that falls under the stewardship of a single vice president who "owns" the subsystem on behalf of the enterprise. A GEM source file describes the architecture of just one of those subsystems. Individual subsystem models may reference elements defined in other subsystem models. In this way, the collection of subsystem models is knit into a single contiguous enterprise model, and an internal web application allows all stakeholders to browse the set of subsystem models as an integrated whole.

Second, a single subsystem model may simultaneously describe the subsystem at various points in the history of its development. Each subsystem declares a set of stages in a build sequence, and each thing and relationship is assigned to the stage in which it is added to (and in some cases dropped from) the subsystem. A request to change the functioning enterprise is made by specifying a new stage in the build sequence of the affected subsystem. Each stage passes through a development life cycle with the following states: proposed, planned for implementation, in development, in quality assurance testing, and in production.

The XML source files for all of the subsystems are stored in a single repository managed by Subversion—an open-source revision control system. Figure 3.7 shows the home page of the dynamic web application SIL has developed for providing a user interface to the repository of enterprise models, and shows all of the subsystems (which are limited to a selection of eight to reduce the size of the graphic) as well as the entire enterprise. The left-hand column names the subsystems that have been modeled; they are grouped under headings for the corporate officer who is steward for the model. The numbers on the right-hand side are rough metrics giving the number of things defined in the models for each column. The five columns in the middle of the page give links for navigating to the models themselves; if the

Repository of Enterprise Models

Federated Core

Pending slivers | Other enterprises

Systems	As is	About to be	Will be	Should be	Could be	Metrics *					
Associate ED for Administration											
Organizational Structure	Production	QA	Development	Planned	Proposed	36	7	7	20	0	5
VP Academic Affairs											
Digital Archiving	Production	QA	Development	Planned	Proposed	13	12	5	10	3	7
Ethnologue	Production	QA	Development	Planned	Proposed	24	24	6	21	9	8
Training Roles	Production	QA	Development	Planned	Proposed	24	1	0	7	0	0
VP Corporate Communications											
Corporate Communications	Production	QA	Development	Planned	Proposed	35	35	2	19	7	0
SIL Apologetics	Production	QA	Development	Planned	Proposed	29	6	2	13	7	5
VP Finance											
PMC	Production	QA	Development	Planned	Proposed	14	8	3	11	1	0
VP Personnel											
Affiliations and Assignments	Production	QA	Development	Planned	Proposed	34	5	0	23	0	0
Complete Enterprise											
Federated Core	Production	QA	Development	Planned	Proposed						

Local intranet   100%

FIGURE 3.7   The GEM Repository of Enterprise Models.

subsystem has at least one build sequence stage in the named life cycle state, then the link is dark and active. The repository application (by adding and dropping model elements based on the life cycle state of the build sequence stages) is able to display the models for each subsystem in each of the possible life cycle states. This helps the enterprise to visualize, discuss, and manage change.

Figure 3.8 is a screenshot showing the result of clicking on the "Development" state link for the *Ethnologue* subsystem that appears in Figure 3.7. The body of the page contains thirty-five links, each of which produces a different view of information in the single GEM language source file. The application is built with Apache Cocoon—an open-source web application framework that uses pipelines of XSLT scripts to transform the XML source file on-the-fly into the requested textual and graphic displays. The top half of the screen gives links to displays that summarize the models over all the columns of the Zachman Framework. The bottom half of the screen gives links to the individual cell models for the top three rows of the Zachman Framework. These are the rows that deal with the ideas that lie behind the subsystem before it is transformed into a technology solution. These are the models that are used by executive leaders and the staff sections they manage. This repository application is aimed at these users; another application, the GEM Workbench, is aimed at IT staff and encompasses all the rows of the Zachman Framework.

	Repository of Enterprise Models					
Powered by Gem	**Ethnologue System** (Development state)					
Scope	Summary scope lists					
Business	Integrated business model: Metrics Integration matrix					
System	Integrated system model: Metrics Integration matrix					
Primitive models by Zachman Framework cell						
	Inventory (What?)	Process (How?)	Network (Where?)	Organization (Who?)	Timing (When?)	Motivation (Why?)
Scope	list	list	list	list	list	list
Business	model G	model G	model G	model G	model G	model G
System	model G	model G	model G	model G	model G	model G
	Copyright © 2007 SIL International					

FIGURE 3.8   Framework for the Ethnologue System in Development State.

Figure 3.9 shows the first page of the HTML document generated as a result of clicking the "model" link in row 2 and column 2. It illustrates the content from Figure 3.5 in its full context. Each of the eighteen "list" and "model" links in the bottom half of Figure 3.8 generates a comparable document. The G icons in the second and third rows are also links; they generate the graphic form of the primitive cell model.

Figure 3.10 shows all six of the graphic models generated for row 2 of the development state of the *Ethnologue* subsystem. These graphs are created by transforming the XML source model into a graph specification in the DOT graphic description language, which is then rendered on-the-fly by Graphviz—an open-source graph visualization package.

Since the XML source file for one subsystem is able to make reference to an element defined in another subsystem, the repository application is able to assemble the entire enterprise model by aggregating the individual subsystem models. This is the effect of clicking on the links for Complete Enterprise at the bottom of Figure 3.7. The result is a screen comparable to Figure 3.8, but that generates the models for the entire enterprise by aggregating the individual subsystem models. For example, Figure 3.11 shows the row 3 data model for all the subsystems that are in production—in other words, it is the logical data model for the Enterprise Information System as it is currently in production. The entities are defined in eight different subsystems, and the graphic, when in color, also color codes the entities by subsystem. This graph, despite being too small here to discern details, still brings to light a current deficiency in the state of development—the six subsystems on the left side of the graph form a contiguous model, but the two subsystems on the right have yet to be integrated with the rest of the enterprise.

ROW 2 PROCESS MODEL FOR ETHNOLOGUE

Architect: Gary Simons
Contributors: Maggie Frank, Ray Gordon, Ray Uchara
Revision date: 2006-04-14
Coverage: Development stage (and all successive stages)

The items in this model are:

> Inventory process: Language Map Inventory
>   World Language Inventory
> Publication Process: Ethnologue Edition
>   Language Survey Report

Alphabetical listing of processes

Ethnologue Edition
A publication process. The process that produces a particular published edition of the catalog of all known living languages of the world.

Relationships
Fed by: Language Map Inventory
Fed by: World Language Inventory

Integrations
Produced at: International Headquarters
Consumed by: Public
Produced by: VP Academic Affairs Office
Timing: Ethnologue Edition Cycle
Motivation: Publish Ethnologue

FIGURE 3.9 A primitive cell model (as text).

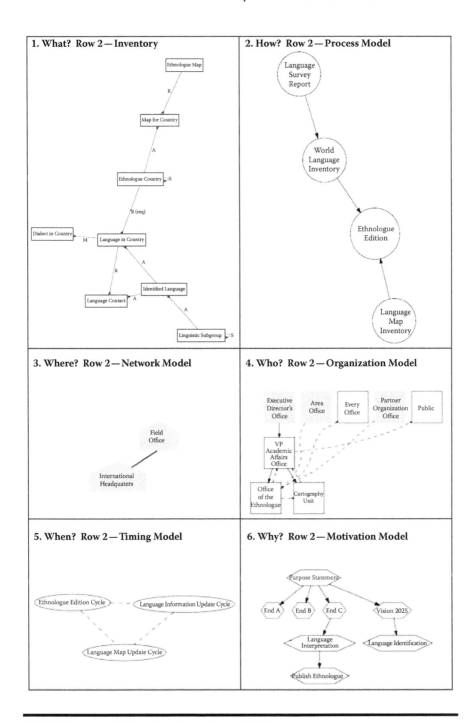

FIGURE 3.10 All six primitive cell models for Row Two (as graphs).

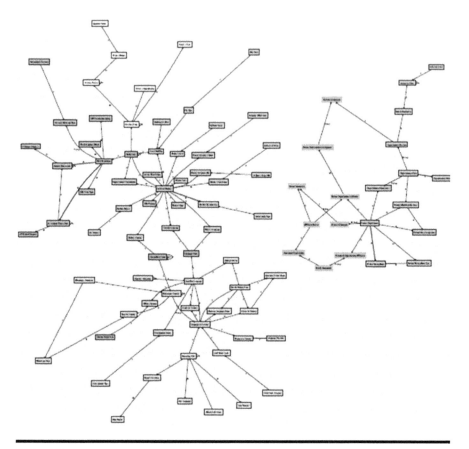

FIGURE 3.11   The Enterprise-wide Row Three data model.

Progress to Date

> In a time of drastic change it is the learners who inherit the
> future. The learned usually find themselves equipped to live
> in a world that no longer exists.
>
> **—Eric Hoffer**

SIL's efforts at reengineering and creating an integrated enterprise information system
are a work in progress. Their enterprise architecture blueprints facilitate communication among the staff of SIL so that the operational aspects of SIL that are managed
by those people, including IT, can be aligned. To date SIL's repository holds eighteen
subsystem models, and each falls under the stewardship of one of their vice presidents.
Originally, they had blueprints for only column 1 (data models) of the Zachman
Framework. The impetus for developing GEM was to get the complete architecture
under control by developing blueprints for the other five columns as well.

	GEM subsystems	*Data entities*	*Modeled in at least n columns of the Zachman Framework*				
			2	*3*	*4*	*5*	*6*
In production	8	178	5	4	3	3	1
Not in production	10	248	9	6	3	3	2
Totals	18	426	14	10	6	6	3
As percent			78%	56%	33%	33%	17%

FIGURE 3.12   Enterprise Architecture Progress and Control at SIL.

Figure 3.12 reports the progress to date in achieving this. This, as well as the entire GEM development effort, represents the work product of a small team consisting of an enterprise architect and a software engineer (both devoting less than half time to the endeavor), plus a few domain specialists who have learned to do the GEM modeling for subsystems in their domain. The two rows of the table separate counts for the eight subsystems that are now part of the in-production integrated Enterprise Information System versus the ten that are in an earlier stage of planning or development. The second column in the table gives a sense of the size of the effort by reporting the number of data entities in the column 1 models. (Note that a large number of the data entities for the subsystems in production are within build sequence stages that are not yet in production; this is why the aggregated model in Figure 3.11 contains many fewer than 178 entities.) The remaining columns show the progress toward modeling the enterprise in all columns of the Zachman Framework: three-quarters of the subsystems are now modeled in two columns, just over half in three columns, one-third in five columns, and only one-sixth in all six columns.

Considering that most enterprises today are fortunate to have even the single data column fully architected, let alone enterprise-wide, SIL stands at the vanguard of what may be a paradigm shift in how enterprises are managed—a change in thought and practice perhaps as significant as those brought about in the Industrial Age by Frederick Taylor's "scientific management" and Joseph Juran's "statistical quality control."[27] And with their enterprise architecture language, tools, methods, and process in place, and with significant organizational learning and success already experienced, SIL's pace and momentum are on the rise.

Lessons Learned

> Someday, you're going to wish you had all those models,
> enterprise-wide, horizontally and vertically integrated, at an
> excruciating level of detail.
>
> **—John Zachman**

Even more than the benefits of creating new tools, processes, methods, innovations, technologies, and intellectual capital while transforming their IT systems, SIL has learned some critical and universal lessons—lessons, perhaps even basic truths, that shed light not only on the practice and value of enterprise architecture but also on some of the fundamental causes of seemingly intractable issues in IT management, such as the perennial quest for alignment.

Among these was the discovery that when the owner speaks directly with the builder (skipping over the row 3 designer), the result is typically a localized stove-piped solution that is not architecturally optimal and thus difficult and costly to integrate and change. That is, the problem of immediate concern is solved but at the cost of adding more complexity to the overall enterprise than was actually necessary. Regrettably, the lack of staff that can function as row 3 architects has been a bottleneck in most of SIL's projects, and it appears this shortage of the architecturally skilled is widespread. Row 3 is a scarce but critical perspective.

The fact that someone has been successful as a software designer (row 4) does not mean they will be successful as an enterprise designer in row 3. It takes someone who can straddle the owner's perspective in row 2 and the builder's perspective in row 4—who can translate the owner's view into a formal logical design that transcends any particular technology for implementing it. Technology designers tend to push a row 4 perspective into row 3 by solving the problem in terms of their preferred technology. The GEM language is giving SIL a way to train people to function in the row 3 role without getting drawn into the details of a row 4 technology solution.

Through GEM, SIL has also learned that having and maintaining "all those models" is possible if they are automatically generated from a single source. When all the primitive models are generated on demand from a single source, they always stay synchronized and in alignment, and enable the enterprise as implemented to be in alignment. In sum, SIL has found that elaborating Zachman's Enterprise Architecture Standards to create a custom modeling language allows an enterprise to gain control of its architecture; but more importantly, to gain control of the actual data, processes, technologies, people, and other resources of which the architecture is a representation. Moreover, having a constrained formal language allows novice modelers to be productive and ensures that all modelers produce comparable results.

But more than all this, SIL has found that the most important result of their enterprise architecture initiative was not the new Enterprise Information System (as they originally thought it would be), but an enterprise change management process that will make it possible for them to use their newly developed enterprise blueprints to manage the never-ending cycle of changes to the enterprise. In other words, enterprise architecture is the key to SIL achieving the design objectives that keep nearly all IT managers up at night—alignment, simplicity, flexibility, speed, and agility.

In order to ensure that this is the result, SIL's EA leadership team recently assigned their chief architect two new highest priorities: (1) developing a plan for finishing the blueprints of all subsystems that are part of the in-production Enterprise Information System (including reverse engineering the models for the legacy subsystems and third-party systems that were integrated without blueprints), and (2) assisting the EA program manager to specify an enterprise change management process that is based on managing the complete blueprints.

Zachman's theory remains confirmed by the practical experience of SIL International, and SIL has realized tangible and intangible benefits as their enterprise architecture efforts are helping them to bridge the chasm between strategy and implementation.[28] SIL has found that their architecture isn't their organization any more than a map is the highway or the blueprints the building. But like maps and blueprints, enterprise architecture is a tool to help us efficiently and effectively get where we want to go, and to keep us from getting lost.

Notes

12. Zachman, John A. 1987. "A Framework for Information Systems Architecture," *IBM Systems Journal*, vol. 26, no. 3, IBM Publication G321-5298, http://www.research. ibm.com/journal/sj/382/zachman.pdf.
13. Zachman, John A. 2001. *The Zachman Framework for Enterprise Architecture: A Primer for Enterprise Engineering and Manufacturing*, Zachman International, http:// www.zachmaninternational.com/2/Book.asp.
14. Zachman, John A. 2007. "Architecture Is Architecture Is Architecture," *EIMInsight*, vol. 1, no. 1, March, Enterprise Information Management Institute. (See Zachman article with same title in Chapter 2, *Ed.*)
15. Zachman 1987.
16. Zachman 2001.
17. Zachman 2007.
18. Zachman, John A. and Sowa, J. F. (1992). "Extending and Formalizing the Framework for Information Systems Architecture," *IBM Systems Journal*, vol. 31, no. 3, IBM Publication G321-5488.
19. Kotter, John P. 1996. *Leading Change.* Harvard Business School Press.
20. Zachman 1987.
21. Zachman 2001.
22. Zachman 2007.
23. Chen, Peter P. 1976. The Entity-Relationship Model: Toward a Unified View of Data, *ACM Transactions on Database Systems*, vol. 1, no. 1, pp. 9-36.

24. Zachman, John A. (2006). "Enterprise Architecture Standards." Zachman International, http://www.zachmaninternational.com/2/Standards.asp. (Also see Zachman's "Framework Standards: What's It All About?" article in Chapter 2, *Ed.*)
25. Zachman 2006.
26. Gordon, Raymond G., Jr. (ed.) 2005. *Ethnologue: Languages of the World* (15th edn.). Dallas: SIL International. Web edition at: http://www.ethnologue.com.
27. Kappelman, Leon A. (2007). "Bridging the Chasm," *Architecture and Governance*, vol. 3, no. 2, http://www.architectureandgovernance.com/articles/09-lastword.asp. (See Kappelman article with same title in Chapter 2, *Ed.*)
28. Kappelman 2007.

Enterprise Architecture: Time for IT to Break Out!

Bruce Ballengee

For IT organizations imprisoned within their enterprise's walls, thinking about and executing enterprise architecture can be a seemingly insurmountable challenge. Enterprise architecture starts with the business and ends with the technology. Architecting a technology platform without equally architecting the business it is intended to support is both costly and quixotic—costly because the business model needs to be analyzed and articulated to assess the goodness of fit of the current-state technical architecture, and quixotic since it becomes nearly impossible to accurately anticipate which future-state technical architecture is needed to support the business. This is the dark side of the long-standing alignment problem between IT and the business.

Stuck in their cells, IT organizations that embrace the value and disciplines of enterprise architecture often choose the path of least resistance: working from the bottom up (technology) in the hope that somehow things will get better because enterprise architecture (the business top) is inherently a good thing to do—hoping that eventually IT will catch up with the business through noble sweat of brow and dint of documentation. Unfortunately, most such efforts die after quarters or years of frustration or never achieve sufficient momentum to succeed.

So where does that leave IT—locked up without a key and no way out? Enterprise architecture is unequivocally a good thing. It is one of the essential prerequisites of successful enterprise-level service-oriented architecture (another very good thing). But business is typically not ready to sit down with IT and listen to how it needs to model itself. Rather, beyond the necessary evil of providing IT enough information to build or buy the IT components it needs, business is concerned merely with the latest quarterly budgets and prioritized projects coming out of the IT governance process.

There is a route of escape for IT. Think of the IT organization itself as a business. Think about "The Business of IT.®"

147

TABLE 3.1 Four Business Success "Musts"

Practice	Companies	Highly Negative	Highly Positive	Principle
Strategy	Winners	7%	82%	Devise and maintain a clearly stated, focused strategy
Strategy	Losers	77%	9%	Devise and maintain a clearly stated, focused strategy
Execution	Winners	4%	81%	Develop and maintain flawless operational execution
Execution	Losers	56%	14%	Develop and maintain flawless operational execution
Culture	Winners	3%	78%	Develop and maintain a performance-oriented culture
Culture	Losers	47%	17%	Develop and maintain a performance-oriented culture
Structure	Winners	3%	78%	Build and maintain a fast, flexible, flat organization
Structure	Losers	50%	14%	Build and maintain a fast, flexible, flat organization

Source: W. Joyce and N. Nohria, *What Really Works: The 4+2 Formula for Sustained Business Success* (New York: HarperCollins, 2003).

It is relatively easy to find executive support in this IT business. The enlightened business leader of IT is the CIO or director of IT. They embrace the value of enterprise architecture; they think in terms of models and ought to be willing to model their business. Once IT makes the simplifying assumption that it is a business, it can free itself from the bars and chains of the business. The business becomes the customer, the supplier, and, sometimes, the competitor. Businesses deal with the separation between themselves, their customers, their suppliers, and their competitors every day. By thinking of itself as a business, IT can now serve the business with greater freedom of thought, and more often than not, freedom of action.

After all, as many an IT organization has discovered over the years, they are a separate business in the minds of the business. Often this realization comes when IT employees are about to be rebadged or released in the wake of the business signing an outsourcing contract. So if the cell door is ajar, is IT ready to step out? Where does IT begin? While there is no "Get out of jail free" card, there are concrete and constructive steps IT can take.

Studies show that the keys to a successful business and "what works" for business also work for IT. There are many well-known studies and books with a high degree of congruence in their conclusions. The four primary "musts" from *What Really Works*[29] are presented in Table 3.1 as one example. Well-known works include *In Search of Excellence,*[30] *Built to Last,*[31] and *Good to Great,*[32] among others.

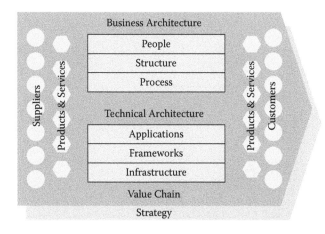

FIGURE 3.13   The Enterprise Architecture Value Chain Framework.[33]

While enterprise architecture plays a crucial and circular role in each practice area, this article focuses on where strategy fits in the enterprise architecture and how strategy affects which enterprise architecture is chosen, layer by layer. Let's begin with a high-level discussion of strategy using a simple high-level enterprise architecture value chain model that we can manipulate. Strategy is how an organization positions itself within a value chain to create unique value, as illustrated in Figure 3.13.

A comprehensive strategy is end-to-end in scope. The value chain runs from the most upstream supplier to the most downstream customer. An effective strategy encompasses all aspects of the organization; the products and services it consumes and produces as well as all layers of its business and technical architectures. IT must not only have its own strategy within the enterprise, but it must also *understand* and extend the enterprise's strategy—the age-old conundrum of IT-business alignment. Most IT organizations must balance between multiple strategies affecting it across the value chain, as illustrated in Figure 3.14.

This complex alignment and balance challenge is compounded by the number of strategy choices available. There are three basic strategies to create value as described by Treacy and Wiersema in *The Discipline of Market Leaders:*[34]

1. *Operational excellence* delivers a combination of quality, price, and ease of purchase that no one else in their market can match.
2. *Product leadership* continually pushes into the realm of the unknown, the untried, or the highly desirable.
3. *Customer intimacy* builds bonds with its customer like those between good neighbors.

While every business works on all three from time to time, the winners are those that narrow their focus to achieve breakthrough performance in a single

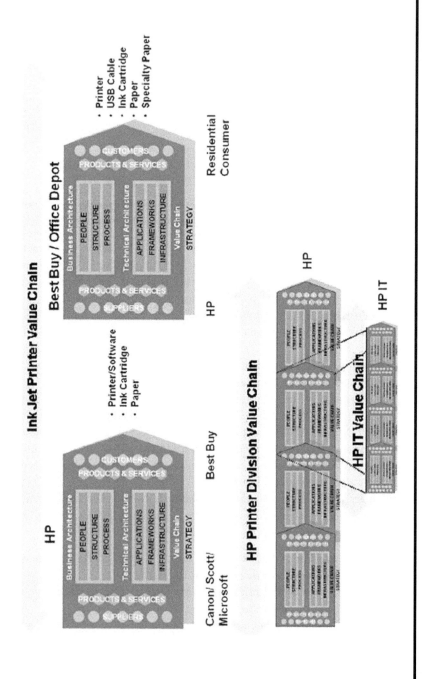

FIGURE 3.14 IT Positioning in the Value Chain.

dimension. Not choosing means complex, hybrid business models that cost more, break more often, and cause more internal conflict. IT must decide which strategic discipline to follow and focus on executing it cohesively across all layers of its enterprise architecture, from business discipline to technical components, as shown in Table 3.2.

Once IT aligns around a strategic discipline, it is appropriate to address how it can use its newly coherent enterprise architecture to create value for its business customers through its application layer. At a strategic level, IT can view its application portfolio as either core or edge solutions. This is demonstrated in Figure 3.15 and illustrated with examples. Examples of core applications are Enterprise Resource Planning (ERP), Manufacturing Execution Systems (MES), Warehouse Management Systems (WMS), Human Resource Information System (HRIS), Customer Relationship Management (CRM), and so on. Examples of edge applications include: visibility (portals for employees, customers, and suppliers, etc.); semantic integrity (Enterprise Application Integration [EAI] and interenterprise integration [FTP, SOA, web services, etc.]); analytics (data marts, database marketing, etc.); and reach (wireless field sales and service, customer alerts, etc.). The distinction between core and edge is critical to strategic discipline.

The key to unlock IT business value for product leadership and customer intimacy is at the edge, rather than in the core. The core is where IT goes to optimize operational excellence. While every IT organization must support both core and edge for its business, it must focus strategically on one or the other.

For operational excellence, focus on core applications and adapting business processes to conform within the standard implementation boundaries of the application suite. For example, if the overall enterprise follows a roll-up strategy of serially acquiring like competitors for increased market share and economies of scale, there can be no greater value IT could deliver than to migrate each successive acquisition as quickly as possible onto a single standardized technical platform from networks to ERP suites.

In the case of product leadership, refine the product or service that the business delivers by leveraging IT to do the end customer's job better. Consider some approaches that have been used successfully:

■ Add business intelligence to the product by adding information collection, reporting, and management capabilities, so that the customer can report on key metrics and make more effective use of the product or service. For example, many ERP vendors already have this in their product offering, or are in the process of adding it.

■ Increase customer visibility, access, and control with web-enabled self-service. For example, HP lets customers reorder ink, and Xerox allows customers to self-diagnose their printer problems over the web.

■ Dis-intermediate various middlemen out of the supply chain. For example, Apple combined the iPod and iTunes to more

TABLE 3.2 IT Strategy—Enterprise Architecture Matrix

Layer	Operational Excellence	Product Leadership	Customer Intimacy
People	• Premium placed on button-down project and vendor managers • Need for testing and documentation reviewers • Culture emphasizes risk avoidance	• Focus on tightly constraining customer demand and rigorously controlling suppliers • Works best with a waterfall development model coupled with outsourced application development	• Relationship management/client management skills are essential • Application architects with good business knowledge are key • Culture stresses individual accountability and risk sharing
Structure	• Inverted pyramid shape • The smallest overall internal organization with extensive use of external resources • Control groups for managing suppliers and service level agreements • Development project organizations may become quite large	• Diamond shape • Strong technology evaluation and postproduction assessment groups track emerging solutions • Boutique suppliers provide small, laser-like solutions with IT providing coordination and project management	• Pyramid shape • Strong customer relationship management groups • Support for a large number of small, cross-functional teams is a differentiator

Process (end to end)	• Focus on tightly constraining customer demand and rigorously controlling suppliers • Works best with a waterfall development model coupled with outsourced application development	• Supply management is essential for feeding the innovation pipeline • Demand management revolves around solution selling—convincing customers to take on IT and business risk for differentiation and competitive advantage • Emphasis is on time to market	• Zeroes in on customer and supplier relationships • Works best with agile development methods, particularly where customer relationships support active involvement with IT—fosters strong customer resistance to outsourcing
Applications	• COTS, with an emphasis on suites for "out of the box" systems integration • No customizations of COTS solutions • SAAS offerings are more acceptable because the business will not be asking IT to integrate and manipulate data across vendors	• Custom applications • Applications from niche vendors • Combine the two to create leading edge applications • Applications are the strategic driver	• Blend of COTS and custom applications • Preference is to pick application vendors that work with selected frameworks • Tailor applications to meet customer needs
Frameworks	• Use the frameworks provided by the application vendor • Reuse frameworks	• Use the most advanced technical functionality to allow advanced application features	• Frameworks support usability that speeds time to market and reduces cost • Frameworks are the key strategic driver
Infrastructure	• Standardization (of products and processes) is the key strategic driver • Standards are those of the application	• Use emerging standards • Have many standards	• Preference for standardization • Implement a widely used infrastructure to gain the greatest flexibility at lower cost

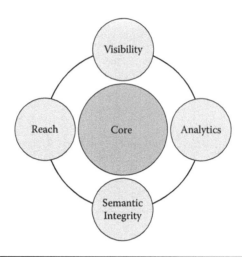

FIGURE 3.15 Core and edge applications.

seamlessly solve the customer's job of listening only to music they like as soon and as cheaply as possible.

For customer intimacy, focus not so much on applications (as they will need to be more customized for each IT customer within the enterprise) as on frameworks like work flow, portal, application servers, EAI, and analytical/reporting tools that provide an 80 percent solution and allow 20 percent to be mass customized by IT for each internal customer.

Finally, the IT strategy can be different from that of the business, so long as it best maximizes business value. Consider two well-known examples. A virtual retailer, Amazon, has a highly customer-intimate, technology-enabled B2C strategy, but consistently pursues an operational excellence–driven technical infrastructure. The end customer's online experience is dependent upon highly responsive/available systems. If Amazon is slow or down, the customer is one or two clicks away from ordering the same item from a ready and willing competitor. A bricks-and-mortar retailer, Wal-Mart is the bastion of operational excellence, yet its IT organization is tightly focused on driving IT product leadership, even to the point of deploying newer technologies such as RFID, which still have kinks to work out. Again, IT delivers high business value because it is through a next generation of supply chain automation that Wal-Mart can maintain its competitive advantage over most of its rivals.

These "prison break" examples used high-level enterprise architecture tools and principles to illustrate how an IT organization should first think of, and then run, itself as a business. There is tremendous value when IT mentally frees itself from the chains of business to serve business far better and more successfully than ever before. But there is another takeaway. Once IT demonstrates to the business the power of using enterprise architecture to remake itself, the business will more likely accept the need of and value for enterprise architecture itself, and ask IT for its assistance to do so. Only when alignment between business and IT has begun, can IT truly deliver the maximum value of enterprise architecture and its progeny, service-oriented architecture. Start planning your Great Escape!

Notes

29. Joyce, W. and Nohria, N. 2003. *What Really Works: The 4+2 Formula for Sustained Business Success*, New York: HarperCollins.
30. Waterman, Jr., R. H., & Peters, T. J. 1983. *In Search of Excellence: Lessons from Americas Best Run Companies*, : New York: Warner Books.
31. Collins, J.C. 1997. *Built to Last: Successful Habits of Visionary Companies*, New York: HarperCollins.
32. Collins, J.C. 2001. *Good to Great: Why Some Companies Make the Leap ... and Others Don't*, New York: HarperCollins.
33. Copyright 1996, 2003, 2007 Bruce Ballengee and Pariveda Solutions, Inc. Permission freely granted to the SIM EA Working Group.
34. Treacy, M. & Wiersema, F. 1997. *The Discipline of Market Leaders: Choose Your Customers, Narrow Your Focus, Dominate Your Market*, Basic Books; Expanded edition.

A Pragmatic Approach to a Highly Effective Enterprise Architecture Program

Larry R. DeBoever, George S. Paras, and Tim Westbrock

The purpose of this article is to describe a holistic and pragmatic approach to enterprise architecture that creates stakeholder value, elicits executive support, and is embraced by its consumers.

Enterprise Architecture and the Value Imperative

The fundamental objective of a business is to create value for stakeholders. Executive teams work hard to determine and validate a business's value drivers and develop a business strategy. They perform SWOT[35] analyses, look for strategic inflection points, examine resource allocation, and search for economies of scale while debating the merits of operational excellence versus customer intimacy.

Business process owners look for value from large-scale BPR efforts, business improvement through eliminating defects by embracing Six Sigma, or a continuous improvement approach such as kaizen. Staff functions also work hard trying to create value—from improved cash management to talent acquisition. All of these roles—executive leadership, business process owners, and staff functions—are striving to create value.

Enterprise architecture (EA) efforts that gain the support of executive leadership, and are viewed as effective both inside and outside the IT organization, create tangible, measurable shareholder value.

A Focus on Reducing Complexity and Increasing Agility

In our experience, EA teams that are viewed as creating meaningful shareholder value almost always have as a primary focus reducing the complexity of IT and business processes across the breadth of the enterprise. Reduced complexity results in increased corporate agility, which is uppermost in the minds of much of today's corporate leadership. In addition, reducing complexity almost always lowers costs, improves quality (due to fewer "touch points"), and accelerates end-to-end processing. The focus of EA on reducing complexity is easy to decompose:

- The goal of business is to create value.
- Value can be created only through change (otherwise you have status quo).
- Complexity in IT systems and infrastructure inhibits change (both proactive and reactive).
- Complexity in business processes inhibits change.
- Because complexity inhibits change, complexity inhibits business value.

To be clear, we do not believe that the goal of EA is to *eliminate* complexity. Not all complexity is bad; in fact, some complexity may be required to provide competitive advantage. Our goal as enterprise architects should be to ensure that complexity is an exception and that there is a valid business case for the desired complexity.

Defining Enterprise Architecture for "Consumption"

We often find that trying to define and explain the discipline of enterprise architecture using an abstract definition to business leadership can be counterproductive. Instead, we have found that describing EA in terms of *outcomes and activities* is much more effective. For example, if we are asked "What is Disney?" we say "Disney is an entertainment company." We don't say, "Disney is a corporation organized under the laws of the state of Delaware."

We *define* enterprise architecture as "a strategic management discipline that creates a single, holistic view of the business processes, systems, information, and technology of the enterprise designed and optimized to create shareholder value by achieving both the long-term business strategy as well as current business objectives."

We typically *describe* enterprise architecture to business leadership as having "a focus on reducing the complexity of IT and business processes across the breadth of the enterprise so a company is much more agile." How does the discipline of enterprise architecture understand complexity? Through models, frameworks, and repositories. How does the discipline of enterprise architecture reduce complexity? Through road maps.

The primary output of enterprise architecture is a road map that evolves the "as-is" business processes, systems, information, and technology of the enterprise from the "current state" to the desired "future state."

Eighteen Pragmatic Insights into Enterprise Architecture

1. It is possible to get the support of executive leadership and the business if the value of EA is effectively demonstrated.
2. There is no single approach to establishing an effective enterprise architecture (EA) program.
3. When done correctly, enterprise architecture is a manifestation of an organization's mission, and the IT strategy that enables that mission.
4. A "mediocre" enterprise architecture that is broadly understood and consistently implemented has much greater value and "hard ROI" than a "great" architecture with brilliant engineering that is neither understood nor embraced.
5. Enterprise architecture can be highly effective despite the lack of a clear business strategy (by "teasing out" business objectives and scenario planning).
6. "Business strategy and required capabilities" must clearly decompose into architecture requirements, which must be clearly supported by architecture principles.
7. The true measure of the effectiveness of an enterprise architecture is the extent to which it changes day-to-day behavior and decision making.
8. Many EA programs fail because they confuse "architecture" with "standards."
9. Picking standards in the absence of a meaningful enterprise architecture is "easy" and "fun" but it avoids the hard work.
10. Many EA efforts fail because they attempt to be all encompassing and drive for perfection.
11. Effective enterprise architecture programs are highly pragmatic and self-evident.
12. Enterprise architecture is a "process" not a "project"; it must be ongoing and organic, just as a healthy organization is always evaluating its strategies and tactics, measuring its performance, and adapting as necessary.
13. An EA framework is less important to success than EA leadership.
14. The development of an enterprise architecture should not be outsourced (but outside resources should be leveraged as required).

15. Producing EA artifacts is not enough. Too many EA teams focus on producing frameworks, diagrams, domain architectures, etc. And when they are done they declare victory.
16. There is a consistent set of critical success factors (CSFs) that characterize effective enterprise architecture efforts, but there are also unique factors that must be identified and considered for each enterprise.
17. Information technology is a fundamental enabler of innovation, but it requires more than procurement and installation to be an effective innovation vehicle.
18. Most EA programs initially focus on technical architecture, but they must continue to evolve to become a significant, long-lasting business value contributor.

Maximizing the Effectiveness of EA Investments

EA teams that struggle to make progress consistently "overinvest" in the same activities and "underinvest" in others. Table 3.3 summarizes some of our key EA investment findings.

TABLE 3.3   Maximizing the Effectiveness of EA Investments

Over Invest	Under Invest
Selecting a framework	Communicating the Enterprise Architecture and how to leverage
Selecting a repository tool	Creating business understanding of the EA
Developing a baseline inventory	Developing an effective EA governance process
Researching EA methodologies and techniques	Taking a highly pragmatic approach to EA issues
Acting as a "Project Architecture Lifeguard"	Developing a clear and concise roadmap
Trying to enforce standards	Evaluation whether EA is impacting day-to-day decision making
Trying to become all-encompassing	Developing EA participation beyond the EA team
Too many permanent EA staff	

The Challenge of "Restarting" Enterprise Architecture Efforts

Today, few organizations are starting enterprise architecture efforts for the first time. Most organizations are on their second or third iteration of EA and are still not satisfied. "Restarting" EA has a number of challenges, including:

- The appetite within the enterprise for another EA effort may be nonexistent.
- The appetite within IT for another EA effort may be hostile.
- Most existing EA artifacts are outdated.
- The EA governance process is ineffective, dormant, or nonexistent.

In researching effective approaches to restarting EA efforts we found that the EA team often does not have a clear idea of what they should do first.

- Should we create internal support first?
- Should we fix governance first?
- Should we talk to executive leadership first?
- Should we implement a repository first?
- Should we look at methodologies first?
- Should we describe the "as-is" architecture first?

EA "restarts" are most successful when the focus is on quick wins, which creates credibility.

Why Bother?

If creating an effective enterprise architecture function is so difficult, why bother? The potential impact of EA is so significant that the importance of EA must be seen in what it can provide to an organization. In our experience, EA, when effective, can have significant impact in a number of areas.

- A process to analyze and plan for change intelligently and consistently across the entire enterprise with full knowledge of the impact of change as well as the consequences of not changing.
- Significant time savings to all areas of the business by saving them from making decisions and completing implementations that are redundant with and/or too narrowly focused to benefit other areas of the enterprise.
- More intelligent investment decisions.
- Extend the life of assets that will continue positive contributions.
- Decrease the number of short-term, high-cost implementations that also tend to increase maintenance costs over time.

■ More agility than competitors, leveraging importance of speedy time-to-market in hypercompetitive markets.

Long-term, we believe that EA will become a key strategic planning function reporting to the VP of corporate strategy with a dotted-line relationship to the CIO. EA would also appear as an agenda item for meetings of the executive committee and the board of directors.

Note

35. Strengths, Weaknesses, Opportunities, Threats analysis is a technique credited to the work of Robert Stewart and Albert Humphrey, who conducted research in the 1960s at the Stanford Research Institute (Ed.).

THE SIM INFORMATION MANAGEMENT PRACTICES SURVEY

4

No one has to change. Survival is optional.

—**W. Edwards Deming**

Introduction

Many important questions and concerns were raised by the members of the SIM Enterprise Architecture Working Group (SIMEAWG) at their first meeting in January 1997 as they began planning their research study into "the state of EA". These included matters such as:

- What is the current state of EA programs, activities, and capabilities?
- What EA-related research has been conducted already?
- How do IT professionals define enterprise architecture?
- What is the scope of EA activities?
- Who participates in EA-related activities?

- What are the purposes, benefits, and risks of doing EA?
- What are the primary enablers and inhibitors of EA programs?
- What are the foundational capabilities for successful EA programs?
- Is there a relationship among EA perceptions and capabilities and other organizational activities such as information system development, system analysis and design, IT governance, and IT project management?

Thus, work began on a research design and a set of survey questions. This chapter describes the process and findings of this collaborative effort of academics, practitioners, consultants, thought leaders, and advisors. Their research revealed a great deal, and thus far resulted in a doctoral dissertation, the publication of several academic papers (including an award winner), and the "Maturity Models" and "Charting the Territory" articles at the end of Chapter 2. But not all their questions were answered, and in many ways their findings led to additional questions and concerns. Such is the nature of research, and in particular what is the first study to take such a comprehensive look at EA perceptions, capabilities, and practices. It is only a beginning, but it is a very important one. We hope that you will find the following report as valuable as we have.

The State of EA: Progress, Not Perfection

Brian Salmans and Leon A. Kappelman

The SIMEAWG initiated in order to establish a baseline to assess the state of EA practices and further the mission of the working group as stated in their charter (see Chapter 5). Specifically, the SIMEAWG wanted to determine the state of EA practices in organizations, develop metrics with which SIM members and other management professionals could benchmark their EA program with other organizations, and begin to track the evolution of EA practices over time. It is hoped that the survey results could also be used in developing a maturity assessment for organizations to self-evaluate and measure the state and progress of their EA programs. Within the context of the Enterprise Wheel hub-and-spoke model that we introduced in Figure 1.1 in Chapter 1, the survey addresses the EA activities and IT activities spokes as well as the EA hub.

Background and Methodology

The SIMEAWG's Information Management Practices Survey was developed and conducted to understand better the state of EA practices in organizations at a particular point in time, and to assess the state of the capabilities in IT organizations to develop EA practices. The survey's demographics and some general IT practices questions were based on a previously conducted survey by the SIM Y2K Working Group.[1] An extensive literature review was also conducted to establish the basis for the survey's EA, alignment, requirements, and maturity questions in drafting the initial survey.

Beginning with the inaugural SIMEAWG meeting in January 2007 and continuing through the spring, a modified Delphi study approach was used with an expert group of EA professionals made up primarily of EAWG members from industry and academia providing insight and recommendations to refine the survey. From this expert group's advice, it was decided to structure the survey so it would not appear as strictly an EA practices survey. This was decided because the expert group believed that many organizations may be doing EA-related activities but not calling them EA. Thus the name of the survey did not include the words *enterprise architecture,* but was called the "SIM Information Management Practices Survey." Moreover, some practices questions used the term *Requirements Analysis and Design* (with a specific definition provided[2]) instead of the term *enterprise architecture.* This reflected the expert group's determination that questions regarding requirements-related practices could serve as a surrogate for at least certain fundamental EA capabilities and practices.

The notion that requirements analysis and design capabilities would provide insights in EA capabilities was based on the belief that within the context of IT professionals and IT organizations, requirements analysis and design capabilities and practices are the foundations of enterprise architecture capabilities and practices. In other words, although IT historically has conducted requirements activities in the context of a particular system development project, EA is basically the expansion of that activity so that it is conducted in the context of the entire enterprise. "EA is requirements on steroids," opines Professor of IT and SIMEAWG Chair Leon Kappelman. Others also contend that EA can be used in the development of information systems and to facilitate communications about IS requirements.[3,4]

Moreover, because of this foundational relationship between requirements (more broadly, requirements analysis and design) and enterprise architecture, it was hypothesized that it was likely that more positive or stronger perceptions of EA would be associated with more positive or stronger requirements capabilities, since both requirements and EA capabilities share many success enablers or characteristics. These include the importance of good communications between the IS group and other organizational components, the availability of subject matter experts on the business side as well as capable analysts/architects on the IT side, the important role of alignment between organizational and IS subsystems within the enterprise, and the importance of senior-leadership engagement.[5,6,7,8,9]

Finally, to satisfy some of the objectives in the SIMEAWG's charter, as well as the curiosity of the EAWG's membership and the value they perceived in doing so, EA maturity models were integrated as a foundational structure of many of the questions within the survey. A variety of EA maturity models were reviewed, with a core of four EA maturity models used to develop and map the survey's questions. This was done in order to attempt to validate and compare the major EA maturity theories in existence at this time. Additionally, the key IT and business alignment enablers and inhibitors posited by Luftman and McLean[10] (2004) were integrated into the survey to reflect the importance of EA to alignment and to reflect this consistent concern of top IT management.[11,12,13,14]

The four primary maturity models utilized in developing the SIMEAWG's survey are described more fully in Brian Salmans's "EA Maturity Models" article in Chapter 2. They are: (1) the Government Accountability Office (GAO) framework for assessing and improving EA management; (2) Carnegie Mellon's Software Engineering Institute's Capability Maturity Model (SEI CMM); (3) the Federal Office of Management and Budget's (OMB) EA Assessment Framework; and (4) the four stages of enterprise architecture developed by Jeanne Ross and her colleagues at MIT's Center for Information Systems Research.[15]

One of the goals of the EAWG was a final survey that would take only ten to fifteen minutes to complete. With this in mind, the questions were winnowed to a final survey of about eighty total questions. The questions were 5-point Likert-type scale anchored with "1" meaning "strongly disagree" to "5" for "strongly agree," "3" being "neutral." "Don't know"-type options were provided as well, and several reverse-scored questions were included to assist in the validation of responses.

An online pilot test of the survey questionnaire by the members of the SIMEAWG was conducted in early June 2007, with the intent that this expert group would develop final recommendations and revisions to present at the second SIMEAWG meeting held in Dallas on 26–27 June 2007. At this meeting the survey instrument was further refined and the final modifications were agreed upon, with the changes being implemented to the survey shortly thereafter. The final survey comprised eighty questions of which fourteen were demographic questions about the respondent, their organization, and their IT department. The initial launch of the survey was in September 2007 using the SIM membership mailing list.

Requests to participate in the survey were sent out entirely by e-mail with each potential respondent receiving a personalized e-mail with an embedded individual hyperlink with which to connect to the web server hosting the online survey. Each message with embedded hyperlink was authenticated at the server, so each hyperlink could not be "used" by more than one respondent, nor could a respondent complete the survey more than once. To attempt to gain maximum participation, we followed a survey distribution method advanced by Dillman (1999)[16] utilizing the following schedule:

Initial survey sent out 4 September 07
First Reminder: 17 September 07
Second Reminder: 12 October 07
Final Reminder: 30 October 07

To encourage participation and accurate responses, each potential participant had an option to include an e-mail address to receive a report of the preliminary research findings. They could then compare their organization to the entire sample and industry. A total of 2,863 survey invitations were sent, with 377 quality responses after data purification (removing responses where over 10 percent of the questions were not answered, and checking response quality with reversed items and consistency checks with duplicative questions). This response rate (13.2 percent) is consistent with other surveys of the SIM membership including the annual member surveys and the SIM Y2K Working Group surveys conducted in 1996, 1997, 1998, and 1999.

Findings

Findings of the survey provide critical insight into how IT professionals view themselves, their profession, and the state of IT and EA practices in their organizations. Some of the findings are reported in "Enterprise Architecture: Charting the Territory for Academic Research," the article that closes Chapter 2. Additional analyses are under way at this time as we develop the follow-up questionnaire to be administered in the near future. A doctoral dissertation utilizing the SIMEAWG's data is nearing completion, and other research papers are in press and in development. The complete question-by-question results of the survey are provided in the second part of this chapter in the Detailed Survey Results (beginning with Table 4.3 and Chart 4.9), and there is a summary by question of the study's main IT and EA practices and perceptions constructs in Table 4.2 at the end of this first part.

The responses to the demographic questions reveal that the average age of the respondents was nearly forty-eight, with each person having an average of about 8.2 years in their organization, and an average of 4.4 years in their present position (see Table 4.5). The level of responsibility of the survey respondents was generally broad-based, with almost 80 percent reporting their responsibility at either an enterprise (63.4 percent) or a business-unit/divisional level (see Table 4.7). The job titles of most of the respondents (as shown in Table 4.3) were chief information officer (26.5 percent), vice president (10.1 percent), or director (32.1 percent). Only 4.2 percent held the title enterprise architect, and about 3 percent chief technology officer. More than 35 percent reported to their chief executive officer (17.5 percent), chief financial officer (12.2 percent), or chief operating officer (6.4 percent); over 38 percent to their CIO (22.1 percent) or vice president (16.2 percent), while 6.1 percent reported to a director and 3.2 percent to their CTO (as shown in Table 4.4).

The vast majority of respondents were with profit-oriented organizations (80.6 percent), with 13.5 percent not-for-profit and 4.5 percent representing the government sector (see Table 4.9). Most of the respondents' organizations were in the United States (86.2 percent, as shown in Table 4.12). Gross revenues of responding organizations were under $100 million for about 18 percent; 31.9 percent had revenues up to $1 billion; 35.4 percent reported revenues ranging from $1 billion to 9.9 billion; and 18 percent had revenues of $10 billion or greater (see Table 4.11). The IT budgets of 12.6 percent of responding organizations were under $1 million,

36.3 percent from $1 billion to 9.9 million, 31.8 percent from $10 million to 99.9 million, and 16 percent $100 million or more (see Table 4.13).

Three findings stand out in our analysis and review of the practices and perceptions current survey results that merit elaboration here because of their importance to the development and management of EA practices and programs. These are that (1) respondents generally believe in the positive potential of EA, but (2) disagree on the scope of EA activities, and thereby basically disagree about the subject matter of EA. More troubling, since as mentioned previously the EAWG sees this as a measure of potentialities to do EA work, (3) respondents rate poorly the quality of their requirements analysis and design practices, and rate their software development practices only marginally better. These three findings are now examined in more detail.

Respondents Generally Believe in the Positive Potential of EA

First of all, our analyses indicate that the respondents generally believe in the potentially positive role of EA. This can be seen by the number of respondents who indicate they agree or strongly agree with various potentialities of EA as asked within the seven questions numbered 19a through 19g that each began with "The purpose/function of enterprise architecture is …" Good examples of this include the following questions:

- 19b "… to facilitate systematic change in an organization" with a mean of 4.02 (out of 5 possible on the 5-point scale from strongly disagree to strongly agree) and over 85 percent of respondents agreeing or strongly agreeing;
- 19d "… as a tool for aligning business objectives with IT initiatives" with a mean of 4.08 and over 80 percent of respondents answering 4 or 5;
- 19e "… to provide a blueprint of an organization's business, data, applications, and technology" with a mean of 4.40 and over 90 percent answering agree or strongly agree;
- 19f "… as a tool for planning" with a mean of 4.25 and nearly 90 percent answering 4 or 5; and
- 19g "… as a tool for decision making" with a mean of 4.13 and more than 84 percent responding agree or strongly agree.

The descriptive statistics of these examples from question 19 are provided here in Chart 4.1 with their histograms. Table 4.2c provides summary statistics for all of the seven individual questions (also referred to here as "items") in question 19 and complete descriptive statistics including histograms in Chart 4.13 in the Detailed Survey Results. Notice in the examples here how skewed the graphs are toward 5, strongly agree, and how few (under 20 percent in all cases) of the responses were 3, neutral or below.

Their answers to question 20 further support the finding that respondents perceive positive potential in EA. These twenty questions (i.e., items) numbered 20a to

CHART 4.1 19. The purpose/function of enterprise architecture is:

CHART 4.1a   19b. … to facilitate systematic change in an organization.

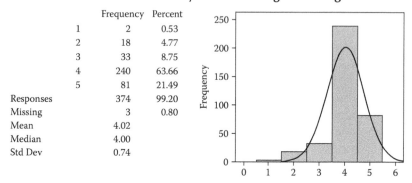

	Frequency	Percent
1	2	0.53
2	18	4.77
3	33	8.75
4	240	63.66
5	81	21.49
Responses	374	99.20
Missing	3	0.80
Mean	4.02	
Median	4.00	
Std Dev	0.74	

CHART 4.1b   19d. … as a tool for aligning business objectives with IT initiatives.

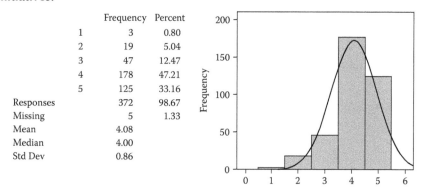

	Frequency	Percent
1	3	0.80
2	19	5.04
3	47	12.47
4	178	47.21
5	125	33.16
Responses	372	98.67
Missing	5	1.33
Mean	4.08	
Median	4.00	
Std Dev	0.86	

CHART 4.1c   19e. … to provide a blueprint of an organization's business, data, applications, and technology.

	Frequency	Percent
1	3	0.27
2	5	1.33
3	21	5.57
4	164	43.50
5	182	48.28
Responses	373	98.94
Missing	4	1.06
Mean	4.40	
Median	4.00	
Std Dev	0.68	

CHART 4.1d   19f. … as a tool for planning.

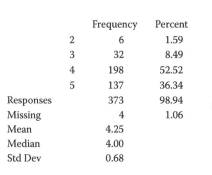
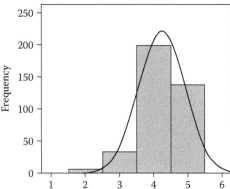

	Frequency	Percent
2	6	1.59
3	32	8.49
4	198	52.52
5	137	36.34
Responses	373	98.94
Missing	4	1.06
Mean	4.25	
Median	4.00	
Std Dev	0.68	

CHART 4.1e   19g. … as a tool for decision making.

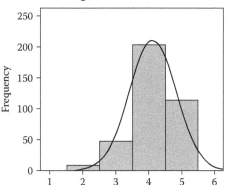

	Frequency	Percent
2	8	2.12
3	48	12.73
4	204	54.11
5	114	30.24
Responses	374	99.20
Missing	3	0.80
Mean	4.13	
Median	4.00	
Std Dev	0.71	

20t asked respondents to select the level to which they agree or disagree that a series of statements were representative of the potential benefits to an organization from practicing enterprise architecture (using the same 5-point scale from strongly disagree to strongly agree). It is noteworthy that the majority of respondents perceived positively the potentialities of EA in all but one of these twenty questions: for question 20o, "EA improves trust in the organization," only 47.5 percent of respondents answered 4 or 5. Examples of strong positive perceptions of EA's potentials include statements such as:

■ 20a "Aligning business objectives with information technology investments" with a mean of 4.14 and more than 83 percent answering agree or strongly agree;
■ 20f "Improved utilization of information technology" with a mean of 4.25 and more than 86 percent answering agree or strongly agree;
■ 20h "Improved interoperability among information systems" with a mean of 4.34 and more than 87 percent answering agree or strongly agree; and

- 20q "More effective use of IT resources" with a mean of 4.02 and more than 78 percent answering agree or strongly agree.

The descriptive statistics of these examples from question 20 are provided here in Chart 4.2 with their histograms. Again, notice here how skewed the graphs are toward 5, strongly agree, and how few (12 percent to 21 percent) of the responses were 3, neutral or below.

Notice also that all four of these questions specifically highlight the potential benefits of EA to specific goals and objectives of the IT department rather than to

CHART 4.2 20. Potential benefits to an organization from doing enterprise architecture:

CHART 4.2a   20a. Aligning business objectives with information technology investments.

	Frequency	Percent
1	2	0.53
2	14	3.71
3	43	11.41
4	185	49.07
5	129	34.22
Responses	373	98.94
Missing	4	1.06
Mean	4.14	
Median	4.00	
Std Dev	0.80	

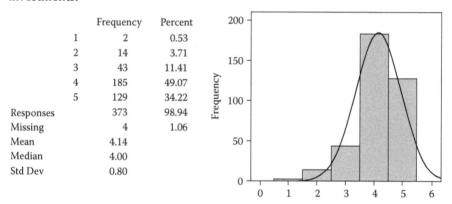

CHART 4.2b   20f. Improved utilization of information technology.

	Frequency	Percent
2	4	1.06
3	43	11.41
4	181	48.01
5	145	38.46
Responses	373	98.94
Missing	4	1.06
Mean	4.25	
Median	4.00	
Std Dev	0.70	

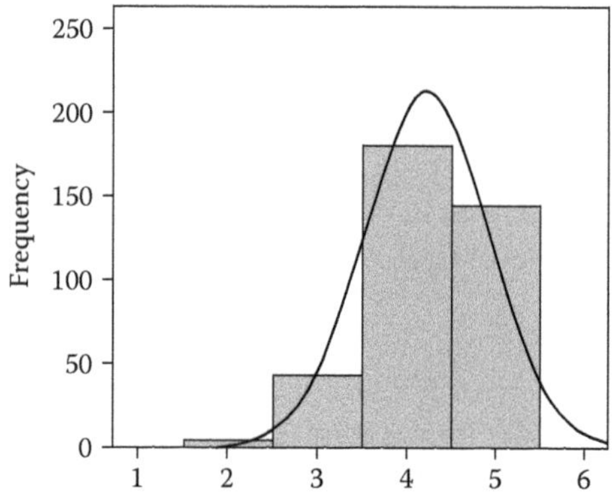

CHART 4.2c   20h. Improved interoperability among information systems.

	Frequency	Percent
2	5	1.33
3	39	10.34
4	154	40.85
5	174	46.15
Responses	372	98.67
Missing	5	1.33
Mean	4.34	
Median	4.00	
Std Dev	0.72	

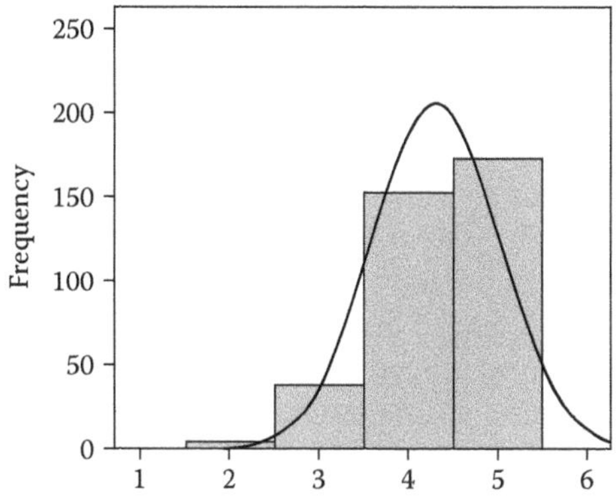

CHART 4.2d   20q. More effective use of IT resources.

	Frequency	Percent
2	10	2.65
3	66	17.51
4	199	52.79
5	95	25.20
Responses	370	98.14
Missing	7	1.86
Mean	4.02	
Median	4.00	
Std Dev	0.74	

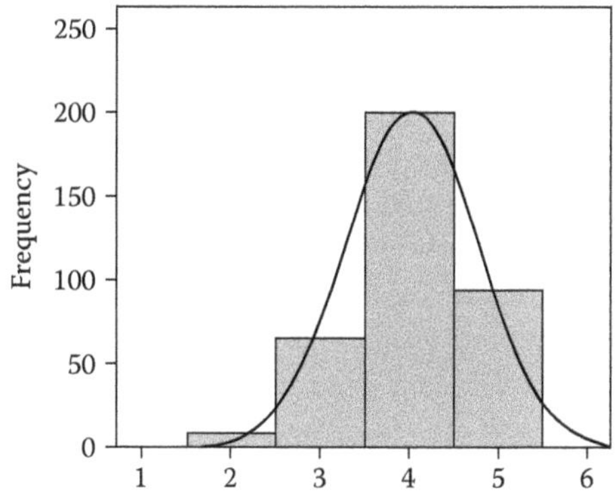

EA's direct benefits to the larger organization. This may indicate that the IT professionals in this sample tend to focus internally, instead of considering ramifications to the greater organization as a whole; although it may simply be that they are more familiar with IT and thus more confident in opining about the potentials of EA closer to home. Nevertheless, all twenty of the potential benefits in question 20 scored favorably (the smallest mean is 3.49 for question 20o that EA "improves trust"). However, in general the responses to the more organizational goals and objectives in question 20 tend to have lower means and histograms more skewed to the left. Table 4.2d provides summary statistics for all twenty of these individual items that make up question 20, and complete descriptive statistics are provided in Chart 4.14 in the Detailed Survey Results.

Nonetheless, the overall positive bias to all of question 20 does point to the conclusion that EA is seen as a viable organizational practice and indicates that IT professionals really do see potential value in EA. However, caution should be exercised in interpreting these results since the respondents may be naïve or simplistic in their understanding of EA as indicated by the next finding.

Respondents Disagree on the Scope of EA Activities

The next finding is related to the bimodal distribution of the responses on question 19a, "The purpose/function of enterprise architecture is: to provide a snapshot in time of an organization," as shown in Chart 4.3. About 46 percent of the respondents disagreed or strongly disagreed with this statement (nearly 64 percent were either neutral or disagreed) while only 35 percent agreed or strongly agreed. The amount of disagreement with the idea that the architecture of an enterprise can provide "a snapshot in time of an organization" is revealing since it seems to indicate that the majority of respondents do not believe that EA is about the enterprise at all. Apparently they believe that EA is only about IT: a belief that may doom their EA and IT efforts to a persistent shortfall of IT-business alignment and an excess of complexity and dis-integration across stovepipes.

Further support of this conclusion comes when comparing this result with responses to question 19e, "The purpose/function of enterprise architecture is: to provide a blueprint of an organization's business, data, applications, and technology." As indicated in Chart 4.4, nearly 92 percent of respondents agreed or strongly agreed with the IT-centric view of EA in question 19e. This particular finding stands out all the more since 19a is the only question in the survey showing such a dichotomous result among the respondents (although, question 18a, "requirements … efforts … are measured," is also bimodal albeit with a more positive skew as shown in Chart 4.12a). More analyses and research are necessary to understand better the significance of this finding, and we intend to dig deeper into it. Of

CHART 4.3   19a. The purpose/function of enterprise architecture is to provide a snapshot in time of an organization.

	Frequency	Percent
1	28	7.43
2	146	38.73
3	67	17.77
4	112	29.71
5	21	5.57
Responses	374	99.20
Missing	3	0.80
Mean	2.87	
Median	3.00	
Std Dev	1.10	

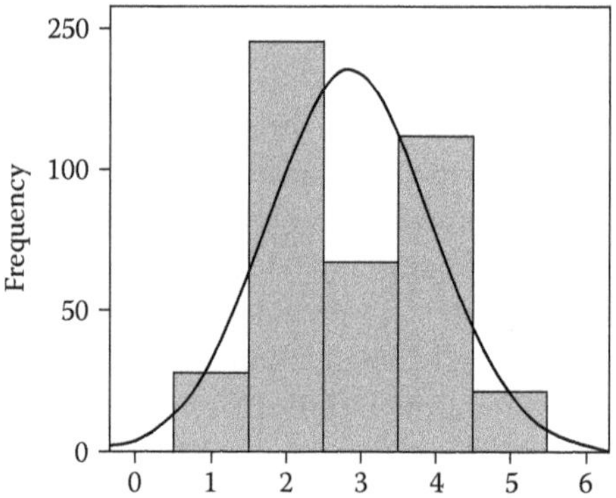

CHART 4.4   19e. The purpose of enterprise architecture is to provide a blueprint of an organization's business, data, applications, and technology.

	Frequency	Percent
1	1	0.27
2	5	1.33
3	21	5.57
4	164	43.50
5	182	48.28
Responses	373	98.94
Missing	4	1.06
Mean	4.40	
Median	4.00	
Std Dev	0.68	

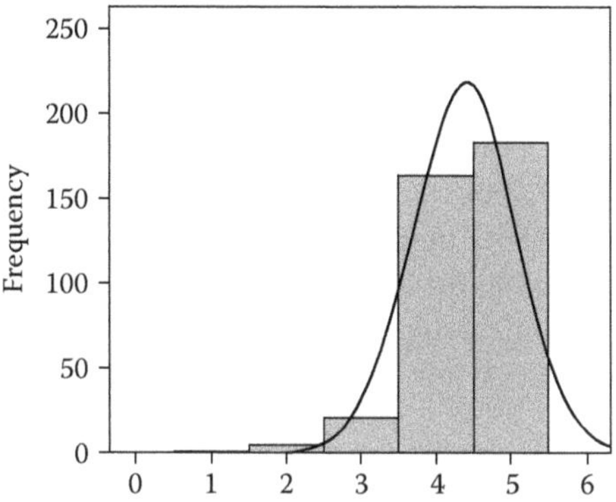

particular interest will be to examine the relationships among responses to questions 19a and 19e and, for example, measures of maturity in EA or IS development practices, industry or respondent demographic differences, or the state of their requirements analysis and design practices.

Additionally, this dichotomous view of EA is further supported when examining the respondents' views of requirements analysis and design practices within their organizations. This is seen in the responses to question 18k, "My organization's requirements analysis and design efforts and activities: are viewed strictly as an IT initiative." As can be seen in Chart 4.5, about 35 percent responded either 1–2 or 4–5 to this statement. Stated another way, just more than one-third of the respondents agreed that their organization's requirements practices were about more than just IT. Might this explain, at least in part, why IT-business alignment appears to be such an elusive and persistent goal for IT professionals?

CHART 4.5   18k. My organization's requirements analysis and design (RA&D) efforts and activities are viewed strictly as an IT initiative.

	Frequency	Percent
1	17	4.51
2	120	31.83
3	97	25.73
4	104	27.59
5	30	7.96
Responses	368	97.61
Missing	9	2.39
Mean	3.03	
Median	3.00	
Std Dev	1.06	

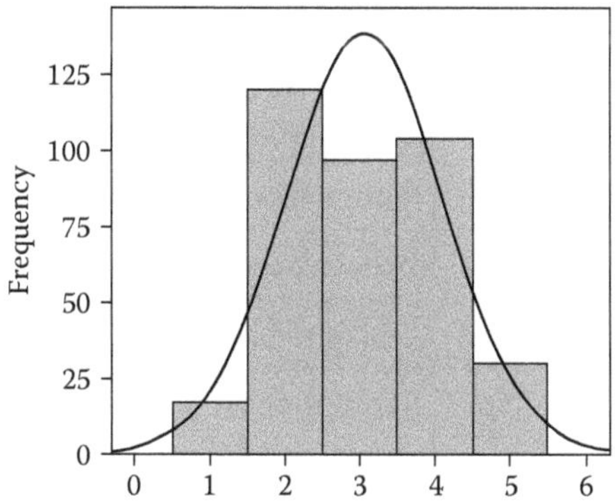

This split among IS professionals as to the purpose and scope of enterprise architecture, and for that matter requirements analysis and design, is significant. It is also in some ways disheartening in that it suggests that the majority of IT professionals responding to our survey aspire only to be great at IT, whether it particularly helps their organizations or not. On the other hand, the more optimistic view is that a third of respondents do seem to believe that EA does hold the potential for a seat at the strategic management table, and we find this encouraging. The SIMEAWG intends to monitor this dichotomy over time and also to do its part to advocate the validity and opportunity inherent in the view that EA is about the entire enterprise. It would seem the term *enterprise* is self-explanatory, but apparently that is not the case.

Respondents Rate the Quality of Their Requirements and Software Development Practices Poorly

The third finding is that developing requirements continues to be a challenge for IT professionals. The fundamental importance and difficulties of getting the requirements right has been a topic of importance among IT professionals at least since Frederick Brooks's 1975 book *The Mythical Man-Month* (discussed in Chapter 2's introduction and Brian Salmans's "EA Maturity Models" article). Getting requirements right is most notably identified with Brooks's contention that requirements are the essence of what IT professionals do, all the rest being accident or risk management. Table 4.1 summarizes the results of the five main research constructs examined in the survey, and Table 4.2 provides summary statistics for each of the individual items used to measure these constructs.

The construct "requirement practices" is operationalized or measured by the fifteen individual questions numbered 18a through 18o, which ask about various aspects of their "requirements analysis and design (RA&D) efforts and activities"

TABLE 4.1   Means of Primary Research Constructs (Rank-Ordered)

Question numbers	Subject/Construct	Mean	See Table	See Chart
19a–19g	Purpose/function of EA	3.92	4.2c	4.13
20a–20t	Potential benefits of EA	3.90	4.2d	4.14
15a–15l	IS development practices	3.68	4.2a	4.9
21a–21j	Use of requirements artifacts	3.53	4.2e	4.15
18a–18o	Requirements practices	3.33	4.2b	4.12
	OVERALL MEAN:	3.67		

TABLE 4.2 Recap by Question for Primary Research Constructs (Rank-Ordered Mean)

	Responses		Mean	Std. Deviation	Scale Avgs.
	Valid	Missing			
TABLE 4.2a: 15. Have IS development processes & procedures for …					
15h. coordination & communications among stakeholders	375	2	3.90	0.92	
15a. establishing customer agreement on requirements	374	3	3.83	1.07	
15i. selecting, contracting, tracking software "suppliers"	367	10	3.83	1.01	
15e. tracking progress & resource use	373	4	3.82	0.93	
15k. tailoring processes to project specifics	368	9	3.76	0.92	
15j. analyzing problems & preventing reoccurrence	372	5	3.75	0.95	
15f. software quality assurance	370	7	3.68	0.99	
15d. estimating all resources	375	2	3.66	1.01	
15c. establishing quality goals w/ customers	374	3	3.55	1.03	
15g. continuous process improvement	371	6	3.51	1.06	
15l. continuous productivity improvements	371	6	3.47	0.98	
15b. identify training needs of IS professionals	370	7	3.42	1.03	
Average of all 15s					3.68
TABLE 4.2b: 18. Requirements analysis & design efforts …					
18n. have IT leadership buy-in & support	371	6	4.18	0.78	
18c. are aligned w/ organization's objectives	373	4	3.90	0.84	

(continued)

TABLE 4.2   Recap by Question for Primary Research Constructs (Rank-ordered Mean) (continued)

	Responses		Mean	Std. Deviation	Scale Avgs.
	Valid	Missing			
18m. contribute directly to business plan goals	370	7	3.78	0.82	
18l. improve our ability to manage risk	367	10	3.61	0.81	
18i. describe "to be"	367	10	3.60	0.91	
18f. have executive support	372	5	3.57	0.99	
18h. describe "as is"	364	13	3.52	0.82	
18e. valued by executive leadership	372	5	3.34	1.04	
18o. are well prioritized by executives	370	7	3.34	1.02	
18g. are characterized by effective communications	373	4	3.21	1.01	
18k. are viewed strictly as an IT initiative	368	9	3.03	1.06	
18d. are highly developed and disciplined	373	4	3.00	1.05	
18a. are measured	370	7	2.99	1.07	
18j. stifle innovation	366	11	2.48	0.91	
18b. are benchmarked to other organizations	368	9	2.36	0.99	
Average of all 18s					3.33

TABLE 4.2c: 19. The purpose/function of enterprise architecture is …

19e. to provide blueprint of data, applications, & technology	373	4	4.40	0.68	

Item	N		Mean	SD	
19f. a tool for planning	373	4	4.25	0.68	
19g. a tool for decision making	374	3	4.13	0.71	
19d. a tool for alignment of business & IT	372	5	4.08	0.86	
19b. to facilitate systematic change	374	3	4.02	0.74	
19c. a tool for communicating objectives	372	5	3.67	0.90	
19a. to provide a snapshot in time of an organization	374	3	2.87	1.10	
Average of all 19s					3.92

TABLE 4.2d: 20. Potential benefits of doing enterprise architecture:

Item	N		Mean	SD
20h. improved IS interoperability	372	5	4.34	0.72
20f. improved utilization of IT	373	4	4.25	0.70
20a. alignment of business & IT investments	373	4	4.14	0.80
20q. more effective use of IT resources	370	7	4.02	0.74
20b. more responsive to change	371	6	3.97	0.80
20i. improved IT ROI	371	6	3.96	0.85
20d. better situational awareness	367	10	3.95	0.71
20p. assists with organizational governance	370	7	3.93	0.77
20g. improved communications & information sharing	371	6	3.92	0.80
20l. improved IS security	369	8	3.92	0.81
20c. less wasted time or $ on nonsupportive projects	373	4	3.92	0.88
20e. more effective at meeting business goals	373	4	3.91	0.77

(continued)

TABLE 4.2 Recap by Question for Primary Research Constructs (Rank-ordered Mean) (continued)

	Responses				
	Valid	Missing	Mean	Std. Deviation	Scale Avgs.
20j. improved communication between organization & IS	369	8	3.82	0.88	
20n. better collaboration within organization	371	6	3.82	0.79	
20k. faster IS development & implementation	369	8	3.80	0.83	
20r. reduced IT complexity	367	10	3.78	1.02	
20t. reduces stovepipes in organization	365	12	3.78	0.84	
20m. standardizes organizational performance measures	364	13	3.69	0.90	
20s. improved communications within organization	368	9	3.67	0.82	
20o. Improves trust in the organization	368	9	3.49	0.85	
Average of all 20s					3.90

TABLE 4.2e: 21. Artifacts of requirements analysis & design:

	Responses				
	Valid	Missing	Mean	Std. Deviation	Scale Avgs.
21h. are approved by owner of business process	361	16	3.84	0.91	
21b. describes transition from "as is" to "to be"	366	11	3.76	0.86	
21g. are approved by CIO	358	19	3.69	1.05	
21f. support strategic business decisions	365	12	3.65	0.89	
21i. are used as basis for IT procurement	363	14	3.60	0.94	
21a. include standards for IS security	362	15	3.58	0.93	
21e. are used to standardize technology	361	16	3.42	0.95	

21d. are kept in a digital repository or database	362	15	3.37	1.02	
21j. are assessed for quality	362	15	3.28	0.96	
21c. are kept current	364	13	3.11	0.95	
Average of all 21s					3.53
Average of all questions:					3.67

TABLE 4.2f: Status to Software Engineering Institute's Capability Maturity Model

16. IS department aspires to SEI's CMM	334	43	2.72	1.06	
17. Aspire or not, what level of SEI's CMM?	365	12	2.15	1.00	

using the definition that "the purpose of ... RA&D is to describe a functional process or a product/service in order to achieve enterprise objectives." Table 4.2b provides summary statistics for all fifteen individual questions in question 18, and complete descriptive statistics including histograms can be found in Chart 4.12 in the Detailed Survey Results.

As indicated in Table 4.1, the overall average of these fifteen question 18 items is the lowest of the five main constructs measured. This is particularly troubling in light of Brooks's view, which we share, that requirements are the essence of IT. In fact, it seems self-evident that no matter how well one builds and deploys an information system, a failure to get the requirements right will invariably result in a failure for the enterprise (although it is acknowledged that on exceptionally rare occasions "lucky breaks" happen, as evidenced by those very uncommon but extant winners of state lotteries). A generally immature state of requirements practices and capabilities in a majority of IT organizations is suggested by the very low responses to questions 18a, 18b, and 18d as shown in Chart 4.6.

The means to the questions in Chart 4.6, on the 1-to-5 scale used on the other questions from strongly disagree to strongly agree, were only 2.99 for 18a (RA&D activities "are measured"), only 2.36 for 18b ("are benchmarked to other organizations"), and 3.00 for 18d ("are highly developed and disciplined")—all basically failing self-reported grades. On a more positive note, question 18c, "are aligned with the organization's objectives," had a mean response of 3.90 as shown in Chart 4.7.

The IT professionals responding to our survey rated their overall IS development activities somewhat poorly, too. This is indicated (and shown in Tables 4.1 and 4.2a) by their responses to the twelve questions numbered 15a to 15l operationalizing the "IS development practices" construct and question 17 ("Whether your IS department aspires to SEI CMM practices or not, at what level would your IS

CHART 4.6 My organization's requirements analysis and design (RA&D) efforts and activities:

CHART 4.6a   18a. ... are measured.

	Frequency	Percent
1	27	7.16
2	114	30.24
3	81	21.49
4	131	34.75
5	17	4.51
Responses	370	98.14
Missing	7	1.86
Mean	2.99	
Median	3.00	
Std Dev	1.07	

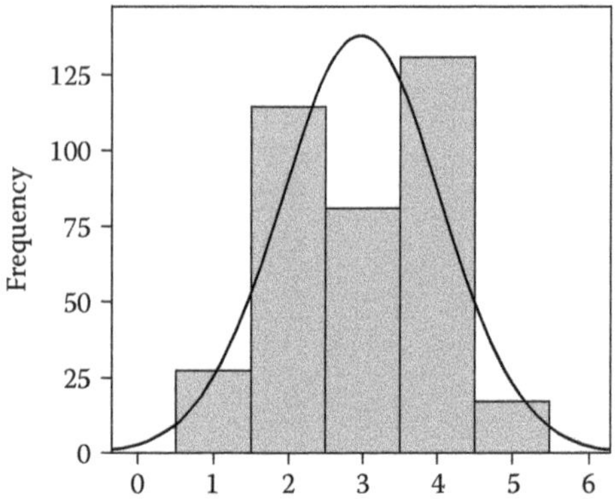

CHART 4.6b   18b. … are benchmarked to other organizations.

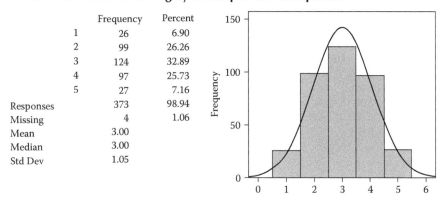

	Frequency	Percent
1	63	16.71
2	171	45.36
3	81	21.49
4	43	11.41
5	10	2.65
Responses	368	97.61
Missing	9	2.39
Mean	2.36	
Median	2.00	
Std Dev	0.99	

CHART 4.6c   18d. … are highly developed and disciplined.

	Frequency	Percent
1	26	6.90
2	99	26.26
3	124	32.89
4	97	25.73
5	27	7.16
Responses	373	98.94
Missing	4	1.06
Mean	3.00	
Median	3.00	
Std Dev	1.05	

organization be assessed?"). Recall from Chapter 2 that the Software Engineering Institute's (SEI) Capability Maturity Model (CMM) is based on five levels of maturity: 1, initial; 2, repeatable; 3, defined; 4, managed; 5, optimizing.

As shown in Chart 4.8, nearly two-thirds rated their IS development practices as either level 1 or 2 on question 17. It would seem a self-rating of 3 would be the preferred "passing" score since a 1 rating indicates no repeatable IS development practices and a 2 rating indicates that, although repeatable software development practices exist, there are inadequate project management practices. An examination of Chart 4.8 indicates that some level of ad hoc chaos is apparently the reported status quo for the nearly 29 percent of respondents self-rating their practices a 1, and some chaos still reigns for the 37 percent rating a 2. Only 19 percent rate their IS development at level 3, and 11 percent rate their CMM level at level 4.

In other words, it appears that the majority of IT professionals are still challenged at performing sufficiently in both the essence (requirements management)

CHART 4.7   18c. My organization's requirements analysis and design (RA&D) efforts and activities are aligned with the organization's objectives.

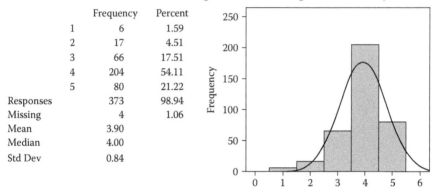

	Frequency	Percent
1	6	1.59
2	17	4.51
3	66	17.51
4	204	54.11
5	80	21.22
Responses	373	98.94
Missing	4	1.06
Mean	3.90	
Median	4.00	
Std Dev	0.84	

CHART 4.8   17. Whether your IS department aspires to SEI CMM practices or not, at what level would your IS organization be assessed?

		Frequency	Percent
Initial	1.00	108	28.65
Repeatable	2.00	140	37.14
Defined	3.00	72	19.10
Managed	4.00	43	11.41
Optimizinig	5.00	2	0.53
Responses		365	96.82
Missing		12	3.18
Mean		2.15	
Median		2.00	
Std Dev		1.00	

and the accident (risk management) of their craft. Simply stated, they are challenged at both aiming and firing their skills and resources. It is especially disconcerting that the professionals responding to our survey rate their IS department's practices so low in these areas given the importance continually emphasized regarding getting the requirements right, software engineering, and project management. Is it any wonder that so many CIOs no longer report to their CEOs—as much as 50 percent fewer than just seven years ago according to some surveys, and down a third in just the past few years;[17] although, recent reports indicate that this downward trend may be reversing.[18]

Nevertheless, it must be noted that significant progress in IS development practices appears to have been made over the past decade. This is evidenced by the fact that in a 1997 study also of SIM members,[19] 70 percent of respondents answered 1, strongly disagree, to whether their "IS department aspires to the software development practices of the Software Engineering Institute's (SEI's) Capability Maturity Model for software development," whereas in the current study less than 9 percent so responded (as shown in Chart 4.10). The 1997 mean for this question was 1.55 while in 2007 it was 2.72 (see Table 4.2f). Progress has clearly been made.

In an effort to further examine the bimodal results to some of the maturity of requirements practices items, we divided the respondents to question 18a into two groups (Group 1—those that responded with either 1 or 2; and Group 2—those that responded with either 4 or 5) and compared them based on their responses on the SEI CMM self-rating question 17. Interestingly, those in Group 1 rated their organizations with a mean of 1.65 while those in Group 2 rated their organizations with a mean of 2.61. For the overall subsample (of those responding 1, 2, 4, or 5) the mean for question 17 was 2.00, and for all respondents 2.15. This provides some support for the hypothesis that organizations that are more mature in their requirements practices are more mature in their IS development practices.

Nevertheless, the generally low scores for requirements analysis and design as operationalized by the fifteen questions in question 18 (see Chart 4.6, Table 4.2b, and Chart 4.12) do suggest an underlying reason why IT-business alignment appears so elusive to IT professionals. The scores also point to some fundamental weaknesses in these critically important requirements activities and skills of IT professionals and perhaps suggest the need for some professional "soul searching" among IT academics, management, and leadership as to whether this is acceptable and, if not, what can be done about it. The low scores for question 17 and the seven questions in question 15, all of which measure IS development capabilities, are equally troubling and provide a further indication of why IT departments may be having credibility and stature problems (see Charts 4.8 and 4.9, Tables 4.2a and 4.2f).

What's Next?

As a summary of findings, Table 4.2 provides a question-by-question rank-ordered recap of all items used in the SIMEAWG survey to operationalize the primary research constructs. The Detailed Survey Results that follow has complete descriptive statistics for every question as well as histograms of the items in Table 4.2.

We consider all the findings presented here, especially those related to EA, as preliminary. The practice of EA is perhaps twenty-five years old, and the Information Age barely sixty. It is still very early in the game. We intend to conduct further, more extensive validation and analysis of the data from the current survey. It is also the intention of the SIMEAWG to update and revise our survey questionnaire as may be indicated by our findings and our ongoing understanding of the subject matter. Future surveys will reexamine the practices examined in this survey as well as explore specific EA practices and the skill requirements of enterprise architects. Subsequent findings will be made available in future publications.

We believe that progress is being made in all areas of IT management, including EA. But much remains to be learned, discovered, and invented. Mistakes will no doubt be made, but only because that is part of the cost of progress. As opined in Chapter 2's "Bridging the Chasm" article, it may be useful to view the evolution of EA through the historical lens of the evolution of the productivity and quality movements that began during the Industrial Age in the nineteenth and twentieth centuries and continue today in the Information Age. One of the founders of the quality movement, W. Edwards Deming, closed a seminar this way: "You have heard the words; you must find the way. It will never be perfect. Perfection is not for this world; it is for some other world. I hope what you have heard here today will haunt you the rest of your life."[20] We hope it will inspire you, too!

Notes

1. Kappelman, L. A. (Editor) (1997). *Year 2000 Problem: Strategies and Solutions from the Fortune 100.* International Thomson Computer Press: Boston.
2. Specifically: "The purpose of requirements analysis and design (RA&D) is to describe a functional process or a product/service in order to achieve enterprise objectives."
3. Chen, P., and Pozgay, A. (2002) Architecture Practice: a fundamental discipline for information systems (2002). *ACIS 2002 Proceedings.* Paper 9.
4. Finkelstein, C. (2004, July 1). System Development Strategies for 21st Century Enterprises. *The Data Administration Newsletter,* pp. 1-9.
5. Luftman, J. (2000) Assessing IT/Business Alignment, *Communications of the Association for Information Systems,* 14 (4), 1-51.
6. Gregor, S., Hart, D., & Martin, N. (2007). Enterprise architectures: enablers of business strategy and IS/IT alignment in government. *Information Technology & People,* 20(2), 96-120.
7. Vaidyanathan, S. (2005). Enterprise architecture in the context of organizational strategy. *BPTrends,* 11, pp. 1-9.
8. Ross, J. W., Peter, W., & Robertson, D. (2006). *Enterprise architecture as strategy:* Harvard Business School Press.
9. McKeen, J., & Guimaraes, T., (1997) Successful strategies for user participation in systems development, *Journal of Management Information Systems,* 14 (2), pp. 133-152.
10. Luftman, J., & McLean, E. R. (2004). Key issues for IT executives. *MIS Quarterly Executive,* 3(2), 89-104.
11. Luftman, J., (2000) Assessing IT/Business Alignment, *Communications of the Association for Information Systems,* 14 (4), 1-51.
12. Gregor, S., Hart, D., & Martin, N. (2007). Enterprise architectures: enablers of business strategy and IS/IT alignment in government. *Information Technology & People,* 20(2), 96-120.
13. Vaidyanathan, S. (2005). Enterprise architecture in the context of organizational strategy. B*PTrends,* 11, pp. 1-9.
14. Ross, J. W., Peter, W., & Robertson, D. (2006). *Enterprise architecture as strategy:* Harvard Business School Press.

15. Ross, J. W., Peter, W., & Robertson, D. (2006). *Enterprise architecture as strategy:* Harvard Business School Press.
16. Dillman, D. A. (1999). *Mail and Internet Surveys – The Tailored Design Method*, 2nd edition, Wiley, New York.
17. Luftman, J. (2008) SIM 2007 *IT Trends Survey Findings*, available to SIM members only at http://simnet.org/Portals/0/Content/Library/SIMposium/luftmanhandout.ppt (5 January 08)
18. Nash, Kim S. (2009). "The State of the CIO '09", *CIO Magazine*, January 1, http://assets.cio.com/documents/cache/pdfs/2009_state_of_the_cio_charts.pdf.
19. Kappelman, L. A. (Editor) (1997). *Year 2000 Problem: Strategies and Solutions from the Fortune 100*. International Thomson Computer Press: Boston.
20. Dr. W. Edwards Deming, Deming Management Seminar, Newport Beach, CA, February 24 to 28, 1986.

Detailed Survey Results

Demographic Questions

Questions about the Individual Respondents

TABLE 4.3   Respondent Job Title

1. Job Title	Frequency	Percent
Chief Executive Officer (CEO)	8	2.13
Chief Information Officer (CIO)	100	26.60
Chief Technology Officer (CTO)	13	3.46
Director	121	32.18
Enterprise Architect	16	4.26
Member of the Board	1	0.27
Vice President	38	10.12
Other	79	21.01
Total	**376**	**100.00**

TABLE 4.4   Title of the Person to Whom the Respondent Reports

2. Job Title	Frequency	Percent
Agency Dir/Secretary/Administrator	10	2.65
Chief Executive Officer (CEO)	66	17.51
Chief Financial Officer (CFO)	46	12.20
Chief Information Officer (CIO)	83	22.07
Chief Operating Officer (COO)	24	6.37
Chief Technology Officer (CTO)	12	3.18
Director	23	6.12
Enterprise Architect	7	1.86
Member of the Board	4	1.06
President	5	1.33
Vice President	61	16.22
Other	35	9.31
Total	**376**	**100.00**

TABLE 4.5   Age, Time in Organization, and Time in Present Position

	Number	Minimum	Maximum	Mean	Std. Deviation
3. Age	370	29	73	47.69	8.55
4. Years in Org	376	0	35	8.16	7.50
5. Years in Pos	375	0	35	4.37	4.26

TABLE 4.6   Highest Level of Education Attained

6. Educational Level	Frequency	Percent
Associate Degree	12	3.18
Bachelor's Degree	140	37.14
Master's Degree	198	52.52

(continued)

TABLE 4.6   Highest Level of Education Attained (continued)

6. Educational Level	Frequency	Percent
High School	1	0.27
PhD, JD, MD, or other terminal degree	16	4.24
Some College	8	2.12
Not Answered	1	0.27
Total	**376**	**100.00**

TABLE 4.7   Level of Responsibility

7. Responsibility	Frequency	Percent
Department	59	15.65
Division/Business Unit	60	15.92
Enterprise-wide	239	63.40
Team/Work Group	17	4.51
Not Answered	1	0.27
Total	**376**	**100.00**

Questions about the Respondents' Organizations

TABLE 4.8   Type of Industry

8. Industry	Frequency	Percent
Agriculture	1	0.27
Banking/Securities/Investments/Finance/Insurance	48	12.73
Business Services (Legal/R&D)	8	2.12
Capital Goods Mfg	14	3.71
Chemical	8	2.12
Construction/Engineering	3	0.80
Consumer Goods Mfg	27	7.16

(continued)

TABLE 4.8   Type of Industry (continued)

8. Industry	Frequency	Percent
Education	18	4.77
Entertainment	4	1.06
Food Service	6	1.59
Government (Fed, State, Local)	14	3.71
Healthcare/Medical/Pharmaceutical/Biotech	42	11.14
Hotels/Tourism/Travel	3	0.80
IT Services Provider/Consultant	33	8.75
Military	2	0.53
Other	68	18.09
Mining/Energy	8	2.12
Printing/Publishing	6	1.59
Real Estate	5	1.33
Retail/Wholesale	32	8.49
Transportation/Distribution/Logistical	14	3.71
Utilities	10	2.65
Not Answered	2	0.53
Total	**376**	**100.00**

TABLE 4.9   Organizational Description

9. Organization Type	Frequency	Percent
Governmental Organization	17	4.51
Not-for-Profit Organization	51	13.53
Profit-Making Corporation	304	80.64
Other	3	0.81
Not Answered	1	0.27
Total	**376**	**100.00**

TABLE 4.10 Number of Employees in Organization

10. Number	Frequency	Percent
Less than 100	35	9.28
100–499	69	18.30
500–999	40	10.61
1,000–4,999	81	21.49
5,000–9,999	50	13.26
10,000–19,999	33	8.75
20,000–29,999	14	3.71
30,000–50,000	20	5.31
Greater than 50,000	31	8.22
Don't Know	3	0.80
Total	**376**	**100.00**

TABLE 4.11 Gross Revenue/Income/Budget of Organization

11. Range in Dollars	Frequency	Percent
Less than $50 million	49	13.00
$50 million–$100 million	19	5.04
$101 million–$500 million	79	20.95
$501 million–$999 million	41	10.88
$1 billion–$4.9 billion	86	22.81
$5 billion–$9.9 billion	25	6.63
$10 billion–$14.9 billion	13	3.45
$15 billion–$24.9 billion	17	4.05
$25 billion–$50 billion	19	5.04
Greater than $50 billion	10	2.65
Don't Know	12	3.18
Not Answered	6	1.59
Total	**376**	**100.00**

TABLE 4.12   Primary Location of Organization

12. Location	Frequency	Percent
Africa	1	0.27
Asia	3	0.80
Europe	8	2.12
North America (other than USA)	29	7.69
South America	1	0.27
United States	325	86.21
Not Answered	9	2.39
Total	376	100.00

Questions about the Respondents' IS Departments

TABLE 4.13   Operating Budget of IT Department

13. Range in Dollars	Frequency	Percent
Less than $100,000	8	2.12
$100,000–$249,999	4	1.06
$250,000–$499,999	17	4.51
$500,000–$999,999	21	5.57
$1 million–$9.9 million	137	36.34
$10 million–$49.9 million	100	26.53
$50 million–$99.9 million	20	5.31
$100 million–$499.9 million	40	10.61
$500 million–$1 billion	10	2.65
Greater than $1 billion	10	2.65
Not Answered	9	2.39
Total	376	100.00

TABLE 4.14   Number of Employees in IT Department

14. Number	Frequency	Percent
Less than 50	147	38.99
50–99	49	13.00
100–499	92	24.40
500–999	33	8.75
1,000–4,999	35	9.28
5,000–9,999	8	2.12
10,000–19,999	2	0.53
Greater than 30,000	6	1.59
Not Answered	4	1.06
Total	**376**	**100.00**

IT and EA Practices and Perceptions Questions

CHART 4.9 15. For software development and/or maintenance, our IS department specifies and uses a comprehensive set of processes and/or procedures for:

CHART 4.9a   15a. ... establishing customer agreement on requirements.

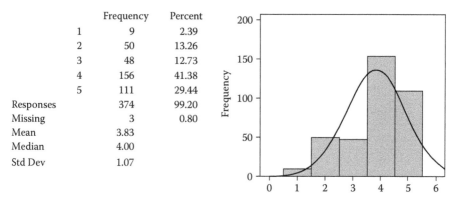

	Frequency	Percent
1	9	2.39
2	50	13.26
3	48	12.73
4	156	41.38
5	111	29.44
Responses	374	99.20
Missing	3	0.80
Mean	3.83	
Median	4.00	
Std Dev	1.07	

CHART 4.9b   15b. ... identifying the training needs of IS professionals.

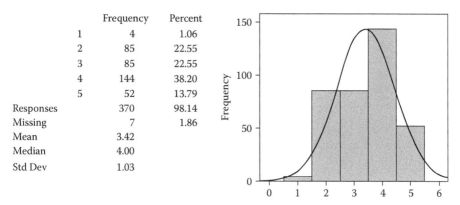

	Frequency	Percent
1	4	1.06
2	85	22.55
3	85	22.55
4	144	38.20
5	52	13.79
Responses	370	98.14
Missing	7	1.86
Mean	3.42	
Median	4.00	
Std Dev	1.03	

CHART 4.9c   15c. ... establishing quality goals with customers.

	Frequency	Percent
1	6	1.59
2	67	17.77
3	83	22.02
4	151	40.05
5	67	17.77
Responses	374	99.20
Missing	3	0.80
Mean	3.55	
Median	4.00	
Std Dev	1.03	

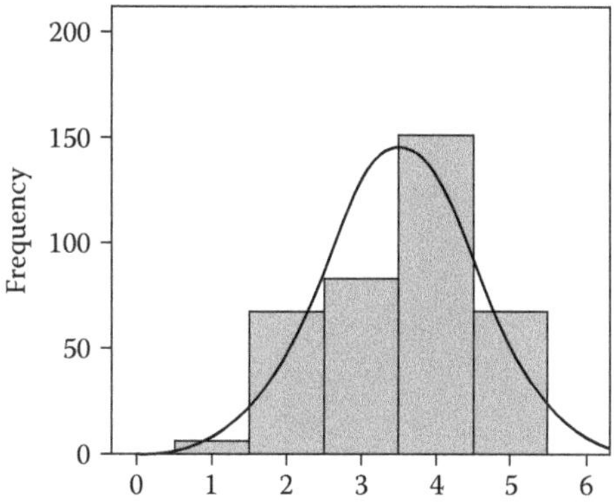

CHART 4.9d   15d. ... estimating all resource needs.

	Frequency	Percent
1	6	1.59
2	67	17.77
3	83	22.02
4	151	40.05
5	67	17.77
Responses	374	99.20
Missing	3	0.80
Mean	3.55	
Median	4.00	
Std Dev	1.03	

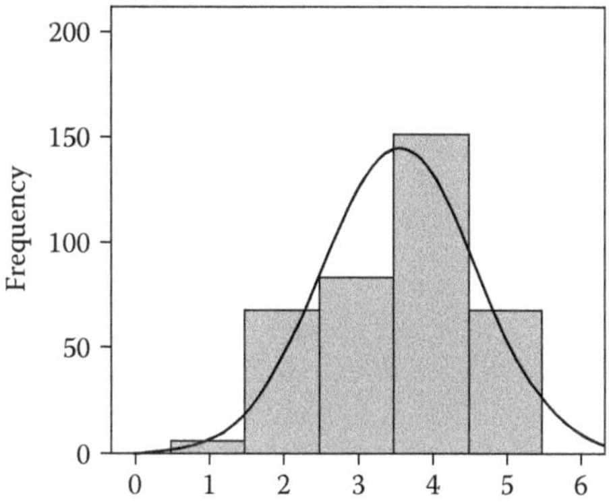

CHART 4.9e   15e. ... tracking progress and resources.

	Frequency	Percent
1	1	0.27
2	44	11.67
3	64	16.98
4	177	46.95
5	87	23.08
Responses	373	98.94
Missing	4	1.06
Mean	3.82	
Median	4.00	
Std Dev	0.93	

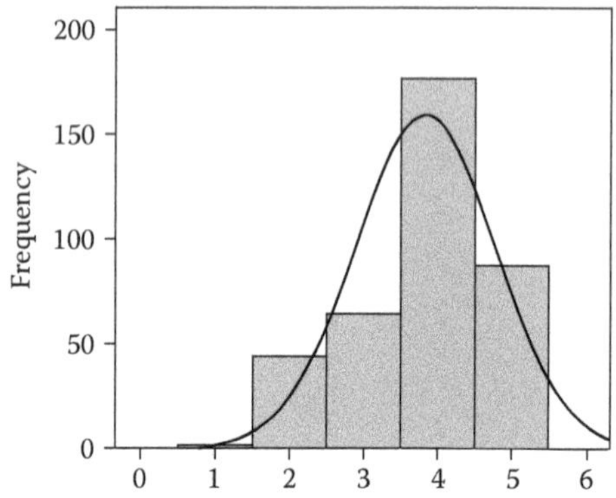

CHART 4.9f   15f. ... software quality assurance.

	Frequency	Percent
1	4	1.06
2	51	13.53
3	80	21.22
4	158	41.91
5	77	20.42
Responses	370	98.14
Missing	7	1.86
Mean	3.68	
Median	4.00	
Std Dev	0.99	

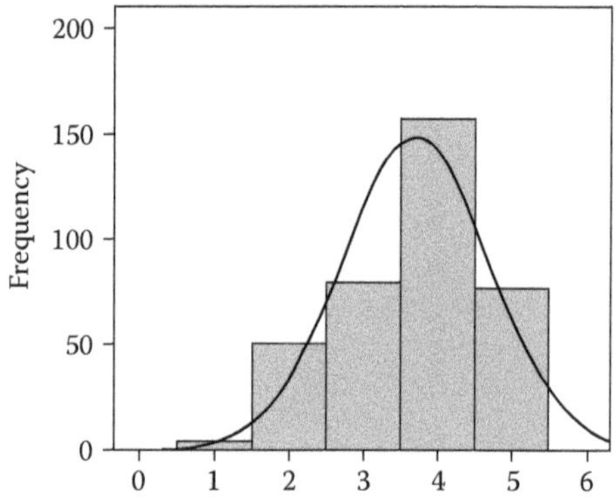

CHART 4.9g   15g. ... continuous process improvement.

	Frequency	Percent
1	8	2.12
2	70	18.57
3	85	22.55
4	142	37.67
5	66	17.51
Responses	371	98.41
Missing	6	1.59
Mean	3.51	
Median	4.00	
Std Dev	1.06	

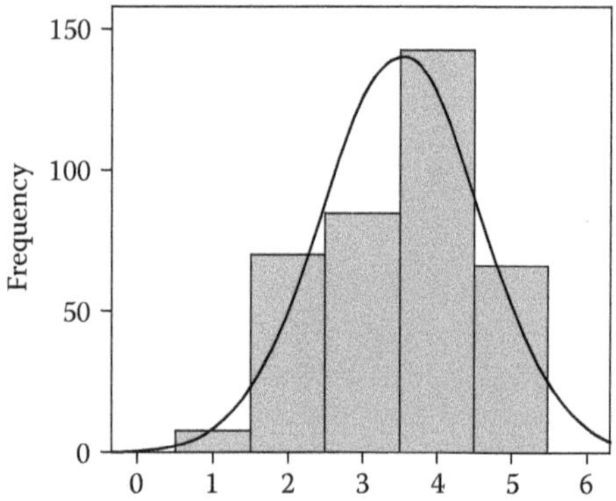

CHART 4.9h 15h. ... coordination and communication among stakeholders.

	Frequency	Percent
1	4	1.06
2	34	9.02
3	54	14.32
4	186	49.34
5	97	25.73
Responses	375	99.47
Missing	2	0.53
Mean	3.90	
Median	4.00	
Std Dev	0.92	

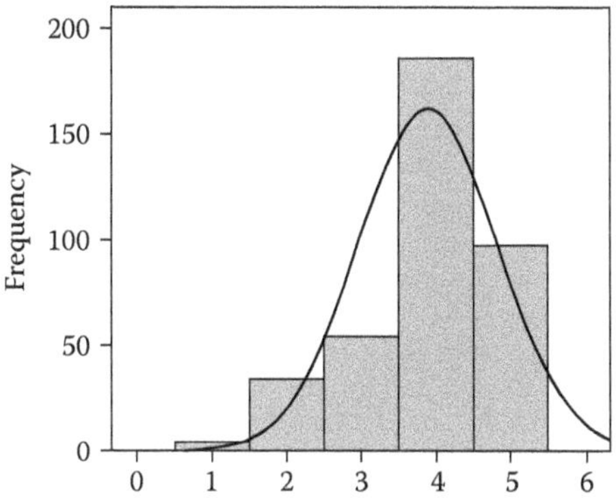

CHART 4-9i: 15i. ... selecting, contracting, tracking, and reviewing software contractors and outsourcers.

	Frequency	Percent
1	5	1.33
2	44	11.67
3	61	16.18
4	157	41.64
5	100	26.53
Responses	367	97.35
Missing	10	2.65
Mean	3.83	
Median	4.00	
Std Dev	1.01	

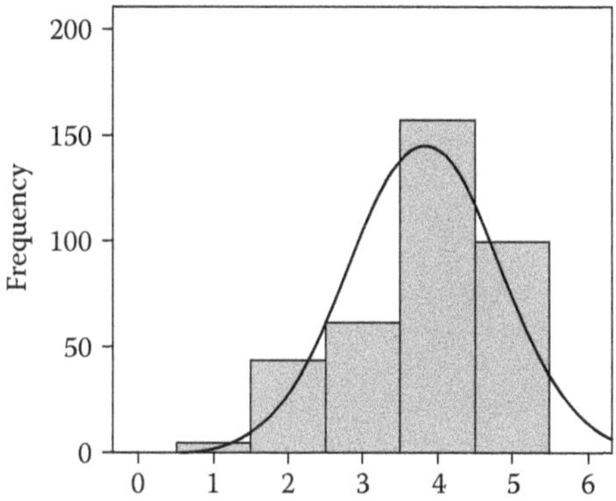

CHART 4-9j: 15j. ... analyzing problems and preventing reoccurrence.

	Frequency	Percent
1	6	1.59
2	37	9.81
3	79	20.95
4	171	45.36
5	79	20.95
Responses	372	98.67
Missing	5	1.33
Mean	3.75	
Median	4.00	
Std Dev	0.95	

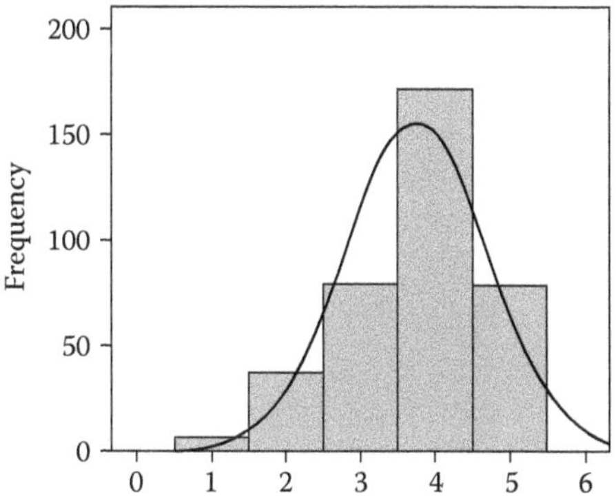

CHART 4-9k: 15k. ... tailoring the process to project specific needs.

	Frequency	Percent
2	45	11.94
3	75	19.89
4	171	45.36
5	77	20.42
Responses	368	97.61
Missing	9	2.39
Mean	3.76	
Median	4.00	
Std Dev	0.95	

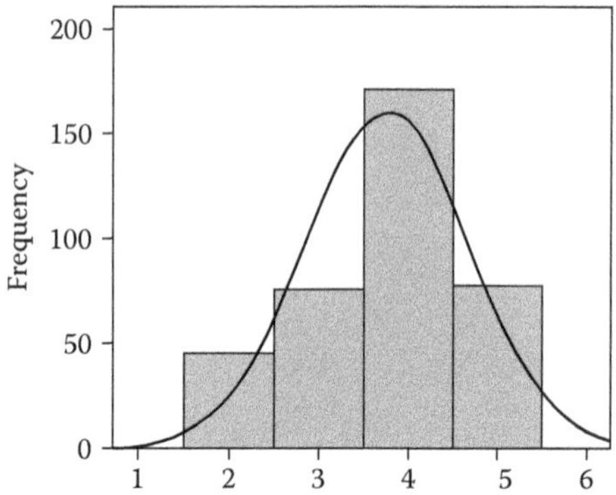

CHART 4-9l: 15l. ... continuous productivity improvements.

	Frequency	Percent
1	5	1.33
2	63	16.71
3	107	28.38
4	144	38.20
5	52	13.79
Responses	371	98.41
Missing	6	1.59
Mean	3.47	
Median	4.00	
Std Dev	0.98	

CHART 4.10   16. This IS department aspires to the software development practices of the Software Engineering Institute's (SEI's) Capability Maturity Model for software development.

	Frequency	Percent
1	33	8.75
2	127	33.69
3	94	24.93
4	60	15.92
5	20	5.31
Responses	334	88.59
Missing	43	11.41
Mean	2.72	
Median	3.00	
Std Dev	1.06	

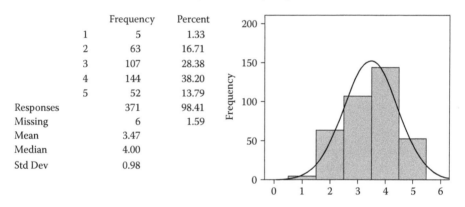

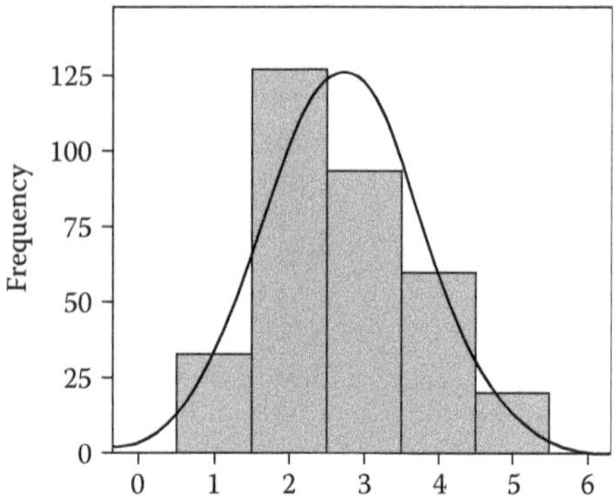

CHART 4.11   17. Whether your IS department aspires to SEI CMM practices or not, at what level would your IS organization be assessed?

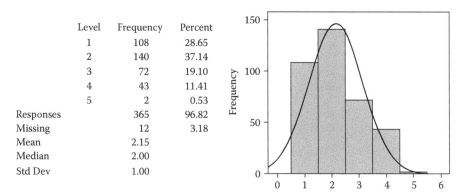

Level	Frequency	Percent
1	108	28.65
2	140	37.14
3	72	19.10
4	43	11.41
5	2	0.53
Responses	365	96.82
Missing	12	3.18
Mean	2.15	
Median	2.00	
Std Dev	1.00	

CHART 4.12 18. Please select the level to which you agree or disagree that each of the following statements is representative of the requirements analysis and design practices in your IT organization.

The purpose of requirements analysis and design (RA&D) is to describe a functional process or a product/service in order to achieve enterprise objectives.

My organization's requirements analysis and design (RA&D) efforts and activities:

CHART 4.12a   18a. ... are measured.

	Frequency	Percent
1	27	7.16
2	114	30.24
3	81	21.49
4	131	34.75
5	17	4.51
Responses	370	98.14
Missing	7	1.86
Mean	2.99	
Median	3.00	
Std Dev	1.07	

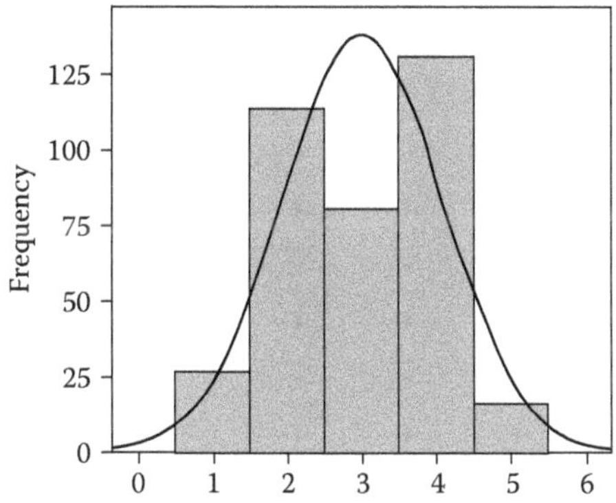

CHART 4.12b 18b. ... are benchmarked to other organizations.

	Frequency	Percent
1	63	16.71
2	171	45.36
3	81	21.49
4	43	11.41
5	10	2.65
Responses	368	97.61
Missing	9	2.39
Mean	2.36	
Median	2.00	
Std Dev	0.987	

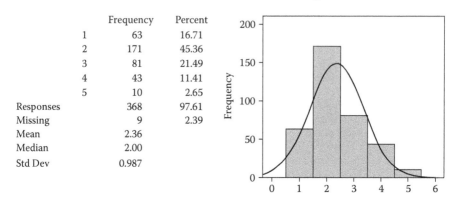

CHART 4.12c 18c. ... are aligned with the organization's objectives.

	Frequency	Percent
1	6	1.59
2	17	4.51
3	66	17.51
4	204	54.11
5	80	21.22
Responses	373	98.94
Missing	4	1.06
Mean	3.90	
Median	4.00	
Std Dev	0.84	

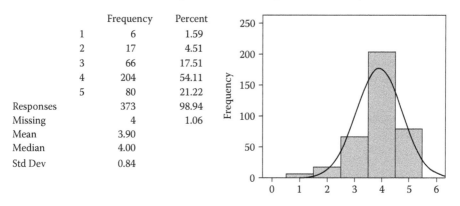

CHART 4.12d 18d. ... are highly developed and disciplined.

	Frequency	Percent
1	26	6.90
2	99	26.26
3	124	32.89
4	97	25.73
5	27	7.16
Responses	373	98.94
Missing	4	1.06
Mean	3.00	
Median	3.00	
Std Dev	1.05	

CHART 4.12e   18e. ... are valued by executive leadership.

	Frequency	Percent
1	16	4.24
2	71	18.83
3	99	26.26
4	144	38.20
5	42	11.14
Responses	372	98.67
Missing	5	1.33
Mean	3.34	
Median	3.50	
Std Dev	1.04	

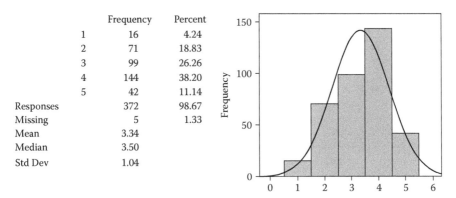

CHART 4.12f   18f. ... have executive leadership buy-in and support.

	Frequency	Percent
1	8	2.12
2	54	14.32
3	88	23.34
4	162	42.97
5	60	15.92
Responses	372	98.67
Missing	5	1.33
Mean	3.57	
Median	4.00	
Std Dev	0.99	

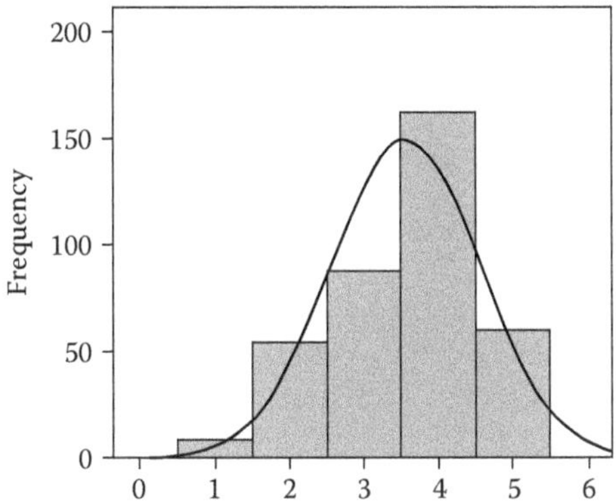

CHART 4.12g   18g. ... are characterized by effective communication between executive leadership and the requirements analysis and design team.

	Frequency	Percent
1	18	4.77
2	75	19.89
3	122	32.36
4	127	33.69
5	31	8.22
Responses	373	98.94
Missing	4	1.06
Mean	3.21	
Median	3.00	
Std Dev	1.01	

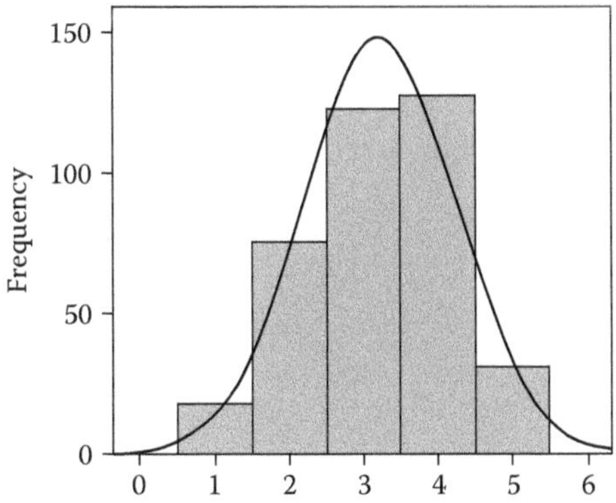

CHART 4.12h   18h. ... describe our present "as is" environment.

	Frequency	Percent
1	5	1.33
2	38	10.08
3	108	28.65
4	190	50.40
5	23	6.10
Responses	364	96.55
Missing	13	3.45
Mean	3.52	
Median	4.00	
Std Dev	0.82	

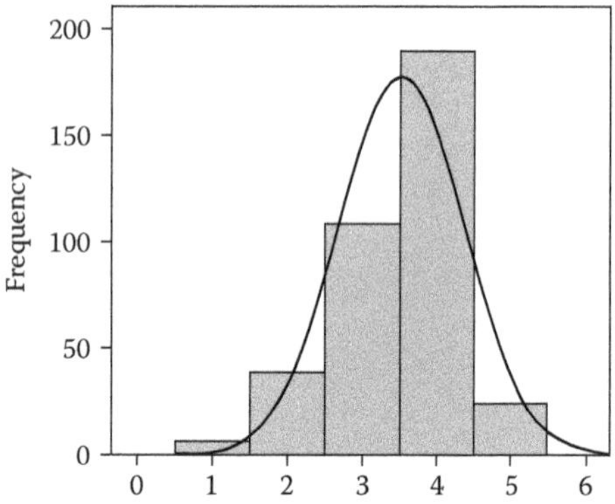

CHART 4.12i   18i. ... describe our "to be" or desired environment.

	Frequency	Percent
1	9	2.39
2	37	9.81
3	91	24.14
4	186	49.34
5	44	11.67
Responses	367	97.35
Missing	10	2.65
Mean	3.60	
Median	4.00	
Std Dev	0.91	

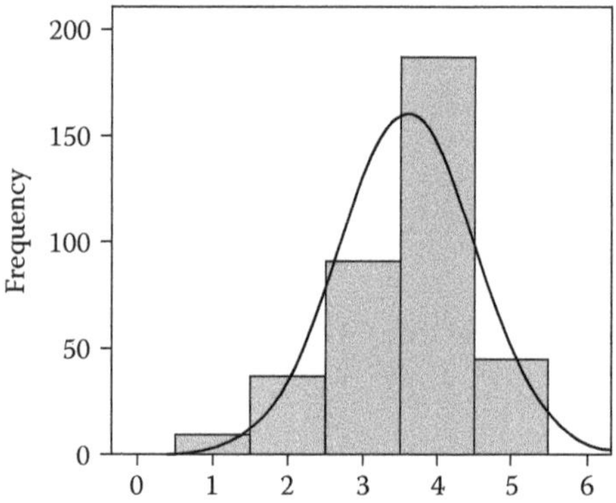

CHART 4.12j   18j. ... do not stifle innovation in our organization. (Question was reverse-coded and worded.)

	Frequency	Percent
1	8	2.12
2	44	11.67
3	101	26.79
4	175	46.42
5	38	10.08
Responses	366	97.08
Missing	11	2.92
Mean	3.52	
Median	4.00	
Std Dev	0.91	

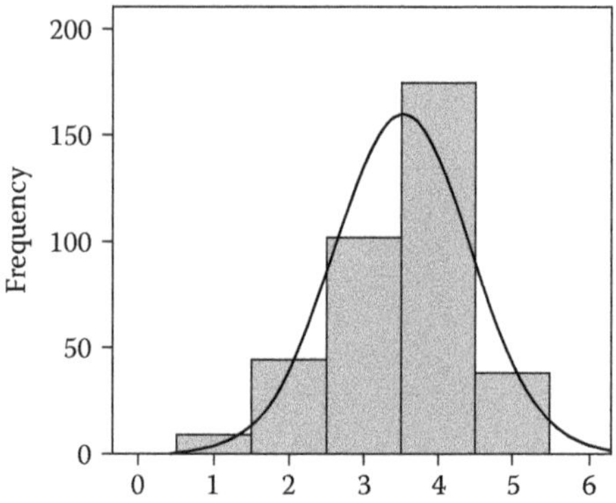

CHART 4.12k   18k. ... are viewed strictly as an IT initiative.

	Frequency	Percent
1	17	4.51
2	120	31.83
3	97	25.73
4	104	27.59
5	30	7.96
Responses	368	97.61
Missing	9	2.39
Mean	3.03	
Median	3.00	
Std Dev	1.06	

CHART 4.12l   18l. ... improve ability to manage risk.

	Frequency	Percent
1	5	1.33
2	29	7.69
3	102	27.06
4	198	52.52
5	33	8.75
Responses	367	97.35
Missing	10	2.65
Mean	3.61	
Median	4.00	
Std Dev	0.81	

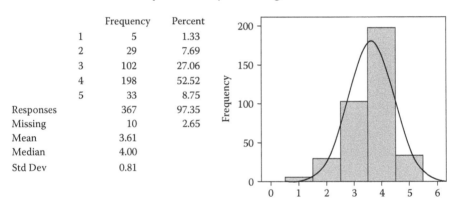

CHART 4.12m   18m. ... contribute directly to the goals and objectives of our business plan.

	Frequency	Percent
1	3	0.80
2	27	7.16
3	73	19.36
4	212	56.23
5	55	14.59
Responses	370	98.14
Missing	7	1.86
Mean	3.78	
Median	4.00	
Std Dev	0.82	

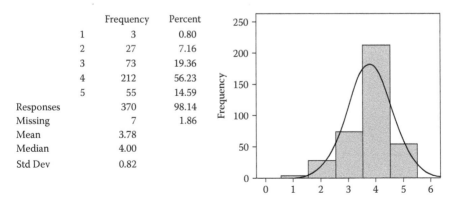

CHART 4.12n **18n. … have IT leadership buy-in and support.**

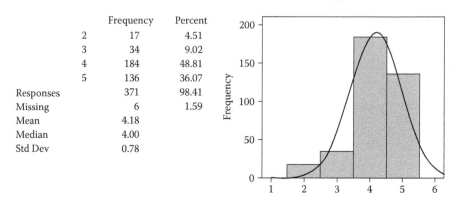

	Frequency	Percent
2	17	4.51
3	34	9.02
4	184	48.81
5	136	36.07
Responses	371	98.41
Missing	6	1.59
Mean	4.18	
Median	4.00	
Std Dev	0.78	

CHART 4.12o **18o. … are well prioritized by executive leadership.**

	Frequency	Percent
1	15	3.98
2	65	17.24
3	113	29.97
4	135	35.81
5	42	11.14
Responses	370	98.14
Missing	7	1.86
Mean	3.34	
Median	3.00	
Std Dev	1.02	

CHART 4.13 19. The purpose/function of enterprise architecture is:

CHART 4.13a   19a. ... to provide a snapshot in time of an organization.

	Frequency	Percent
1	28	7.43
2	146	38.73
3	67	17.77
4	112	29.71
5	21	5.57
Responses	374	99.20
Missing	3	0.80
Mean	2.87	
Median	3.00	
Std Dev	1.10	

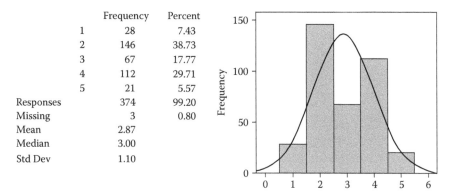

CHART 4.13b   19b. ... to facilitate systematic change in an organization.

	Frequency	Percent
1	2	0.53
2	18	4.77
3	33	8.75
4	240	63.66
5	81	21.49
Responses	374	99.20
Missing	3	0.80
Mean	4.02	
Median	4.00	
Std Dev	0.74	

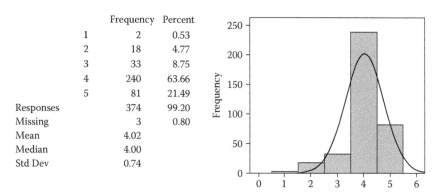

CHART 4.13c   19c. ... as a tool for communicating organizational objectives.

	Frequency	Percent
1	2	0.53
2	45	11.94
3	87	23.08
4	179	47.48
5	59	15.65
Responses	372	98.67
Missing	5	1.33
Mean	3.67	
Median	4.00	
Std Dev	0.90	

CHART 4.13d 19d. … as a tool for aligning business objectives with IT initiatives.

	Frequency	Percent
1	3	0.80
2	19	5.04
3	47	12.47
4	178	47.21
5	125	33.16
Responses	372	98.67
Missing	5	1.33
Mean	4.08	
Median	4.00	
Std Dev	0.86	

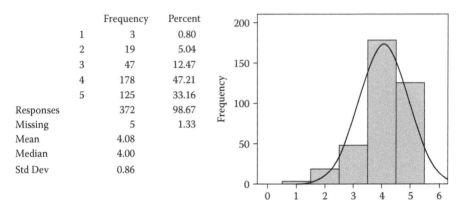

CHART 4.13e 19e. … to provide a blueprint of an organization's business, data, applications, and technology.

	Frequency	Percent
1	1	0.27
2	5	1.33
3	21	5.57
4	164	43.50
5	182	48.28
Responses	373	98.94
Missing	4	1.06
Mean	4.40	
Median	4.00	
Std Dev	0.68	

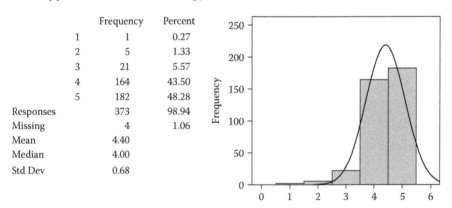

CHART 4.13f 19f. … as a tool for planning.

	Frequency	Percent
2	6	1.59
3	32	8.49
4	198	52.52
5	137	36.34
Responses	373	98.94
Missing	4	1.06
Mean	4.25	
Median	4.00	
Std Dev	0.68	

CHART 4.13g 19g. ... as a tool for decision making.

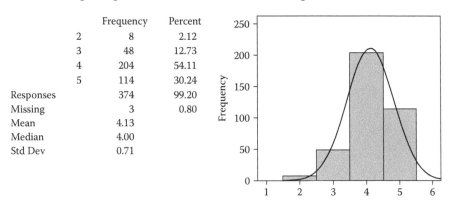

	Frequency	Percent
2	8	2.12
3	48	12.73
4	204	54.11
5	114	30.24
Responses	374	99.20
Missing	3	0.80
Mean	4.13	
Median	4.00	
Std Dev	0.71	

CHART 4.14 20. Please select the level to which you agree or disagree that each of the following statements is representative of the potential benefits to an organization from doing enterprise architecture.

Potential benefits of doing EA:

CHART 4.14a 20a. Aligns business objectives with information technology investments.

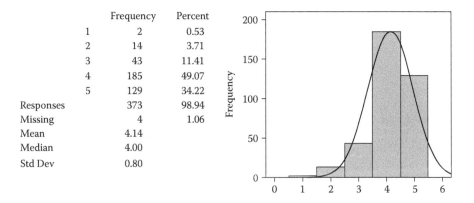

	Frequency	Percent
1	2	0.53
2	14	3.71
3	43	11.41
4	185	49.07
5	129	34.22
Responses	373	98.94
Missing	4	1.06
Mean	4.14	
Median	4.00	
Std Dev	0.80	

CHART 4.14b   20b. More responsive to change.

	Frequency	Percent
2	20	5.31
3	63	16.71
4	195	51.72
5	93	24.67
Responses	371	98.41
Missing	6	1.59
Mean	3.97	
Median	4.00	
Std Dev	0.80	

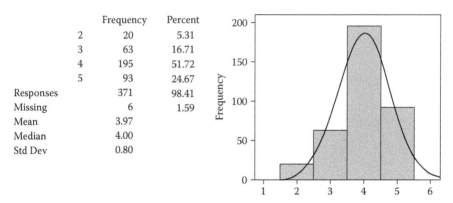

CHART 4.14c   20c. Less wasted time or money on projects which do not support business goals or objectives.

	Frequency	Percent
1	1	0.27
2	29	7.69
3	69	18.30
4	175	46.42
5	99	26.26
Responses	373	98.94
Missing	4	1.06
Mean	3.92	
Median	4.00	
Std Dev	0.88	

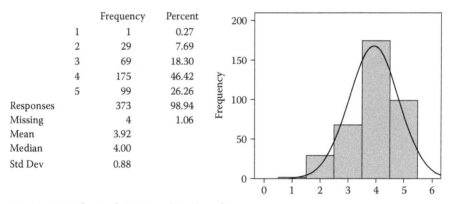

CHART 4.14d   20d. Better situational awareness.

	Frequency	Percent
2	11	2.92
3	71	18.83
4	212	56.23
5	73	19.36
Responses	367	97.35
Missing	10	2.65
Mean	3.95	
Median	4.00	
Std Dev	0.71	

CHART 4.14e   20e. More effective at meeting business goals.

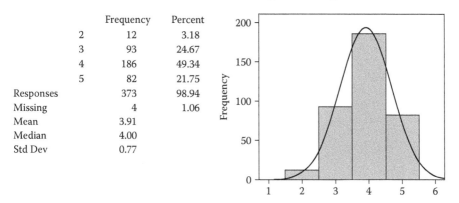

	Frequency	Percent
2	12	3.18
3	93	24.67
4	186	49.34
5	82	21.75
Responses	373	98.94
Missing	4	1.06
Mean	3.91	
Median	4.00	
Std Dev	0.77	

CHART 4.14f   20f. Improves utilization of information technology.

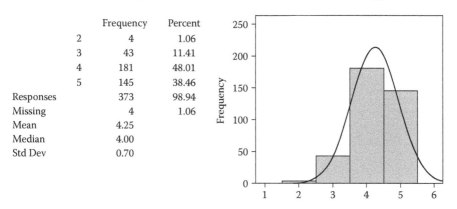

	Frequency	Percent
2	4	1.06
3	43	11.41
4	181	48.01
5	145	38.46
Responses	373	98.94
Missing	4	1.06
Mean	4.25	
Median	4.00	
Std Dev	0.70	

CHART 4.14g   20g. Improves organizational communications and information sharing.

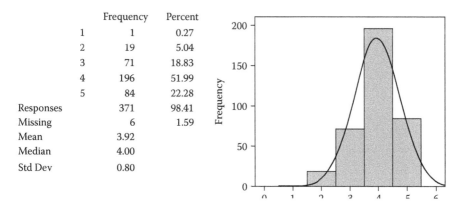

	Frequency	Percent
1	1	0.27
2	19	5.04
3	71	18.83
4	196	51.99
5	84	22.28
Responses	371	98.41
Missing	6	1.59
Mean	3.92	
Median	4.00	
Std Dev	0.80	

CHART 4.14h   20h. Improves interoperability among information systems.

	Frequency	Percent
2	5	1.33
3	39	10.34
4	154	40.85
5	174	46.15
Responses	372	98.67
Missing	5	1.33
Mean	4.34	
Median	4.00	
Std Dev	0.72	

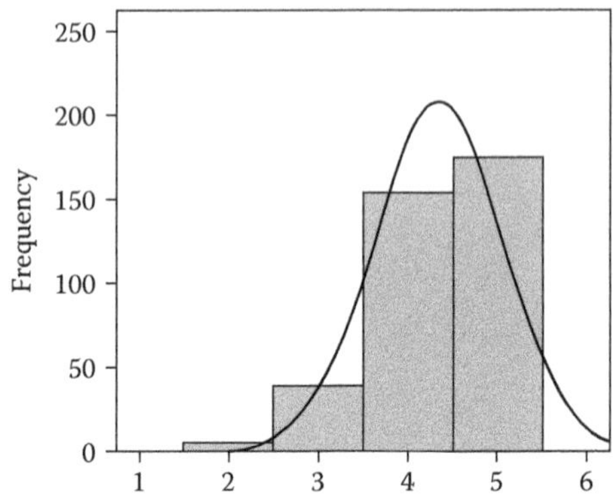

CHART 4.14i   20i. Improves ROI from IT spending.

	Frequency	Percent
1	2	0.53
2	16	4.24
3	80	21.22
4	168	44.56
5	105	27.85
Responses	371	98.41
Missing	6	1.59
Mean	3.96	
Median	4.00	
Std Dev	0.85	

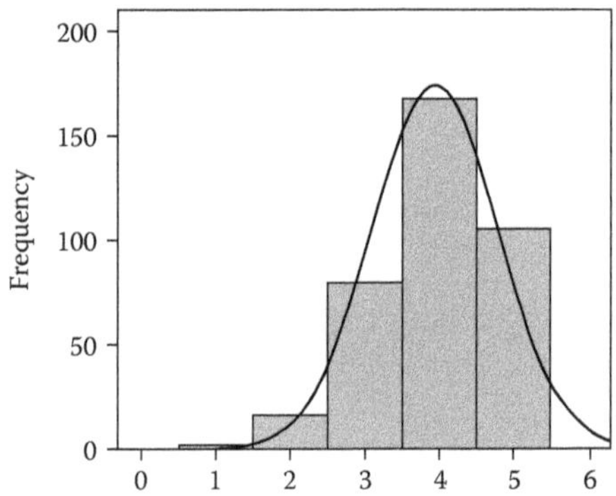

CHART 4.14j   20j. Improves communications between the organization and the information systems department.

	Frequency	Percent
2	30	7.96
3	93	24.67
4	160	42.44
5	86	22.81
Responses	369	97.88
Missing	8	2.12
Mean	3.82	
Median	4.00	
Std Dev	0.88	

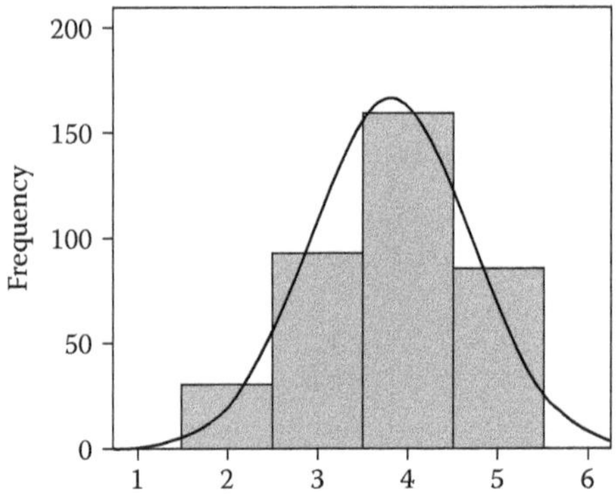

CHART 4.14k   20k. Faster development and implementation of new information systems.

	Frequency	Percent
1	1	0.27
2	19	5.04
3	109	28.91
4	165	43.77
5	75	19.89
Responses	369	97.88
Missing	8	2.12
Mean	3.80	
Median	4.00	
Std Dev	0.83	

CHART 4.14l   20l. Improves information systems security across the business.

	Frequency	Percent
2	15	3.98
3	91	24.14
4	170	45.09
5	93	24.67
Responses	369	97.88
Missing	8	2.12
Mean	3.92	
Median	4.00	
Std Dev	0.81	

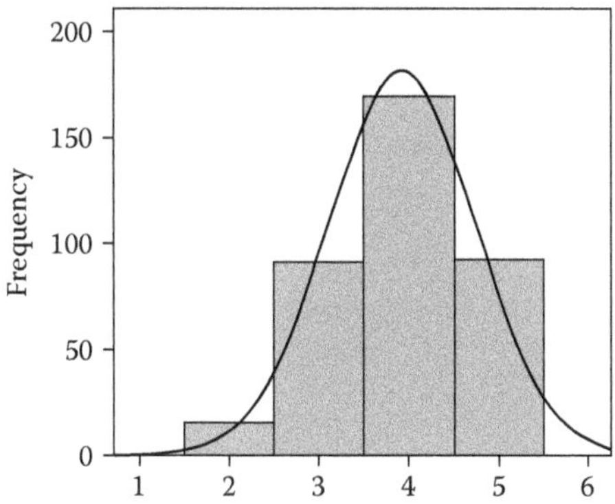

CHART 4.14m   20m. Standardizes organizational performance measures.

	Frequency	Percent
1	1	0.27
2	39	10.34
3	97	25.73
4	162	42.97
5	65	17.24
Responses	364	96.55
Missing	13	3.45
Mean	3.69	
Median	4.00	
Std Dev	0.90	

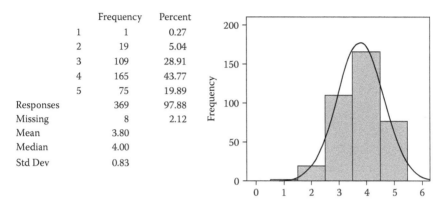

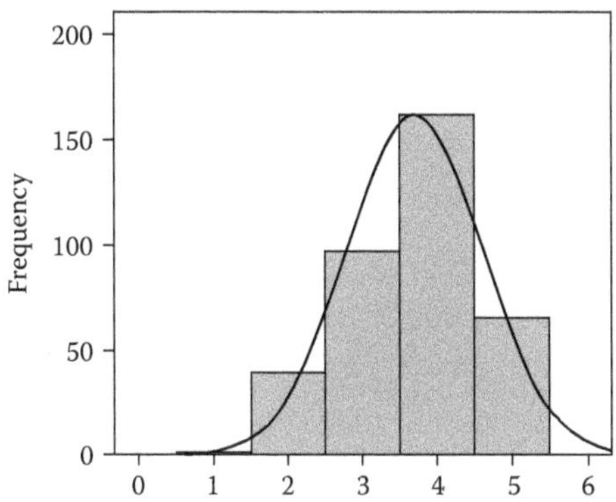

CHART 4.14n   20n. Better collaboration within organization.

	Frequency	Percent
1	1	0.27
2	20	5.31
3	89	23.61
4	197	52.25
5	64	16.98
Responses	371	98.41
Missing	6	1.59
Mean	3.82	
Median	4.00	
Std Dev	0.79	

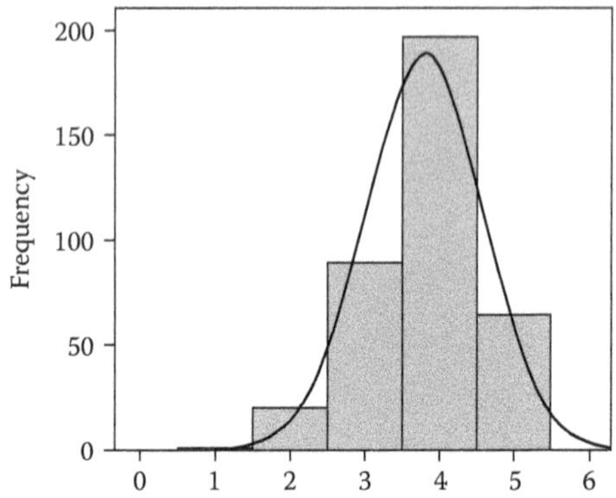

CHART 4.14o   20o. Improves trust in the organization.

	Frequency	Percent
2	44	11.67
3	141	37.40
4	141	37.40
5	42	11.14
Responses	368	97.61
Missing	9	2.39
Mean	3.49	
Median	3.00	
Std Dev	0.85	

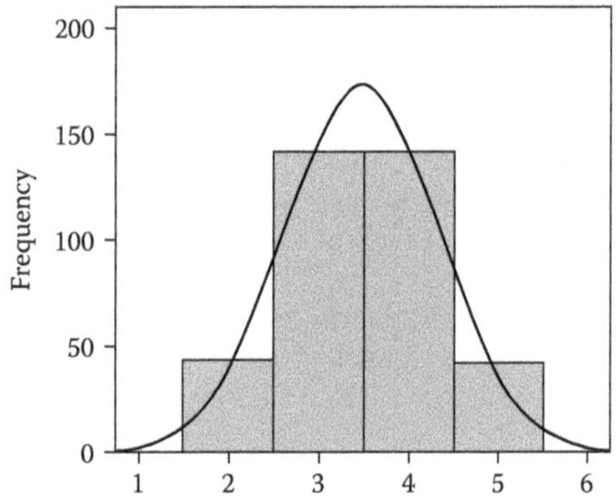

CHART 4.14p   20p. Assists with organizational governance.

	Frequency	Percent
1	1	0.27
2	13	3.45
3	79	20.95
4	195	51.72
5	82	21.75
Responses	370	98.14
Missing	7	1.86
Mean	3.93	
Median	4.00	
Std Dev	0.77	

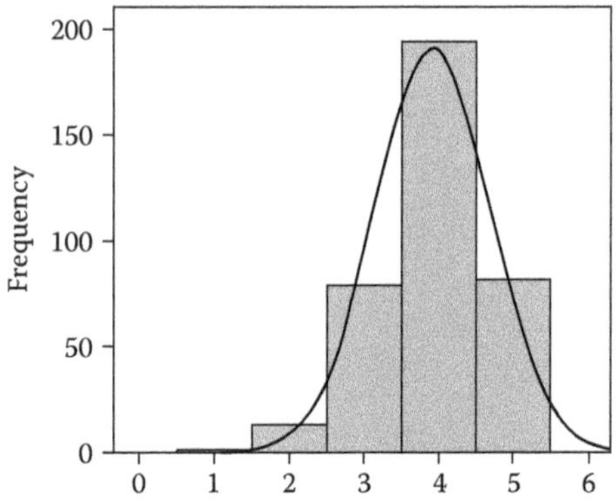

CHART 4.14q   20q. More effective use of IT resources.

	Frequency	Percent
2	10	2.65
3	66	17.51
4	199	52.79
5	95	25.20
Responses	370	98.14
Missing	7	1.86
Mean	4.02	
Median	4.00	
Std Dev	0.74	

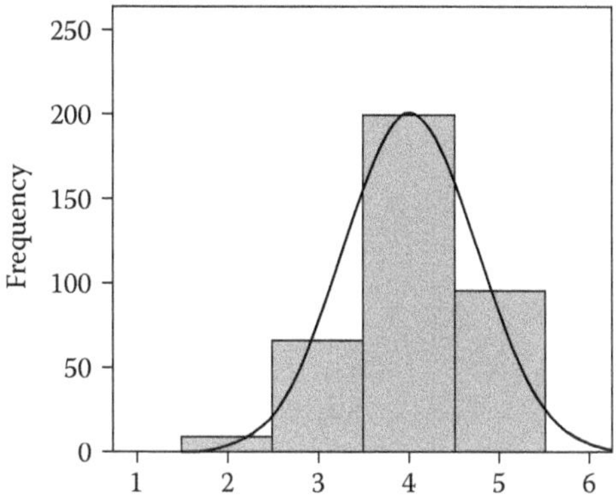

CHART 4.14r   20r. Reduces IT complexity.

	Frequency	Percent
1	6	1.59
2	44	11.67
3	74	19.63
4	145	38.46
5	98	25.99
Responses	367	97.35
Missing	10	2.65
Mean	3.78	
Median	4.00	
Std Dev	1.01	

CHART 4.14s   20s. Improves communications within organization.

	Frequency	Percent
1	2	0.53
2	27	7.16
3	113	29.97
4	175	46.42
5	51	13.53
Responses	368	97.61
Missing	9	2.39
Mean	3.67	
Median	4.00	
Std Dev	0.82	

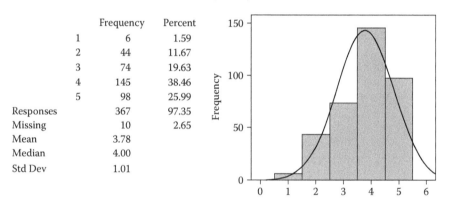

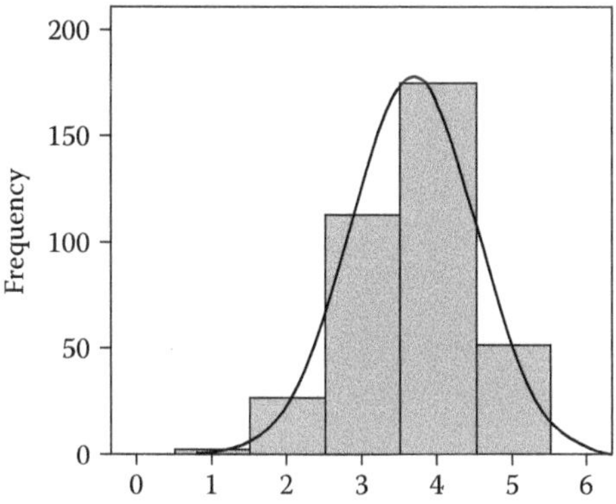

CHART 4.14t 20t. Reduces organizational stovepipes.

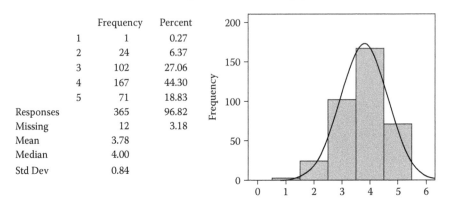

	Frequency	Percent
1	1	0.27
2	24	6.37
3	102	27.06
4	167	44.30
5	71	18.83
Responses	365	96.82
Missing	12	3.18
Mean	3.78	
Median	4.00	
Std Dev	0.84	

CHART 4.15: 21. The outcomes or products of my organization's requirements analysis and design (RA&D) activities:

CHART 4.15a 21a. … include standards for information systems security.

	Frequency	Percent
1	5	1.33
2	55	14.59
3	68	18.04
4	192	50.93
5	42	11.14
Responses	362	96.02
Missing	15	3.98
Mean	3.58	
Median	4.00	
Std Dev	0.93	

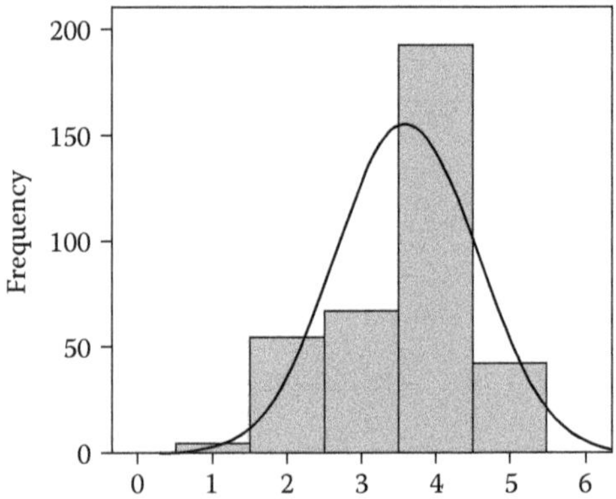

CHART 4.15b   21b. ... describe our transition from "as is" to "to be".

	Frequency	Percent
1	3	0.80
2	35	9.28
3	66	17.51
4	205	54.38
5	57	15.12
Responses	366	97.08
Missing	11	2.92
Mean	3.76	
Median	4.00	
Std Dev	0.86	

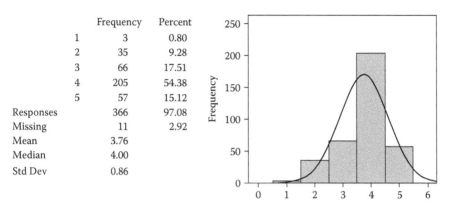

CHART 4.15c   21c. ... are kept current.

	Frequency	Percent
1	7	1.86
2	105	27.85
3	114	30.24
4	117	31.03
5	21	5.57
Responses	364	96.55
Missing	13	3.45
Mean	3.11	
Median	3.00	
Std Dev	0.95	

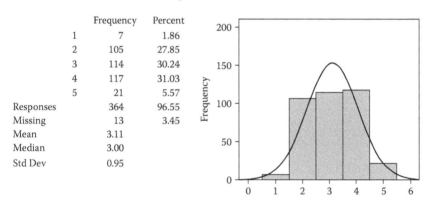

CHART 4.15d   21d. ... are kept in a digital repository or database.

	Frequency	Percent
1	8	2.12
2	83	22.02
3	75	19.89
4	159	42.18
5	37	9.81
Responses	362	96.02
Missing	15	3.98
Mean	3.37	
Median	4.00	
Std Dev	1.02	

CHART 4.15e   21e. ... are used to standardize our technologies.

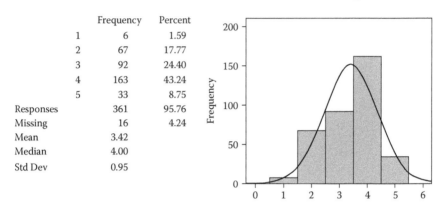

	Frequency	Percent
1	6	1.59
2	67	17.77
3	92	24.40
4	163	43.24
5	33	8.75
Responses	361	95.76
Missing	16	4.24
Mean	3.42	
Median	4.00	
Std Dev	0.95	

CHART 4.15f   21f. ... are used to support strategic business decisions.

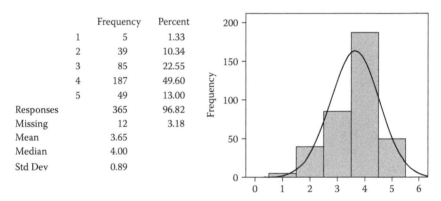

	Frequency	Percent
1	5	1.33
2	39	10.34
3	85	22.55
4	187	49.60
5	49	13.00
Responses	365	96.82
Missing	12	3.18
Mean	3.65	
Median	4.00	
Std Dev	0.89	

CHART 4.15g   21g. ... are approved by the CIO.

	Frequency	Percent
1	8	2.12
2	55	14.59
3	56	14.85
4	159	42.18
5	80	21.22
Responses	358	94.96
Missing	19	5.04
Mean	3.69	
Median	4.00	
Std Dev	1.05	

CHART 4.15h 21h. ... are approved by the owner of the relevant business processes.

	Frequency	Percent
1	1	0.27
2	38	10.08
3	63	16.71
4	174	46.15
5	85	22.55
Responses	361	95.76
Missing	16	4.24
Mean	3.84	
Median	4.00	
Std Dev	0.91	

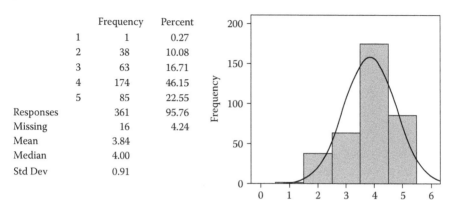

CHART 4.15i 21i. ... are used as the basis for IT procurement.

	Frequency	Percent
1	6	1.59
2	48	12.73
3	81	21.49
4	178	47.21
5	50	13.26
Responses	363	96.29
Missing	14	3.71
Mean	3.60	
Median	4.00	
Std Dev	0.94	

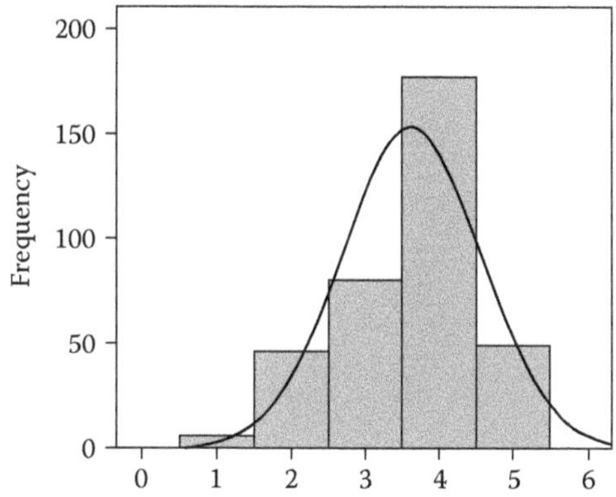

CHART 4.15j 21j. ... are assessed for their quality.

	Frequency	Percent
1	7	1.86
2	77	20.42
3	119	31.56
4	126	33.42
5	33	8.75
Responses	362	96.02
Missing	15	3.98
Mean	3.28	
Median	3.00	
Std Dev	0.96	

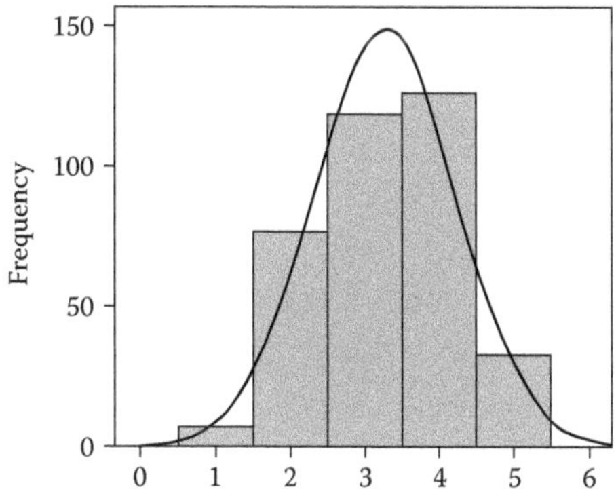

REFERENCES AND RESOURCES 5

"Never let formal education get in the way of your learning."

—**Mark Twain**

Introduction

This chapter is intended to serve as a resource guide to support those wishing to learn more about Enterprise Architecture (EA). It is intended only as a beginning, a starting point. It contains references to many readings and other materials, additional sources of information on EA, as well as a reading list, a website list, and a glossary of EA-related terms. This chapter begins with information about the Society for Information Management (SIM) and the SIM Enterprise Architecture Working Group (SIMEAWG).

Disclaimer

Our attorneys and risk managers asked us to tell you that this resource guide is not purported to be complete. It is provided as a starting point. The information provided here was gathered from numerous sources, and though we have tried to verify it, we can make no guarantee as to the accuracy or completeness of the materials referenced in this resource guide, nor do we endorse the documentation referenced herein. Users of this guide are responsible for checking the accuracy and suitability of all information, products, services, and the like themselves. In any event, the editor, authors, and their organizations shall not incur any liability by providing the following information. This is simply a guide to materials available on this topic. We hope that it is useful to you.

The Society for Information Management (SIM)

Since 1968, the Society for Information Management (SIM) has inspired the minds of the most prestigious IT leaders in the industry. Highly regarded as the premier network for IT leadership, SIM is a community of thought leaders who share experiences and rich intellectual capital, and who explore future IT direction.

Vision

To be recognized as the community that is most preferred by IT leaders for delivering vital knowledge that creates business value and enables personal development.

Mission

SIM is an association of senior IT executives, prominent academicians, selected consultants, and other IT thought leaders, built on the foundation of local chapters, who come together to share and enhance their rich intellectual capital for the benefit of its members and their organizations. SIM members strongly believe in and champion:

- The alignment of IT and business as a valued partnership.
- The creation and sharing of best practices.
- The effective, efficient, and innovative business use of information technology to continuously bring to market valuable products and services.

- IT management and leadership skills development that enables our members growth at each stage of their career.
- The replenishment and education of future IT leaders including a strong role in influencing university curriculums and continuing education.
- Working with the IT industry to shape its direction.
- Policies and legislation that stimulate innovation, economic development, healthy competition, and IT job creation.
- Serving our communities and the industry through giving and outreach.

What Does SIM Offer?

Recognizing the unique needs of the industry, SIM collects the intellectual capital of IT leaders nationwide and offers the resources you need to do business better, including:

- **Face-to-face meetings/networking** – Annual SIMposium conference, Advance Practices Council (APC) meetings, Regional Leadership Forums (RLF), chapter meetings, working groups, communities of interest, and CIO roundtables bring you face-to-face with other key industry executives to share knowledge and network about topics pertinent to IT leaders.
- **Online tools** – On-demand webinars and archived webcasts, an online library featuring nearly fifty white papers, working group deliverables, past conference presentations, and much more to bring best practices of other IT leaders straight to your desktop.
- **Publications** – *SIM News*—a compilation of association news, articles of interest, interviews, and industry insights—and *MIS Quarterly Executive* (MISQE)—a quarterly publication dedicated to publishing high-quality articles, case studies, and research reports.
- **More resources/programs** – SIM offers a wealth of knowledge with these resources and more. Visit http://simnet.org for additional information.

Inside SIM

Strategic direction for the organization is provided by SIM's elected executive board. SIM's standing committees are key to developing initiatives that fulfill the strategic goals of the association. Supporting the organization and fulfilling day-to-day management responsibility is SIM's professional staff.

The SIM Enterprise Architecture Working Group

The following is an abridged excerpt from the SIMEAWG's proposal as adopted by the SIM executive board in October 2006. The complete original document, which in effect serves as the charter and mission statement of the EAWG, is available online at http://eawg.simnet.org.

Background

Can IT afford not to seize the opportunity to be "the keeper of all the knowledge" about the enterprise? It could be no more than an historical accident that IT has been afforded first chance at this critical responsibility, largely due to the fact that we have done a reasonably good job managing the technical architecture of the enterprise. If we believe that information is power, then the potential is high for internal turf struggles and political machinations concerning who gets managerial responsibility for all of the information about the enterprise. In short, who will "own" the enterprise architecture for an organization? Being the keeper of the EA has the potential to ensure IT's seat at the strategic table. The purpose of this Working Group is to help make that happen.

Mission of the Working Group

The SIM Enterprise Architecture Working Group will identify and share processes, methods, tools, concepts, and best practices to enable IT organizations to understand, create, and manage EA in partnership with the business. This will in turn help these same IT organizations substantially enhance the way they manage change, reduce complexity, reengineer processes, plan, strategize, govern, manage projects, and deliver value. The Working Group will achieve these objectives by:

1. Developing a common understanding of what "EA" is and why it is important to the organization.
2. Proposing materials for the CIO to use to make EA simple to comprehend and verbalize to his or her peers and others in the enterprise.
3. Determining, through a survey of SIM membership (and other groups if possible), the current state of EA practices. These metrics can then serve as benchmarks so SIM members can determine how their organizations compare with others. This may also include a methodology for an organization to "self-survey" itself against the collective metrics.
4. Understanding the challenges and opportunities for the CIO's organization in leading EA.
5. Sharing how organizations have successfully implemented and managed EA.
6. Identifying EA best practices including the critical initiatives and enabling processes for the successful leadership and management of EA.
7. Making its findings and recommendations available through publications and presentations.

Bibliography, Suggested Readings, and Websites

Bibliography and Suggested EA Readings

This is but a starting point. There can be little doubt that we left out many useful readings about enterprise architecture, and included others of only peripheral interest. We simply hope that what we have provided here is useful to you.

Abbott, J., J. Hutchins, and D. Schoch "Roles and Delegation of Authority (R/DA) System." *IEEE Internet Computing* (1999).

Adelman, S., and L. Moss. *Data Warehouse Project Management.* Boston: Addison Wesley Longman, 2000.

Anthony, R. N. *Planning and Control Systems: A Framework for Analysis.* Cambridge, MA: Harvard University Press, 1965.

Appleton, D. S. *Killer Business Models and Business Rules.* Oakton, VA: Appleton Company, 2002.

———. *Principles of Information Asset Management.* Oakton, VA: Appleton Company, 2002.

———. *PROBE: Principles of Business Engineering.* Manhattan Beach, CA: Talon Press, 1994.

Assimakopoulos, N. A., and A. N. Riggas. "Designing a Virtual Enterprise Architecture Using Structured Systems Dynamics." *Human Systems Management* 25 (2006): 13–29.

Babers, C. *The Enterprise Architecture Sourcebook Volume One: Process and Products.* El Paso, TX: Charles Babers, 2006.

Babichuk, B., and M. Eulenberg. *An Information Architecture Framework.* GUIDE Project 1234 (1989).

Bahrami, A., A. Sadowski, S. Beahrami, B. Co, and W. A. Seattle. (1998). "Enterprise Architecture for Business Process Simulation." *Simulation Conference Proceedings* (Winter 1998): 2.

Baltzan, P., and A. Phillips. *Business-Driven Information Systems.* New York: McGraw-Hill/Irwin, 2007.

Beam, W. R., J. D. Palmer, and A. P. Sage. (1987). "Systems Engineering for Software Productivity." *IEEE Transactions on Systems, Man and Cybernetics* 17, no. 2 (1997): 163–86.

Beckner, S. G., and S. T. Norman. *Air Force Architecture Development Guide.* Colorado Springs: MITRE Corp. 1998.

Beecham, S., T. Hall, and A. Rainer. "Defining a Requirements Process Improvement Model." *Software Quality Journal* 13, no. (2005): 247–79.

Belasco, J., and R. Stayer. *Flight of the Buffalo: Soaring to Excellence, Learning to Let Employees Lead.* New York: Warner Books, 1993.

Bernanke, B. S. Commencement address at MIT, June 9, 2006, http://web.mit.edu/newsoffice/2006/comm-bernanke.html.

Bernard, S. A. *An Introduction to Enterprise Architecture,* 2nd ed. Bloomington, IN: AuthorHouse, 2005.

Bernus, P., L. Nemes, and G. Schmidt. *Handbook on Enterprise Architecture.* Berlin: Springer-Verlag, 2003.

Berry, D. M. (2004). *The Inevitable Pain of Software Development: Why There Is No Silver Bullet.* Lecture Notes in Computer Science, 50–74. Earlier version available at http://se.uwaterloo.ca/~dberry/FTP_SITE/tech.reports/painpaper.pdf.

Bischoff, J. *Data Warehouse: Practical Advice from the Experts.* New York: Prentice Hall, 1997.

Bittler, R. S., and G. Kreizman. *Gartner Enterprise Architecture Process: Evolution 2005.* Gartner Report ID No. G00130849, October 2005.

Blumenthal, S. C. *Management Information Systems: A Framework for Planning and Development.* New York: Prentice Hall, 1969.

Boar, B. *Constructing Blueprints for Enterprise IT Architectures.* New York: Wiley, 1998.

Boh, W. F., and D. Yellin. "Using Enterprise Architecture Standards in Managing Information Technology." *Journal of Management Information Systems* 23, no. 3 (2006): 163–207.

Bohn, R. E. "The Impact of Process Noise on VLSI Process Improvement." *IEEE Transactions on Semiconductor Manufacturing* 8, no. 3(1995): 228–38.

Boulding, K. E. *The Image.* Ann Arbor: University of Michigan Press, 1956.

Brackett, M. H. *Data Sharing: Using a Common Data Architecture.* New York: Wiley, 1994.

———. *The Data Warehouse Challenge: Taming Data Chaos.* New York: Wiley, 1996.

The British Computer Society. *The International IT Professional Practice Programme,* 2007, http://www.bcs.org.

Brooks, F. *The Mythical Man-Month,* 20th anniversary ed. Boston: Addison-Wesley Longman, 1995.

Browne, G. J. "An Empirical Investigation of User Requirements Elicitation: Comparing the Effectiveness of Prompting Techniques." *Journal of Management Information Systems* 17, no. 4 (2001): 223–49.

Bruce, T. A. *Designing Quality Databases with IDEF1X Information Models.* New York: Dorset House, 1992.

———. "Simplicity and Complexity in the Zachman Framework." *Database Newsletter* 20, no. 3 (1992): 3–11.

———. *Zachman's Framework: Still Going, and Going ....* TABSET, 1992. 1-415-848-8916.

Buckl, S., A. M. Ernst, J. Lankes, K. Schneider, and C. M. Schweda. "A Pattern Based Approach for Constructing Enterprise Architecture Management Information Models." 8. *Internationale Tagung Wirtschaftsinformatik* 8, no. 2 (2007): 145–62.

Burgess, B., and T. Hokel. *A Brief Introduction to the Zachman Framework.* Breckenridge, CO: Framework Software, 1994.

Burlton, R. T. *Business Process Management: Profiting from Process.* Indianapolis, IN: Sams Publishing, 2001.

Callon, M. "Some Elements of a Sociology of Translation: Domestication of the Scallops and the Fishermen." In *Power, Action and Belief: A New Sociology of Knowledge,* ed. J. Law, 197–225. London: Routledge and Kegan Paul, 1986.

Callon, M., and B. Latour. "Unscrewing the Big Leviathan: How Actors Macro-Structure Reality and How Sociologists Help Them to Do So." In *Advances in Social Theory and Methodology: Towards an Integration of Micro and Macro-Sociologies,* ed. K. D. Knorr-Cetina and A. V. Cicourel, 277–303. London: Routledge and Kegan Paul, 1981.

Cane, S. "Measuring the Impact of Enterprise Architecture." *Issues in Information Systems* 8, no. 2 (2007): 437–42.

Carbone, J. A. *IT Architecture Toolkit.* New York: Prentice Hall PTR, 2004.

Chen, P. P. "The Entity-Relationship Model: Toward a Unified View of Data." *ACM Transactions on Database Systems* 1 (1976): 9–36.

Cheng, B. H. C., and J. M. Atlee. *Research Directions in Requirements Engineering.* Washington, DC: IEEE Computer Society Press, 2007.

Chief Information Officers Council.. *Federal Enterprise Architecture Framework,* version 1.1, September 1999.

———. *A Practical Guide to Federal Enterprise Architecture,* version 1.0, February 2001. http://www.gao.gov/bestpractices/bpeaguide.pdf.

Chrissis, M. B., M. Konrad, and S. Shrum. *CMMI: Guidelines for Process Integration and Product Improvement.* Boston: Addison-Wesley Professional, 2003.

Clark, B. K. "Quantifying the Effects of Process Improvement on Effort." *IEEE Software* 17 (2000): 65–70.

Clinger–Cohen Act of 1996. Title 40, U.S. Code 40, U.S.C. 1401 (formerly, the Information Technology Management Reform Act of 1996 [ITMRA]), 10 February 1996.

Collett, S. "Hot Skills, Cold Skills." *Computerworld* (17 July 2006). http://computerworld.com/action/article.do?command=viewArticleBasic&articleId=112360.

Collins, J. C. *Good to Great: Why Some Companies Make the Leap ... and Others Don't.* New York: Collins Business, 2001.

Collins, J. C., and J. I. Porras. *Built to Last: Successful Habits of Visionary Companies.* New York: HarperBusiness, 1994.

Cook, M. A. *Building Enterprise Information Architectures: Reengineering Information Systems.* Upper Saddle River, NJ: Prentice Hall, 1996.

Curtis, B., W. E. Hefley, and S. A. Miller. *People Capability Maturity Model (P-CMM),* version 2.0. Pittsburgh: Software Engineering Institute, 2001.

Damian, D., and J. Chisan. "An Empirical Study of the Complex Relationships between Requirements Engineering Processes and Other Processes That Lead to Payoffs in Productivity, Quality, and Risk Management." *IEEE Transactions on Software Engineering* 32, no. 8 (2006): 433–53.

Daneva, M., and P. van Eck. *What Enterprise Architecture and Enterprise Systems Usage Can and Cannot Tell about Each Other.* CTIT Technical Report No. TR-CTIT-06-02 (2006), 1–15.

Davis, G. "Strategies for Information Requirements Determination." *IBM Systems Journal* 21, no. 1 (1982): 4–30.

DeMarco, T. *Structured Analysis and System Specification.* New York: Yourdon Press, 1978.

DeMarco, T., and T. Lister. "Both Sides Always Lose: The Litigation of Software-Intensive Contracts." *Cutter IT Journal* 11, no. 4 (1998): 5–9.

Dion, R., and S. Raytheon. "Process Improvement and the Corporate Balance Sheet." *IEEE Software* 10, no. 4 (1993): 28–35.

Doucet, G., J. Gotze, P. Saha, and S. Bernard. *Coherency Management: Architecting the Enterprise for Alignment, Assurance, and Agility.* Unpublished manuscript, 2009.

Drucker, P. F. *Management: Tasks, Responsibilities, and Practices.* New York: Harper & Row, 1973.

———. *Managing for the Future: The 1990's and Beyond.* New York: Dutton, 1992.

———. *Managing in Turbulent Times.* New York: Harper & Row, 1980.

———. *The New Realities.* New York: Harper & Row, 1989.

———. "The Next Information Revolution." *Forbes ASAP* 24 (1998): 47–58.

———. *The Post Capitalist Society.* New York: Harper Business, 1994.

———. *The Practice of Management.* New York: Harper & Row, 1954.

Duggan, E. W. "Silver Pellets for Improving Software Quality." *Information Resources Management Journal* 17, no. 2 (2004): 1–21.

Duggan, E. W., and H. Reichgelt. *The Panorama of Information Systems Quality.* Toronto, Canada: Idea Group Publishing.

El Sawy, O., A. Malhotra, S. Gosain, and K. Young. "IT-Intensive Value Innovation in the Electronic Economy: Insights from Marshall Industries." *MIS Quarterly* 23, no. 3 (1999): 305–35.

Ekstedt, M. *Enterprise Architecture as a Means for IT Management.* EARP Working Paper 2004-02. Department of Industrial Information and Control Systems, KTH, 2004. Available at http://www.ics.kth.se/Publikationer/Working%20Papers/EARP-WP-2004-02.pdf.

El Emam, K., and N. H. Madhavji. "The Reliability of Measuring Organizational Maturity." *Software Process Improvement and Practice* 1 (1995): 3–26.

Estep, C. K. (1988). *The Software Planning Guide.* San Ramon, CA: Chevron Information Technology Company, 1988.

Fatolahi, A., and F. Shams. "An Investigation into Applying UML to the Zachman Framework." *Information Systems Frontiers* 8, no. 2 (2006): 133–43.

Federal Chief Information Officers Council, F. A. W. G. *Architecture Alignment and Assessment Guide,* October 2000.

———. *Federal Enterprise Architecture Framework (FEAF),* version 1.1, September 1999.

———. *Smart Practices in Capital Planning,* October 2000.

Finkelstein, C. "Enterprise Integration Using Enterprise Architecture." In H. Linger et al., Eds. *Constructing the Infrastructure for the Knowledge Economy: Methods and Tools, Theory and Practice,* 43–82. New York: Kluwer Academic/Plenum, 2004.

———. *An Introduction to Information Engineering.* Boston: Addison-Wesley, 1989.

———. *Strategic Systems Development.* Boston: Addison-Wesley, 1992.

———. "System Development Strategies for 21st Century Enterprises." *The Data Administration Newsletter,* 1 July 2004, 1–9.

———. *Enterprise Architecture for Integration: Rapid Delivery Methods and Technologies.* Boston: Artech House, 2006.

———. "Why Is Enterprise Architecture Important?" *The Data Administrator Newsletter,* 1 April 2007, 1–14.

Finkelstein, C., and P. Aiken. *Building Corporate Portals with XML.* New York: McGraw-Hill, 1999.

Finkelstein, C., and J. Martin. *Information Engineering,* vols. 1 and 2. Englewood Cliffs, NJ: Prentice Hall, 1981.

Fletcher, A., J. Guthrie, P. Steane, G. Roos, and S. Pike. (2003). "Mapping Stakeholder Perceptions for a Third Sector Organization." *Journal of Intellectual Capital* 4, no. 4 (2003): 505–27.

Ford, G., and N. Gibbs. *A Mature Profession of Software Engineering.* Technical Report No. CMU/SEI-96-TR-004 ESC-TR-96-004, January 1996. http://www.sei.cmu.edu/pub/documents/96.reports/pdf/tr004.96.pdf.

Forrester, J. *Industrial Dynamics.* Cambridge, MA: MIT Press, 1965.

Fowler, M. *Patterns of Enterprise Application Architecture.* Boston: Addison-Wesley Professional, 2003.

Freedom of Information Act (FOIA). 5 U.S.C. §552 (1996), a. a. b. P. L., 110 Stat. 3048.

Gammelgård, M., M. Simonsson, and Å. Lindström, (2007). "An IT Management Assessment Framework: Evaluating Enterprise Architecture Scenarios." *Information Systems and eBusiness Management,* 5, no. 4 (2007): 415.

Garlan, D., and D. Perry. "Introduction to the Special Issue on Software Architecture." *IEEE Transactions on Software Engineering,* 21, no. 4 (1995): 269–74.

Gill, H. S., and P. C. Rao. *The Official Guide to Data Warehousing.* New York: Que, 1996.

Glass, R. L. "The Realities of Software Technology Payoffs. *Communications of the ACM* 42, no. 2 (1999): 74–79.

Goethals, F. G., M. Snoeck, W. Lemahieu, and J. Vandenbulcke. "Management and Enterprise Architecture Click: The FAD(E)E Framework." *Information Systems Frontiers* 8, no. 2 (2006): 67–86.

Goikoetxea, A. "A Mathematical Framework for Enterprise Architecture Representation and Design." *International Journal of Information Technology and Decision Making* 3, no. 1 (2004): 5–32.

Goldenson, D. R., K. El-Emam, J. Herbsleb, and C. C. Deephouse. "Empirical Studies of Software Process Assessment Methods." *Elements of Software Process Assessment and Improvement* 10, no. 1 (1996): 177–218.

Goldman, S. L., R. N. Nage, and K. Priess. *Agile Competitors and Virtual Corporations: Strategies for Enriching the Customer.* New York: Van Nostrand Reinhold, 1995.

Gordon, R. G., Jr., ed. *Ethnologue: Languages of the World,* 15th ed. Dallas, TX: SIL International, 2005. Web edition at: http://www.ethnologue.com.

Gottschalk, K. D., S. Graham, H. Kreger, and J. Snell. "Introduction to Web Services Architecture." *IBM Systems Journal* 41 (2002): 170–77.

Goulielmos, M. "Outlining Organisational Failure in Information Systems Development." *Disaster Prevention and Management: An International Journal* 12, no. 4 (2003): 319–27.

Greer, R. C. *A Model for the Discipline of Information Science.* Emporia State University Conference on "The Intellectual Foundations of Information Professionals: Criteria for New Educational Programs," 1984.

Gregor, S., D. Hart, and N. Martin. "Enterprise Architectures: Enablers of Business Strategy and IS/IT Alignment in Government." *Information Technology & People* 20, no. 2 (2007): 96–120.

Greiner, L. "Evolution and Revolution as Organizations Grow." *Harvard Business Review* 50, no. 4 (1972): 37–46.

Grigoriu, A. *An Enterprise Architecture Development Framework: The Business Case, Best Practices and Strategic Planning for Building Your Enterprise Architecture.* Victoria, BC, Canada: Trafford Publishing, 2006.

Hackos, J. A. T. (1997). "From Theory to Practice: Using the Information Process-Maturity Model as a Tool for Strategic Planning." *Technical Communication* 44, no. 4 (1997): 369–80.

Hagan, P., ed. *MITRE Enterprise Architecture Body of Knowledge,* 2004. http://www.mitre.org/tech/eabok/.

Halbleib, H. (2004). "Requirements Management." *Information Systems Management* 21, no. 1(2004): 8–21.

Hall, J. *Application Partitioning and Integration with SSADM.* Norwich: United Kingdom Government Centre for Information Systems, 1994.

———. *Distributed Systems: Application Development.* Norwich: United Kingdom Government Centre for Information Systems, 1990.

———. *Reuse in SSADM Using Object Orientation.* Norwich: United Kingdom Government Centre for Information Systems, 1994.

Hall, T., S. Beecham, and A. Rainer. "Requirements Problems in Twelve Software Companies: An Empirical Analysis." *IEEE Proceedings-Software* 149, no. 5 (2002): 153–60.

Halpin, T. A. *Information Modeling and Relational Databases.* New York: Morgan Kaufmann, 2001.

Hammer, M., and J. Champy. *Reengineering the Corporation.* New York: Harper, 1993.

Hanseth, O., E. Jacucci, M. Grisot, and M. Aanestad. "Reflexive Standardization: Side Effects and Complexity in Standard Making." Special issue, *MIS Quarterly* 30 (August 2006): 563–81.

Harter, D. E., and S. A. Slaughter. "Process Maturity and Software Quality: A Field Study." In *Proceedings of the Twenty-First International Conference on Information Systems,* 407–11. Brisbane, Queensland, Australia: Association for Information Systems, 2000.

Hay, D. C. *Requirements Analysis: From Business Views to Architecture.* Upper Saddle River, NJ: Prentice Hall PTR, 2003.

———. "UML Misses the Boat." *EssentialStrategies.Com,* 2008.

Hay, D., and K. A. Healy. *GUIDE Business Rules Project Final Report,* October 1997.

Healy, K. *GUIDE Business Rules Project Final Report.* Model Systems, 1995.

———. *YADMD (Yet Another Data Modeling Document, or A Bigot's Guide to Fundamentals of Automation Support for Semantic Data Modeling).* Model Systems, 1995.

Henderson, J. C., and N. Venkatraman. "Strategic Alignment: Leveraging Information Technology for Transforming Organizations." *IBM Systems Journal* 32, no. 1 (1993): 4–23.

Henning, R. "Use of the Zachman Architecture for Security Engineering." In *Proceedings of the 19th National Information Systems Security Conference,* 398–409. Baltimore, MD: U.S. Department of Commerce, NIST, 1996.

Hilliard, R. *Impact Assessment of IEEE 1471 on the Open Group Architecture Framework,* 2000. Retrieved 29 January 2003 from http://www.opengroup.org/architecture/togaf7/procs/p1471-togafimpact.pdf, 1–11.

Hinssen, P. *Business/IT Fusion. How to Move Beyond Alignment and Transform IT in Your Organization.* Gent, Belgium: Mach Media NV/SA, 2009.

Hirvonen, A., and M. Pulkkinen. A Practical Approach to EA Planning and Development: The EA Management Grid. In *Proceedings of the 7th International Conference on Business Information Systems,* ed. W. Abramowicz, 284–302. Poznan, Poland: Springer, 2004.

Hite, R. C., G. D. Kutz, and United States General Accounting Office. *Information Technology Observations on Department of Defense's Draft Enterprise Architecture.* Washington, DC: U.S. General Accounting Office, 2003.

Hite, R. C. "Information Technology, the Federal Enterprise Architecture, and Agencies' Enterprise Architectures Are Still Maturing." Testimony before the Subcommittee on Technology, Information Policy, Intergovernmental Relations, and the Census, Committee on Government Reform, House of Representatives. *Testimony, GAO-04-798 T.* Washington, DC: U.S. General Accounting Office, 2004.

Hite, R. C., United States Department of Defense, and United States General Accounting Office. *DOD Business Systems Modernization Limited Progress in Development of Business Enterprise Architecture and Oversight of Information Technology Investments: Congressional Defense Committees.* Washington, DC: U.S. General Accounting Office, 2004.

Hoogervorst, J. "Enterprise Architecture: Enabling Integration, Agility and Change." *International Journal of Cooperative Information Systems* 13, no. 3 (2004): 213–33.

Hudson, D. L. *Practical Model Management Using CASE Tools.* London: QED, 1993.

Humphrey, W. S. "Characterizing the Software Process: A Maturity Framework." *IEEE Software, IEEE,* 5, no. 2 (1988): 73–79.

Humphrey, W. S. *Managing the Software Process.* Boston: Addison Wesley, 1990.

Hutchings, A. F., and S. T. Knox. "Creating Products Customers Demand." *Communications of the ACM* 38, no. 5 (1995): 72–80.

IEEE Standard 1471-2000. *IEEE Recommended Practice for Architectural Description of Software-Intensive Systems,* 2004. http://standards.ieee.org/reading/ieee/std_public/description/se/1471-2000_desc.html.

IEEE Standard 610.12. *IEEE Standard Glossary of Software Engineering Terminology,* 1990. http://ieeexplore.ieee.org/xpls/abs_all.jsp?tp=&isnumber=4148&arnumber=159342&punumber=2238.

Inmon, W. H. (1989). *Advanced Topics in Information Engineering.* London: QED, 1989.

———. *Data Architecture: The Information Paradigm.* London: QED, 1989.

Inmon, W. H., J. A. Zachman, and J. Geiger. *Data Stores, Data Warehousing, and the Zachman Framework.* New York: McGraw-Hill, 1997.

International Federation for Information Processing (IFIP). *WCC 2008 Declaration on ICT Professionalism and Competences.* 20th World Computer Congress, Milan, Italy, 2008.

IT Governance Institute. *Board Briefing on IT Governance.* Rolling Meadows, IL: Information Systems Audit and Control Foundation, 2001.

Ives, B., S. L. Jarvenpaa, and R. O. Mason. "Global Business Drivers: Aligning Information Technology to Global Business Strategy." *IBM Systems Journal* 32, no. 1 (2004): 143–61.

Iyer, B., and R. Gottlieb. "The Four-Domain Architecture: An Approach to Support Enterprise Architecture Design." *IBM Systems Journal* 43, no. 3 (2004): 587–97.

James, G. A., R. Handler, A. Lapkin, and N. Gall. *Gartner Enterprise Architecture Framework: Evolution 2005.* Gartner Report ID No. G00130855, 2005.

Janssen, M., and K. Hjort-Madsen. *Analyzing Enterprise Architecture in National Governments: The Cases of Denmark and the Netherlands.* 40th Hawaii International Conference on Systems Science (HICSS-40), Waikoloa, Hawaii, 2007.

Johnson, P., M. Ekstedt, E. Silva, and L. Plazaola. "Using Enterprise Architecture for CIO Decision-Making: On the importance of theory." In *Proceedings of the 2nd Annual Conference on Systems Engineering Research (CSER),* 1–12. Los Angeles: Stevens Institute, 2004.

Jones, C. *Best Practices in Software Engineering.* New York: McGraw-Hill, forthcoming.

———. "Defense Software Development in Evolution." *Crosstalk: The Journal of Defense Software Engineering ,* 25, no. 11 (2002): 26–29.

————. *Measuring Defect Potentials and Defect Removal Efficiency.* Boston: Software Productivity Research, 2008.

Jones, C. *Software Assessments, Benchmarks, and Best Practices.* Boston: Addison Wesley Longman, 2000.

————. "Variations in Software Development Practices." *IEEE Software* 20, no. 6 (2003): 22–27.

Jonkers, H., M. Lankhorst, and R. Van Buuren. "Concepts for Modeling Enterprise Architectures." *International Journal of Cooperative Information Systems* 13, no. 3 (2004): 257–87.

Jonkers, H., M. M. Lankhorst, H. W. L. ter Doest, F. Arbab, H. Bosma, and R. J. Wieringa. "Enterprise Architecture: Management Tool and Blueprint for the Organisation. *Information Systems Frontiers* 8, no. 2 (2006): 63–66.

Joyce, W., and N. Nohria. *What Really Works: The 4+2 Formula for Sustained Business Success.* New York: HarperCollins, 2003.

Kaisler, S. H., F. Armour, M. Valivullah, and U.S. Senate. "Enterprise Architecting: Critical Problems." In *System Sciences, 2005. HICSS'05. Proceedings of the 38th Annual Hawaii International Conference on,* 224b–224b. LOCATION: PUBLISHER, 2005.

Kamata, M. I., and T. Tamai. "How Does Requirements Quality Relate to Project Success or Failure?" 15th IEEE International Requirements Engineering Conference. *IEEE Xplore* (2007): 69–79.

Kaner, C. (1997). *Computer Malpractice.* http://www.badsoftware.com/malprac.htm. (Originally published in *Software QA* 3, no. 4 (1997): 23–27.)

Kantor, R. M. *The Change Masters.* New York: Simon & Schuster, 1984.

————. *When Giants Learn to Dance.* New York: Simon & Schuster, 1989.

Kappelman, L. A. "Bridging the Chasm." *Architecture and Governance Magazine* 3, no. 2 (2007): 28.

————. "Enterprise Architecture: Not Just Another Management Fad." *Align Journal* (March/April 2007): 24–27.

————. *Year 2000 Problem: Strategies and Solutions from the Fortune 100.* Boston: International Thomson Computer Press, 1997.

Kappelman, L. A., R. McKeeman, and L. Zhang. "Early Warning Signs of IT Project Failure: The Dominant Dozen." *Information Systems Management* 23, no. 4 (2006): 31–36.

Kappelman, L., T. McGinnis, A. Pettit, A. Salmans, and A. Sidorova. "Enterprise Architecture: Charting the Territory for Academic Research." In *Proceedings of the Fourteenth Americas Conference on Information Systems,* Toronto, Ontario, Canada, 2008. Available at http://aisel.aisnet.org/amcis2008/162.

Keen, P. G. W. "Information Technology and the Management Difference: A Fusion Map." *IBM Journal of Research and Development* 32, no. 1 (1993): 17–39.

Khoury, G., S. Simoff, and J. Debenham. *Modelling Enterprise Architectures: An Approach Based on Linking Metaphors and Ontologies.* Paper presented at the Proceedings of the 2005 Australasian Ontology Workshop – vol. 58.

Kiernan, C. Client Server: Learning from History. In *Microsoft: Database Programming and Design,* 46–53. San Francisco: Miller Freeman, 1993.

Kim, J., and J. Lee. "Business as Buildings: Metrics for the Architectural Quality of Internet Businesses. *Information Systems Research* 13, no. 3 (2002): 239–54.

King, W. R. Creating a Strategic Capabilities Architecture. *Information Systems Management* 12, no. 1 (1995): 67–69.

Koch, C. "A New Blueprint for the Enterprise." *CIO Magazine,* March 1, 2005. http://www. cio.com/archive/030105/blueprint.html.

Koenig, M. E. D. *Business Process Redesign and the Productivity Paradox.* New York: Long Island University, 1993.

Koenig, M. E. D. *The Productivity Paradox: Real or Apparent.* New York: Long Island University, 1993.

Kotter, J. P. *Leading Change.* Cambridge, MA: Harvard Business School Press, 1996.

Kuilboer, J. P., and N. Ashrafi. "Software Architecture: How Are the Boundaries Defined?" In *Proceedings of the Workshop on Object-Oriented Technology,* 65–66. London: Springer-Verlag, 1999.

Land, M., E. Proper, M. Waage, J. Cloo, and C. Steghuis. *Enterprise Architecture: Creating Value by Informed Governance.* Berlin: Springer, 2008.

Langenberg, K., and A. Wegmann. *Enterprise Architecture: What Aspects Is Current Research Targeting?* EPFL Technical Report IC/2004/77, 2004.

Lankhorst, M., et al. *Enterprise Architecture at Work: Modelling, Communication and Analysis.* Berlin: Springer-Verlag, 2005.

Latour, B. *Reassembling the Social: An Introduction to Actor-Network-Theory.* New York: Oxford University Press, 2005.

———. "Where Are the Missing Masses? The Sociology of Some Mundane Artifacts. In *Shaping Technology/Building Society,* ed. W. E. Bijker and J. Law, 225–28. Cambridge, MA: MIT Press, 1992.

Law, J. *Networks, Relations, Cyborgs: On the Social Study of Technology,* 2000. http://www. lancs.ac.uk/vass/sociology/research/resalph.htm.

Law, J. *Ordering and Obduracy,* 2003. http://www.lancs.ac.uk/fass/sociology/papers/law-ordering-and-obduracy.pdf.

Layman, B. (2005). "Implementing an Organizational Software Process Improvement Program." *IEEE Software Engineering* 2 (2005): 279–88.

Lewis, T. "Surviving in the Software Economy." *Upside* March/April (1996): 67–78.

Leyden, P. "On the Edge of the Digital Age: The Historic Moment." *Minneapolis Star Tribune,* June 4, 1995.

Lindström, Å., P. Johnson, E. Johansson, M. Ekstedt, and M. Simonsson. "A Survey on CIO Concerns: Do Enterprise Architecture Frameworks Support Them?" *Information Systems Frontiers* 8, no. 2 (2006): 81–90.

Loosley, C. "Separation and Integration in the Zachman Framework." *Database Newsletter* 2, no. 1 (1992): 3–9.

Loosley, C., and F. Douglas. *High Performance Client Server: A Guide to Building and Managing Robust Distributed Systems.* New York: Wiley, 1998.

Loosley, C., and C. Gane. "Information Systems Modeling." *InfoDB* 4, no. 4 (1991): 21–33.

Luftman, J. (2000). "Assessing Business-IT Alignment Maturity." *Communications of the Association for Information Systems* 4, no. 14 (2000): 1–51.

———. *IT-Business Strategic Alignment Maturity Assessment,* 7 October 2003. http://www. simnet.org/Content/NavigationMenu/Resources/Library/Download_Page3res/ ITBusinessAlignment.pdf.

———. *SIM 2007 IT Trends Survey Findings,* 2007. Available to SIM members only at *http://simnet.org/Portals/0/Content/Library/SIMposium/luftmanhandout.ppt.*

Luftman, J., and T. Brier. "Achieving and Sustaining Business-IT Alignment." *California Management Review* 42, no. 1 (1999): 109–38.

Luftman, J. N., P. R. Lewis, and S. H. Oldach. "Transforming the Enterprise: The Alignment of Business and Information Technology Strategies." *IBM Systems Journal* 32, no. 1 (1993): 198–209.

Luftman, J. and E. R. McLean. "Key Issues for IT Executives." *MIS Quarterly Executive* 3, no. 2 (2004): 89–104.

Maier, M., and E. Rechtin. *The Art of Systems Architecting.* Boca Raton, FL: CRC Press, 2000.

Malhotra, Y. *Enterprise Architecture: An Overview.* Syracuse, NY: BRINT Institute, 1996.

Margolius, I. *Architects + Engineers = Structures.* Chichester, UK: Wiley, 2002.

Marks, E., and M. Bell. *Service-Oriented Architecture: A Planning and Implementation Guide for Business and Technology.* New York: Wiley, 2006.

McConnell, S. "Software Engineering Principles." *IEEE Software* 16, no. 2 (1999): 6–8.

McGahan, A., and M. E. Porter. "How Much Does Industry Matter Really?" *Strategic Management Journal* 18 (1997): 15–30.

McGovern, J., S. Ambler, M. Stevens, J. Linn, V. Sharon, and L. Jo. *A Practical Guide to Enterprise Architecture.* New York: Prentice Hall PTR, 2003.

McKee, R. L., and J. Rodgers. "N-Ary Versus Binary Data Modeling: A Matter of Perspective." *Data Resource Management* 3, no. 4 (1992): 22–32.

McMenamin, S. M., and J. F. Palmer. *Essential Systems Analysis.* New York: Yourdon Press, 1984.

McNurlin, B. C., and R. H. Sprague. *Information Systems Management in Practice.* New York: Pearson, 2006.

Miller, D. "Enterprise Client/Server Planning." *Information Systems Management* 14, no. 2 (1997): 7–15.

Mitchell, R. K., B. R. Agle, and D. J. Wood. "Toward a Theory of Stakeholder Identification and Salience: Defining the Principle of Who and What Really Counts." *Academy of Management Review* 22, no. 4 (1997): 853–88.

Mintzberg, H. *The Rise and Fall of Strategic Planning.* New York: Simon & Schuster, 1994.

Monteiro, E. "Monsters: From Systems to Actor-Networks." In *Planet Internet,* ed. K. Braa, C. Sorenson, and B. Dahlbom, 239–49. Lund, Sweden: Studentlitteratur, 2000.

Morabito, J., I. Sack, and A. Bhate. *Organizational Modeling: Innovative Architectures for the 21st Century.* Englewood Cliffs, NJ: Prentice Hall PTR, 1999.

Nadeau, L. "Object Oriented Techniques: An Information Architect's Perspective." *InfoDB Magazine,* 16, no. 3 (2001).

Nadeau, L., and J. Rodgers. "Evaluating Tools: Case Studies." *Computer Decisions,* March 1988.

Naisbitt, J. *Megatrends.* New York: Warner Books, 1982.

———. *Reinventing the Corporation.* New York: Warner Books, 1985.

Nelson, R. "Project Retrospectives: Evaluating Project Success, Failure, and Everything In Between." *MIS Quarterly Executive* 4, no. 3 (2005): 361–72.

Newton, T. "Creating the New Ecological Order? Elias and Actor-Network Theory." *Academy of Management Review* 27, no. 4 (2002): 523–40.

Nidumolu, S. R., and M. R. Subramani. "The Matrix of Control: Combining Process and Structure Approaches to Managing Software Development." *Journal of Management Information Systems* 20, no. 3 (2003): 159–96.

Nohria, N., W. Joyce, and B. Roberson. "What Really Works." *Harvard Business Review* 81, no. 7 (2003): 42–52.

Nolan, R. L. "Managing the Crises in Data Processing." *Harvard Business Review* 57, no. 2 (1979): 115–26.

———. *Managing the Data Resource Function.* St. Paul, MN: West, 1974.

North, E., J. North, and S. Benade. "Information Management and Enterprise Architecture Planning—A Juxtaposition." *Problems and Perspectives in Management* 4 (2004): 166–79.

Nuseibeh, B., and S. Easterbrook. "Requirements Engineering: A Roadmap." *Communications of the ACM,* 38, no. 5 (2000): 35–46.

Office of Management and Budget (OMB). *The Data Reference Model,* version 2.0. Federal Enterprise Architecture Program Management Office, Office of Management of Budget, November 2005.

———. *FEA Consolidated Reference Model Document,* version 2.1. Federal Enterprise Architecture Program Management Office, Office of Management of Budget, December 2006.

———. *FEA Practice Guidance.* Federal Enterprise Architecture Program Management Office, Office of Management of Budget, December 2006.

———. *Management of Federal Information Resources,* Circular No. A-130, November 2005. http://www.whitehouse.gov/omb/circulars/a130/a130trans4.html.

O'Rourke, C., N. Fishman, and W. Selkow. *Enterprise Architecture Using the Zachman Framework.* Florence, KY: Thompson Course Technology, 2003.

Parker, B. G. *Presentation on Enterprise-Wide Data Management Process Improvement.* Arlington, VA: Paladin Integration Engineering, 2007.

Pascal, F. The Dangerous Illusion: Denormalization, Performance and Integrity. *Fabian Pascal Information Management Magazine,* June 2002: 1–5.

Paulk, M., C. Weber, B. Curtis, and M. Chrissis. *The Capability Maturity Model,* version 1. Boston: Addison Wesley Professional, 1993.

Peak, D. A. "The Expert Opinion: An Interview with John Zachman." *Journal of Information Technology Cases and Applications* 4, no. 3 (2002): 86–94.

Pereira, C. M., and P. Sousa. "A Method to Define an Enterprise Architecture Using the Zachman Framework." In *Proceedings of the 2004 ACM Symposium on Applied Computing,* 1366–71. New York: ACM.

Perks, C., and T. Beveridge. *Guide to Enterprise IT Architecture.* New York: Springer-Verlag, 2003.

Persson, A., and J. Stirna. "Why Enterprise Modelling? An Explorative Study into Current Practice." In *Advanced Information Systems Engineering,* ed. K. R. Dittrich, A. Geppert, and M. C. Norrie, 465–68. Berlin: Springer, 2001.

Peters, T. J. *Liberation Management.* New York: Knopf, 1992.

———. *The Tom Peters Seminar.* New York: Vintage Books.

Peters, T. J., and R. H. Waterman. *In Search of Excellence: Lessons from America's Best-Run Companies.* New York: HarperCollins, 2004.

Porter, M. *Competitive Advantage.* New York: Macmillan, 1985.

Pulkkinen, M., and A. Hirvonen. "EA Planning, Development and Management Process for Agile Enterprise Development." In *System Sciences, 2005. HICSS'05. Proceedings of the 38th Annual Hawaii International Conference on,* 1–10. Washington, DC: IEEE Computer Society, 2005.

Radice, R. A., N. K. Roth, A. O'Hara, and W. A. Ciarfella. "A Programming Process Architecture." *IBM Systems Journal* 24, no. 2 (1985): 79–90.

Ramchandani, C., A. Dziewulski, J. Iannuzzi, R. Menzel, P. Rothschild, and M. Tiemann. *Advancing Enterprise Architecture Maturity.* Fairfax, VA: Industry Advisory Council.

Realizing the Potential of Information Resources: Information, Technology, and Services. Track 1: Strategic Planning. Boulder, CO: CAUSE Exchange Library, 1996.

Reich, B. H., and I. Benbasat. "Measuring the Linkage between Business and Information Technology Objectives." *MIS Quarterly* 20, no. 1 (1996): 55–71.

Reifer, D. J. "The CMMI: It's Formidable." *The Journal of Systems & Software* 50, no. 2 (2000): 97–98.

Rico, D. "A Framework for Measuring ROI of Enterprise Architecture." *Journal of Organizational and End User Computing* 18, no. 2 (2006): i–xii.

Rogoway, P. "How to Reap the Business Benefit from SPI: Adding SPICE While Preserving the CMM." Motorola, Tel Aviv, SPI Newspaper, European Software Process Improvement, SPI and Assessments, 1–5.

Rohloff, M. "Enterprise Architecture: Framework and Methodology for the Design of Architecture in the Large." In *ECIS 2005 Proceedings*. 2005. Paper 113. http://aisel.aisnet.org/ecis2005/113.

Rood, M. A. "Enterprise Architecture: Definition, Content, and Utility." In *Enabling Technologies: Infrastructure for Collaborative Enterprises*, 106–11. Washington, DC: IEEE Computer Society, 1994.

Rosemann, M., and T. de Bruin. "Towards a Business Process Management Maturity Model." In *Proceedings of the 13th European Conference on Information Systems (ECIS 2005)*, 26. Regensburg, Germany, 2005.

Ross, J. "Creating a Strategic IT Architecture Competency: Learning in Stages." *MIS Quarterly Executive* 2, no. 1 (March 2003): 31–43.

Ross, J. W. *Stop Aligning IT with the Business*. Presentation at the Milwaukee SIM Chapter, March 7, 2007. https://www.simnet.org/Portals/0/Content/Chapters/Wisconsin/Documents/Ross_Milwaukee_SIM_March_2007.pdf.

Ross, J. W., C. M. Beath, and D. L. Goodhue. *Developing Long Term Competitiveness Through Information Technology Assets*. CISR Working Paper #290, Center for Information Systems Research, Sloan School of Management, Massachusetts Institute of Technology, WP 3878-95, 1995.

Ross, J. W., P. Weill, and D. Robertson. *Enterprise Architecture as Strategy: Creating a Foundation for Business Execution*. Boston: Harvard Business School Press, 2006.

Ross, R. G. *The Business Rule Book: Classifying, Defining and Modeling Rules*. Boston: Database Research Group, 1997.

———. *Business Rule Concepts: The New Mechanics of Business Information Systems*. Houston, TX: Business Rule Solutions, 1998.

———. "An Interview with John A. Zachman." *Database Newsletter* 17, no. 5 (1989): 112–118.

———. "Rules for the Zachman Framework Architecture." *Database Newsletter* 19, no. 4 (1991): 15–23.

———. "The Zachman Architecture Framework: Reflections from the Trenches." *Database Newsletter* 21, no. 1 (1993).

———. "Zachman Framework Extensions: An Update." *Database Newsletter* 19, no. 4 (1991): 45–51.

Saha, P. *Handbook of Enterprise Architecture in Practice*. Hershey, PA: IGI Global, 2007.

———. "A Real Options Perspective to Enterprise Architecture as an Investment Activity." *Journal of Enterprise Architecture* 2, no. 3 (2006): 32–52.

Salmans, B., L. Kappelman, and R. Pavur. *Validating Determinants of Information Systems Maturity Model*. Southwest Decision Sciences Institute Conference, University of North Texas, February 2009.

Sarker, S., S. Sarker, and A. Sidorova. "Understanding Business Process Change Failure: An Actor-Network Perspective." *Journal of Management Information Systems* 23, no. 1 (Summer 2003): 51–86.

Sauer, C., and L. Willcocks. "Strategic Alignment Revisited: Connecting Organizational Architecture and IT Infrastructure." In *System Sciences, 2004. Proceedings of the 37th Annual Hawaii International Conference on Systems Software,* 232–41. Washington, DC: IEEE Computer Society, 2004.

Savage, G. T., T. W. Nix, C. J. Whitehead, and J. D. Blair. "Strategies for Assessing and Managing Organizational Stakeholders." *Academy of Management Executive* 5, no. 2 (1991): 61–75.

Sawyer, P., I. Sommerville, and S. Viller. "Capturing the Benefits of Requirements Engineering." *IEEE Software* 16, no. 2 (1999): 78–85.

———. "Improving the Requirements Process." In *Proceedings of the Fourth International Workshop on Requirements Engineering: Foundations of Software Quality REFSQ'98,* ed. E. Dubois, L. Opdahl, and K. Pohl, 71–84. Pisa, Italy.

Saxe, J. G. (1873). "The Blind Men and the Elephant." In *The Poems of John Godfrey Saxe,* Boston: James Osgood and Co., 77–78. (Poem first appeared in 1863, New York: Whittlesey House.)

Schekkerman, J. *The Economic Benefits of Enterprise Architecture: How to Quantify and Manage the Economic Value of Enterprise Architecture.* Victoria, BC, Canada: Trafford, 2005.

———. *Enterprise Architecture Good Practices Guide.* Victoria, BC, Canada: Trafford.

———. *How to Survive in the Jungle of Enterprise Architecture Frameworks: Creating or Choosing an Enterprise Architecture Framework.* Victoria, BC, Canada: Trafford.

Schelp, J., and M. Stutz. "A Balanced Scorecard Approach to Measure the Value of Enterprise Architecture." In *Proceedings of the Second Workshop on Trends in Enterprise Architecture Research,* ed. M. Laqnkhorst and P. Johnson, 5–11. 2007. http://www.via-nova-architectura.org/files/TEAR2007/Schelp.pdf.

Schmidt, R., K. Lyytinen, M. Keil, and P. Cule. "Identifying Software Project Risks: An International Delphi Study." *Journal of Management Information Systems* 17, no. 4 (2001): 5–26.

Schon, D. A. "From Technical Rationality to Reflection-in-Action." In *Adult and Continuing Education: Major Themes in Education,* 56–73. ed. Peter Jarvis. London: Routledge, 2003.

Senge, P. M. *The Fifth Discipline: The Art and Practice of the Learning Organization.* New York: Doubleday, 1990.

Seow, S. P. S. *The Zachman Framework for Enterprise Architecture: Finding Out More.* Simon P. S. Seow and the Analyst, 2000. http://www.theanalyst.com.

Sessions, R. *A Comparison of the Top Four Enterprise Architecture Methodologies.* May 2007. http://msdn2.microsoft.com/en-us/architecture/bb466232.aspx.

———. "Interview with John Zachman." *Perspectives of the International Association of Software Architects* 6 (2007).

Sherwood, J., A. Clark, and D. Lynas. *Enterprise Security Architecture,* 1–23. Gilroy, CA: CMP Books, 2005.

Shpilberg, D., S. Berez, R. Puryear, and S. Shah. "Avoiding the Alignment Trap in IT." *MIT Sloan Management Review* 49, no. 1 (2007): 51–73.

SIM IT Complexity Reduction Working Group. *Enterprise Architecture Requirements for Information Technology Vendors.* October 1999. http://www.simnet.org/Content/NavigationMenu/Resources/Download_Page32/ICRWhitepaper.pdf.

Sledgianowski, D., and J. Luftman. "IT-Business Strategic Alignment Maturity." *Journal of Cases on Information Technology* 7, no. 2 (2005): 102–20.

Sledgianowski, D., J. N. Luftman, and R. R. Reilly. "Development and Validation of an Instrument to Measure Maturity of IT Business Strategic Alignment Mechanisms." *Information Resources Management Journal* 19 (2006): 3–18.

Sommerville, I., and J. Ransom. "An Empirical Study of Industrial Requirements Engineering Process Assessment and Improvement." *ACM Transactions on Software Engineering and Methodology (TOSEM)* 14, no. 1 (2005): 85–117.

Sowa, J. F., and J. A. Zachman. "Extending and Formalizing the Framework for Information Systems Architecture." *IBM Systems Journal* 31, no. 3 (1992): 590–616.

Spewak, S. H., with S. C. Hill. *Enterprise Architecture Planning: Developing a Blueprint for Data, Applications, and Technology.* New York: Wiley, 1992.

Spund, L. *VITAL: Virtually Integrated Technical Architecture Lifecycle.* Cupertino, CA: Apple Computer, 1992.

Stalk, G., Jr., and T. M. Hout. *Competing Against Time.* New York: The Free Press, 1990.

Steghuis, C., M. Daneva, P. van Eck. "Correlating Architecture Maturity and Enterprise Systems Usage Maturity to Improve Business/IT Alignment." In *Proceedings of REBNITA 2005. First International Workshop on Requirements Engineering for Business Need and IT Alignment, Paris, France,* 64–73. In: *Journal of Systems and Software* 80, no. 3. (2005).

Strano, C., and Q. Rehmani. "The Role of the Enterprise Architect." *Information Systems and E-Business Management* 5, no. 4 (2007): 379–96.

Swanson, B., and C. Beath. Reconstructing The Systems Development Organization. *MIS Quarterly, 13,* no. 3 (1989): 293–304.

Tasker, D. *Fourth Generation Data: A Guide to Data Analysis for New and Old Systems.* Englewood Cliffs, NJ: Prentice Hall, 1989.

———. *The Problem Space.* Sydney, Australia: Electronic publication, 1993.

Theuerkorn, F. *Lightweight Enterprise Architectures.* Boca Raton, FL: CRC Press, 2005.

Thomas, R., II, R. A. Beamer, and P. K. Sowell. *Civilian Application of the DoD C4ISR Architecture Framework: A Treasury Department Case Study.* Paper presented at the Proceedings of the 5th International Command and Control Research and Technology Symposium, Canberra, Australia, October 2000.

Toffler, A. *Future Shock.* New York: Bantam Books, 1970.

———. *Powershift.* New York: Bantam Books, 1990.

———. *The Third Wave.* New York: Morrow, 1980.

Treacy, M. *The Discipline of Market Leaders: Choose Your Customers, Narrow Your Focus, Dominate Your Market.* Cambridge, MA: Perseus Books, 1995.

Tucker, C., and D. Aron. *Applying Enterprise Architecture.* Gartner Report No. COM-20-2071. September 2005. Retrieved from http://www.commonperu.com/html/eventos/2006/cio/ppt/gartner/GARTNER_Applying_Enterprise_Architecture.pdf.

Tucker, R. L., T. Zueshow, and J. Lehmann. "Enterprise-CASE Environment." *EDS Technical Journal* 7, no. 1 (1993): 56–59.

Tudor, J. K. *Information Security Architecture: An Integrated Approach to Security in the Organization.* Boca Raton, FL: CRC Press, 2006.

U.S. Customs Service. *Enterprise Architecture Blueprint,* August 1999.

———. *Systems Development Life Cycle,* October 1998.

U.S. Department of Defense. Joint Publication 1-02, April 2001, http://www.dtic.mil/doctrine/jel/new_pubs/jpl_02.pdf.

————. *Technical Architecture Framework for Information Management (TAFIM)*, vols. 1–8, version 2.0. Reston, VA: DISA Center for Architecture, 1994.

U.S. Department of Defense, C. I. A. W. G. *DoD C4ISR Architecture Framework*, version 2.0, 18 December 1997.

U.S. Government Accountability Office (GAO). *Business Modernization: Some Progress Made Toward Implementing GAO Recommendations Related to NASA's Integrated Financial Management Program*. GAO-05-799R, September 2005.

————. (2007). *Business Systems Modernization Strategy for Evolving DOD's Business Enterprise Architecture Offers a Conceptual Approach, but Execution Details Are Needed: Report to Congressional Committees*, 2007. http://purl.access.gpo.gov/GPO/LPS82927.

————. *DOD Business Systems Modernization: Long-Standing Weaknesses in Enterprise Architecture Development Need to Be Addressed*. GAO-05-702, July 2005.

————. *Enterprise Architecture: Leadership Remains Key to Establishing and Leveraging Architectures for Organizational Transformation*, GAO-06-831, August 2006. http://www.gao.gov/new.items/d06831.pdf.

————. *Executive Guide: Measuring Performance and Demonstrating Results of IT Investments*. GAO-AIMD-98-89, March 1998.

————. *Information Technology: Enterprise Architecture Use Across the Federal Government Can Be Improved*. GAO-02-6, February 2002. http://www.gao.gov/new.items/d026.pdf.

————. *A Framework for Assessing and Improving Enterprise Architecture Management*, version 1.1. GAO-03-584G, April 2003. http://www.gao.gov/.

————. *Homeland Security: Progress Continues, but Challenges Remain on Department's Management of Information Technology*. Testimony before Congressional Subcommittees, Randolph C. Hite, Director, Information Technology Architecture and Systems Issues, March 2006.

————. *Information Technology: FBI Is Taking Steps to Develop an Enterprise Architecture, but Much Remains to Be Accomplished*. GAO-05-363, September 2005.

————. *Information Technology: The Federal Enterprise Architecture and Agencies' Enterprise Architectures Are Still Maturing*. GAO Testimony Before the Subcommittee on Technology, Information Policy, Intergovernmental Relations and the Census, Committee on Government Reform, House of Representatives, March 2004.

————. (February 1997). *Information Technology Investment Evaluation Guide: Assessing Risks and Returns. A Guide for Evaluating Federal Agencies' IT Investment Decision-Making*, April 2003.

————. *Information Technology Investment Management: A Framework for Assessing and Improving Maturity*.

U.S. Treasury Department (July 2000). *Enterprise Architecture Framework (TEAF)*. July 2000. http://www.eaframeworks.com/TEAF/teaf.doc.

————. *Treasury Information Systems Architecture Framework (TISAF)*. 3 January 1997.

U.S. Treasury Department, C. I. O. C. *Treasury Enterprise Architecture Framework (TEAF)*, version 1.0, 3 July 2000.

Vaidyanathan, S. "Enterprise Architecture in the Context of Organizational Strategy." *BPTrends, 11* (2005): 1–9.

van der Raadt, B., J. F. Hoorn, and H. van Vliet. "Alignment and Maturity Are Siblings in Architecture Assessment." In *Advanced Information Systems Engineering*, ed. O. Pastor and J. Falcão e Cunha, 357–71. Berlin: Springer, 2005.

van der Raadt, B., J. Soetendal, M. Perdeck, H. van Vliet, V. Universiteit, and N. Amsterdam. "Polyphony in Architecture." In *26th International Conference on Software Engineering, ICSE 2004. Proceedings,* 533–42. Edinburgh, Scotland: IEEE, 2004.

Venkatesh, V., H. Bala, S. Venkatraman, and J. Bates. "Enterprise Architecture Maturity: The Story of the Veterans Health Administration." *MIS Quarterly Executive* 6, no. 2 (2007): 79–90.

Versteeg, G., and H. Bouwman. "Business Architecture: A New Paradigm to Relate Business Strategy to ICT." *Information Systems Frontiers* 8, no. 2 (2006): 91–102.

von Halle, B. "Architecting in a Virtual World." *Database Programming and Design.* (November 1996): 13–18. http://www.dbpd.com/vault/9611arch.htm.

———. *Business Rules Applied.* New York: Wiley, 2001.

von Halle, B., and D. Kull. *Handbook of Data Management.* Boca Raton, FL: Auerbach Publications, 1993.

Wagter, R., M. van den Berg, J. Luijpers, and M. van Steenbergen. *Dynamic Enterprise Architecture: How to Make It Work.* Hoboken, NJ: Wiley, 2005.

Wallace, L., M. Keil, and A. Rai. "How Software Project Risk Affects Project Performance." *Decision Sciences* 35, no. 2 (Spring 2004): 289–321.

Walsham, G. "Actor-Network Theory and IS Research: Current Status and Future Prospects." In *Information Systems and Qualitative Research,* ed. A. S. Lee, J. Liebenau, and J. I. DeGross, 466–80. London: Chapman & Hall, 1997.

Walsham, G., and S. Sahay. "GIS for District-Level Administration in India: Problems and Opportunities." *MIS Quarterly* 23, no. 1 (1999): 39–66.

Walton, M. *The Deming Management Method.* New York: Putnam, 1986.

Wasserman, A. I., P. Freeman, and M. Porcella. "Characteristics of Software Development Methodologies." In *Information System Design Methodologies: A Feature Analysis,* ed. T. W. Olle, H. G. Sol, and C. Tully, 37–62. New York: North-Holland, 1983.

Wegmann, A., P. Balabko, L. S. Lê, G. Regev, and I. Rychkova. *A Method and Tool for Business-IT Alignment in Enterprise Architecture.* Paper presented at the 17th CAiSE Forum, Porto, Portugal, June 2005.

Wieringa, R. J., H. M. Blanken, M. M. Fokkinga, and P. W. P. J. Grefen. "Aligning Application Architecture to the Business Context." In *Advanced Information Systems Engineering,* 1028–29. Berlin: Springer, 2003.

Willbanks, L. (2008). "This Old House: Using Enterprise Architecture to Upgrade Old IT Systems." *IT Professional Magazine* 10, no. 2 (2008): 64–65.

Wilson, D. W. (1997). *Maturity Models in IS Development in Managing IT Resources and Applications in the World Economy.* Paper presented at the 8th IRMA International Conference, 1997.

Winter, R., and R. Fischer. *Essential Layers, Artifacts, and Dependencies of Enterprise Architecture.* EDOC Workshop on Trends in Enterprise Architecture Research (TEAR 2006), 17 October 2006, Hong Kong.

Winter, R., and J. Schelp. "Enterprise Architecture Governance: The Need for a Business-to-IT Approach." In *Proceedings of the 2008 ACM Symposium on Applied Computing,* 548–52. New York: ACM, 2008.

Womack, J., J. Jones, and D. Roos. *The Machine That Changed the World.* New York: Harper Perennial, 1991.

Xia, W., and G. Lee "Complexity of Information Systems Development Projects: Conceptualization and Measurement Development." *Journal of Management Information Systems* 22, no. 1 (2003): 45–83.

————. "Grasping the Complexity of IS Development Projects." *Communications of the ACM* 47, no. 5 (2004): 68–74.

Yeo, K. T. "Critical Failure Factors in Information System Projects." *International Journal of Project Management* 20, no. 3 (2002): 241–46.

Young, C. "The Unexpected Case for Enterprise IT Architectures." Gartner Research Report No. SPA-12-7101, 1–5, 2001.

Yourdon, E. *Classics in Software Engineering.* New York: Yourdon Press, 1979.

————. *Death March,* 2nd ed. New York: Prentice Hall PTR, 2003.

————. *Techniques of Program Structure and Design.* Englewood Cliffs, NJ: Prentice Hall, 1975.

Zachman, J. A. "All the Reasons Why You Can't Do Architecture: We Has Met the Enemy and He Is Us." *DataToKnowledge Newsletter* 28, nos. 4–5 (2000).

————. "Architecture Is Architecture Is Architecture." *EIMInsight Magazine* 1, no. 1 (2007): 1–9. Also at http://zachmaninternational.com/index.php/ea-articles/26-articles/68-architecture-is-architecture.

————. "Building the Enterprise: An Infusion of Honesty." *DataToKnowledge Newsletter* 28–29, nos. 6–1 (2000–2001).

————. "Business Systems Planning and Business Information Control Study: A Comparison." *IBM Systems Journal* 21, no. 1 (1982): 31.

————. "Conceptual, Logical, Physical: It Is Simple." *DataToKnowledge Newsletter,* 29, no. 3 (2001).

————. "Data Warehouse: Architecture or Silver Bullet?" *DataToKnowledge Newsletter* 27, no. 3 (1999).

————. "Enterprise Architecture Artifacts Versus Application Development Artifacts." *DataToKnowledge Newsletter* 28, nos. 2 & 3 (2000).

————. "Enterprise Architecture: The Issue of the Century." *Database Programming and Design* 10, no. 3 (1997): 44–53.

————. "Enterprise Architecture: Issues, Inhibitors, and Incentives." *DataToKnowledge Newsletter* 27–28, no. 1 (1999–2000).

————. "Enterprise Architecture: Looking Back and Looking Ahead." *Database Newsletter* 27, no. 3 (1998): 1–9.

————. *Enterprise Architecture Standards,* version 2.01, 2007. Available by free registration at http://www.zachmaninternational.com/2/Standards.asp.

————. "Enterprise Architecture: Straight from the Shoulder." In *Proceeding of Enterprise Architecture Conference Europe.* London, June 9–11, 2003. Available also at http://www.damauk.org/John%20Zachman%20-%20Straight%20from%20the%20Shoulder.pdf.

————. "Fatal Distractions." *DataToKnowledge Newsletter* 29, nos. 4–5 (2001).

————. *The Framework for Enterprise Architecture: Background, Description and Utility.* Zachman International, 1996. http://zachmaninternational.com.

————. "The Framework for Enterprise Architecture and the Search for the Owner's View of Business Rules." *DataToKnowledge Newsletter* 27, no. 1 (1998). http://brcommunity.com/a376.php.

————. "Framework Fundamentals: A Letter to Management." *Business Rules Journal,* 4, no. 2 (Feb 2003): 1–11.

————. "Framework Fundamentals: Level of Detail." *Business Rules Journal* 4, no. 2 (Feb 2003): 11–15.

————. "Framework Fundamentals: Questions from the OMG." *Business Rules Journal* 4, no. 2 (Feb 2003): 15–18.

————. "A Framework for Information Systems Architecture." *IBM Systems Journal* 26, no. 3 (1987): 276–92.

————. *Framework Standards: What's It All About?* Zachman International, 2005. http://zachmaninternational.com/index.php/home-article/19#maincol.

————. *Frameworks, Reference Models, and Matrices.* Zachman International. 2001. http://zachmaninternational.com.

————. "Integration of Systems Planning, Development, and Maintenance Tools and Methods." In *Information Management Directions: The Integration Challenge,* 29–45, NIST Special Publication 500-167. New York: ACM, 1989.

————. "Life Is a Series of Trade-Offs and Change Is Accelerating." *DataToKnowledge Newsletter* 27, nos. 1–2 (1999).

————. "Packages Don't Let You Off the Hook." *DataToKnowledge Newsletter* 27, no. 4–5 (1999).

————. "The Physics of Knowledgement." *DataToKnowledge Newsletter* 26 (1998).

————. "Security and the Zachman Framework." *DataToKnowledge Newsletter* 29, no. 6 (2001).

————. "Yes Virginia, There IS an Enterprise Architecture." *DataToKnowledge Newsletter* 26, no. 6 (1998).

————. "You Can't 'Cost-Justify' Architecture." *DataToKnowledge Newsletter* 29, no. 3 (2001).

Zachman, J. A. *The Zachman Framework™: A Concise Definition,* Zachman International, 2008. http://zachmaninternational.com/index.php/the-zachman-framework/26-articles/13-the-zachman-framework-a-concise-definition.

————. *The Zachman Framework: A Primer for Enterprise Engineering and Manufacturing* Zachman International, 2003. "The Zachman eBook" is available at http://zachman international.com/index.php/home-article/15#maincol.

Zachman, J. A., and J. F. Sowa. "Extending and Formalizing the Framework for Information Systems Architecture." *IBM Systems Journal* 31, no. 3 (1992): 590–616.

Zarvic, N., and R. Wieringa. "An Integrated Enterprise Architecture Framework for Business-IT Alignment." In *Proceedings of Workshop of Business/IT Alignment and Interoperability (BUSITAL'06) at CAiSE,* 6, 262–70. London, 2006.

Zdun, U., and P. Avgeriou. "A Catalog of Architectural Primitives for Modeling Architectural Patterns." *Information and Software Technology* 50, nos. 9–10 (2008): 1003–34

Websites: Some EA-Related Internet Sites

This is a starting point. There is no doubt that we are unaware of many useful websites about enterprise architecture. We have attempted to keep this list noncommercial, but probably have done that imperfectly, too. We simply hope that what we have provided here is useful to you.

Architecture & Governance Magazine – http://www.architectureandgovernance.com

Center for the Advancement of the Enterprise Architecture Profession – http://caeap.org

Clive Finkelstein – http://www.ies.aust.com/

DAMA - Data Management Association International – http://www.dama.org

EA Interest Group – http://www.eaig.org

Enterprise Architecture Center of Excellence (EACOE) – http://eacoe.org/index2.shtml

Enterprise Architecture Page on IS World – http://users.iafrica.com/o/om/omis-ditd/denniss/text/entparch.html

Enterprise Information Management Institute – http://www.eiminstitute.org

Enterprise-wide Information Technology Architectures (EWITA) – http://www.ewita.com

Federal Chief Information Officer Council – http://www.cio.gov

Federal Enterprise Architecture Certification (FEAC) Institute – http://www.feacinstitute.org/

General Accounting Office, *Information Technology Investment Management: A Framework for Assessing and Improving Process Maturity, Exposure Draft, Version 1,* GAO/AIMD-10.1.23, May 2000 – http://www.gao.gov/special.pubs/10_1_23.pdf

General Accounting Office, *Measuring Performance and Demonstrating Results of Information Technology Investments,* AIMD-98-89, March 1998 – http://www.gao.gov/special.pubs/ai98089.pef

General Services Administration, Office of Information Technology – http://www.itpolicy.gsa.gov

Institute for Enterprise Architecture Developments – http://www.enterprise-architecture.info/

International Enterprise Architects Consortium and Architecture Center – http://www.ieac.org

Interoperability Clearinghouse – http://www.ichnet.org/

Intervista Institute – http://www.intervista-institute.com/km/km-videos.html

John F. Sowa – http://www.jfsowa.com/

Journal of Enterprise Architecture – http://www.aeajournal.org

Leon A. Kappelman, Ph.D. – http://courses.unt.edu/kappelman/

Linguistic Indexes on the Internet – http://www.sil.org/linguistics/other_indexes.html

Linguistics, Natural Language, and Computational Linguistics Meta-index – http://nlp.stanford.edu/links/linguistics.html

National Association of State CIOs (NASCIO) Enterprise Architecture Program Toolkit & Resources – http://www.nascio.org/

National Institutes of Health Enterprise Architecture – http://enterprisearchitecture.nih.gov/

Object Management Group – http://www.omg.org

OMB Circular A.130, Management of Federal Information Resources, Revised, 30 November 2000 – http://www.whitehouse.gov/OMB/circulars/a130/a130.html

OMB Memorandum M-00-07, Incorporating and Funding Security in Information Systems Investments, 28 February 2000 – http://www.whitehouse.gov/OMB/memoranda/m00-07.html

OMB Memorandum M-97-16, Information Technology Architectures, 18 June 1997 – http://www.whitehouse.gov/OMB/memoranda/m97-16.html

OMB, Proposed revision of OMB Circular No. A.130, in Federal Register, Vol. 65, No. 72, 13 April 2000, pages 19933–39 – http://www.whitehouse.gov/omb/fedreg/rev-a130.pdf

SIL International – http://www.sil.org/sil/

SIMEAWG – Society for Information Management (SIM) Enterprise Architecture Working Group (EAWG) – http://eawg.simnet.org

Society for Information Management (SIM) – http://simnet.org

Software Engineering Institute (SEI) Architecture Technology Page – http://www.sei.cmu.edu

Steven Spewak Enterprise Architecture Planning Home Page – http://www.eap.com

The Open Group Architecture Framework (TOGAF) Technical Reference Model – http://www.opengroup.org/togaf

Unified Modeling Language (UML) – http://www.omg.org/uml

U.S. CIO Council Architecture & Infrastructure Committee – http://www.cio.gov/index.cfm?function=eastatement

U.S. Department of Veterans Affairs – http://www.va.gov/oirm/architecture/

U.S. General Services Administration Technology Strategy Overview – http://www.gsa.gov/Portal/gsa/ep/channelView.do?pageTypeId=17113&channelId=24659

U.S. Government Accountability Office (GAO) – http://gao.gov

U.S. Office of Management and Budget (OMB) – http://www.whitehouse.gov/omb/

Workflow Management Coalition – http://www.wfmc.org/

Wycliffe International – http://wycliffe.net

Zachman eBook Bibliography – http://www.zachmaninternational.com/index.php/home-article/16

Zachman Framework Applied to Administrative Computing Services – http://apps.adcom.uci.edu/EnterpriseArch/Zachman/

Zachman International – http://www.zachmaninternational.com

Enterprise Architecture Glossary

Larry Burgess, Thiagarajan Ramakrishnan,
Brian Salmans, and Leon A. Kappelman

One would expect an emerging and evolving field like enterprise architecture to have an emerging and evolving vocabulary. Often we include multiple definitions of the same term; and though we realize that this may result in some ambiguity and even confusion, we believe that such is the nature of a discipline that is converging from many different directions, practices, and disciplines. We have unintentionally overlooked some useful terms and definitions related to enterprise architecture and no doubt included others of only peripheral importance. This glossary, like this book, is a starting point on a long journey. We have tried our best to provide something useful to you.

Application Architecture: A comprehensive description or design of an application, either established or planned (may include middleware options, data gateways, and software infrastructures).[1] See also "Software Architecture" and "Architecture Domains."

Application Architecture: The architecture of a specific application.[19]

Architect: One whose responsibility is the creation and/or maintenance of an architectural description.[19]

Architectural Artifact: A specific document, report, analysis, model, or other tangible that contributes to an architectural description.[19]

Architectural Artifact: The relevant documentation, models, diagrams, depictions, and analyses, including a baseline repository, and standards and security profiles.[4]

Architectural Description: One or more architectural products (i.e., artifacts) that make up some or all of an architecture.

Architectural Framework: A skeletal structure that defines suggested architectural artifacts, describes how those artifacts are related to each other, and provides generic definitions for what those artifacts might look like.[19]

Architectural Methodology: Any structured repeatable approach to accomplishing some or all of the tasks related to architecture. Can include process descriptions, deliverable artifacts, methods, and tools.

Architectural Process: A defined series of actions directed to the goal of producing either an architecture or an architectural description.[19]

Architectural Taxonomy: A categorization or classification scheme or concept for organizing architectural artifacts, processes, methods, and/or tools.

Architecture: A framework or structure that portrays the elements and relationships among the elements of the subject force, system, or activity.[3] (The term "Architecture" sometimes refers to the process and sometimes to the product of that process. See also "Architecture Process" and "Architecture Product." – Editor)

Architecture: The description of a complex system—generally its purpose, structure, components, and their corresponding relationships, with varying levels of detail, often at a particular time, either today (for example, "our current network architecture") or as a target in the future. May include principles and values (this definition applies to buildings, landscapes, or wherever architecture is applied).[1]

Architecture: The series of guidelines—standards, processes, methodologies, or policies and rules—that are intended to direct the behavior of designers as they build or acquire new systems, functionality, or capabilities. Ideally derived from a conceptual framework with goals, principles, and values—to create an organizing logic. May be analogous to a building code.[1] (I believe John Zachman might call this the architecture described in the Profession Framework.[27] – Editor)

Architecture: The set of descriptions about something.[16]

Architecture: The set of descriptive representations about an object.[6]

Architecture: A set of design artifacts, or descriptive representations, that are relevant for describing an object such that it can be produced to requirements (quality) as well as maintained over the period of its useful life (change).[6]

Architecture: The fundamental organization of a system embodied in its components, their relationships to each other and to the environment, and the principles guiding its design and evolution.[20]

Architecture Capability Maturity Model: A parallel to the use of the capability maturity model as applied to software development. The model often consists of five stages of maturity—starting out as an "infant" and progressing to an "adult" who had acquired productive wisdom. Each stage must be entered before progressing on to the next in the normal pattern. Its purpose is to assess where you are, where you would like to be, and the steps necessary to follow to attain the goal.[1] (The subject of EA maturity models is discussed in Brian Salmans's article in Chapter 2—in particular, the GAO's five-stage EA maturity model,[28] which is an adaptation of the Software Engineering Institute's Capability Maturity Model for software development. – Editor)

Architecture Domains: A descriptive means of dividing a major topic, such as architecture, into several cohesive subdivisions. In EA a common use of high-level domains would include business architecture, information architecture, and technical architecture. The latter two are sometimes subdivided, for example: information architecture consisting of data architecture, application architecture, integration architecture, and point-of access architecture; and technical architecture consisting of infrastructure architecture, security architecture, and system management architecture.[1]

Architecture "Evergreening": This refers to keeping the architecture relevant and up-to-date all of the time.[1]

Architecture Model: A representation of the real thing in another form.[1] See also "Artifact" and "Architecture Product."

Architecture Ownership: Ownership means taking responsibility for or taking on the task of establishing a process, including governance, education, dissemination, and compliance with the architecture.[1] (Can also refer to the ownership of the object of the architecture [for example, the business process owner] who by definition owns the architecture of that object. – Editor.)

Architecture Portfolio: The use of the word "portfolio" implies categorization or classifying different elements into useful groups. An architecture portfolio can mean many things, such as grouping standards by type of technology, applications by business function, or components by life cycle stage.[1]

Architecture Process: Creating and maintaining an architecture is a continuing process that requires a series of activities, including: a statement of the relevant business goals and drivers for architecture, documentation of the current architecture, a view of the current and emerging technologies, creation of the target architecture, a governance process to select the appropriate standards and processes, a method to publish the guides and provide education, and a means to establish the measurement of compliance.[1] (The term "Architecture" sometimes refers to the process and sometimes to the product of that process. Modifying the noun architecture with another noun is more precise, as in this case with "process." See also "Architecture Product." – Editor)

Architecture Product: The structure of components, their interrelationships, and the principles and guidelines governing their design and evolution over time.[7]

Architecture Product: The graphics, models, and/or narrative that depict the enterprise environment and design.[12] See also "Artifact."

Architecture Repository: A database for architectural artifacts. See Gary Simons's article in Chapter 3 for an example. Commercial tools for EA are emerging and evolving but are at a fairly rudimentary state when compared to repositories for building or product architectures in terms of availability, flexibility, and interconnectivity of artifacts as well as decision support and change analysis.

Architecture Repository: An information system used to store and access architectural information and the relationships among the information elements, and to create and store architecture artifacts.[2]

Architecture Return On Investment (ROI): Studies indicate that operational costs are lower in enterprises with sound architecture programs, but it is difficult to isolate architecture as the causal force.[1]

Architecture Review: At several possible stages of the creation of a new system or capability, it is appropriate to perform a review of the new design to determine whether it has been created in compliance with the architecture.[1]

Architecture Traceability: To achieve optimal performance from an architecture, it should provide guidance that is directly linked to sound strategies—both business and technological. An important test, when a technical choice has been made, is that the reason for the choice is traceable back to the business drivers whenever possible, and not be chosen because it is considered "cool" by the technology staff[1] (in the context of Zachman's Enterprise Framework, confirming that lower row decisions are consistent [aligned] with upper rows. – Editor).

Artifact: An abstract representation of some aspect of an existing or to-be-built system, component, or view. Examples of individual artifacts are a graphical model, structured model, tabular data, and structured or unstructured narrative. Individual artifacts may be aggregated.[2]

"As-Is" or "Today" Architecture: A description of the information system(s) in place today—including conceptual, logical, and physical aspects as they exist. This is often an inventory of applications, platforms, and networks documented in a variety of ways. Planned or not, it is what you have.[1]

"As-Is" Architecture: The current state of an enterprise's architecture (see "Baseline Architecture").[2]

Baseline Architecture: The set of products that portray the existing enterprise, the current business practices, and technical infrastructure. Commonly referred to as the "as-is" architecture.[5]

Baseline Architecture: Representation of the cumulative "as-built" or baseline of the existing architecture. The current architecture has two parts: the current business architecture, which defines the current business needs being met by the current technology; and the current design architecture, which defines the implemented data, applications, and technology used to support the current business needs.[4]

Baseline Architecture: The technology currently in place. Same as "as-is" or today architecture.[1]

Blueprint: This is a frequent metaphor in enterprise architecture due to its relationship to the products of building architecture and construction.[1]

Bottom-Up Architecture: This represents a strategy to initiate or organize an architectural effort that starts at the bottom with the component parts to be used. The focus is on selection and use of standard piece parts, which can be assembled into various components, services, or functions that will enable a solution. This is a comparatively straightforward effort but is limited in potential payoff since the result may be standardization but not tight alignment with the business strategy or drivers.[1] See also "Top-Down Architecture." A descriptor for an architecture process.

Business Architecture: A component of the current and target architectures and relates to the federal mission and goals. It contains the content of the business models and focuses on the federal business areas and processes responding to business drivers. The business architecture defines federal business processes, federal information flows, and information needed to perform business functions.[4]

Business Architecture: This represents the business view—often in the form of the overall value chain for an enterprise, which may then be divided into a series of business functions or departments. These may then be defined as a series of business processes, with each process potentially divided into activities, and then further broken down into tasks. None of these steps necessarily involves the use of technology.[1] See also "Architecture Domains."

Business Architecture: An architecture that deals specifically with business processes and business flow.[19]

Business Drivers: Business drivers are the needs and goals important to the success of the business that may influence the nature or personality of the architecture. This is where architecture must start. Simple examples of drivers include low cost, fast time to market, high flexibility or agility, high security against failure or improper access, and great ease of use.[1] (Sometimes called "design objectives," these are basically represented first in the upper rows of column 6 in the context of the Zachman Enterprise Framework. – Editor)

Business Needs/Goals: See "Business drivers."[1]

Business Reference Model (BRM): An FEA term that gives a business view of the various functions of the federal government.[19]

Business Service Segment: An FEA term that refers to a segment that is foundational to most, if not all, political organizations, such as financial management.[19]

C4ISR: A specific framework for architecture developed for use within the U.S. Department of Defense and since superseded by the DoDAF (Department of Defense Architecture Framework).

Capital Planning and Investment Control (CPIC): It is the same as capital programming and is a decision-making process for ensuring the information technology (IT) investments integrate strategic planning, budgeting, procurement, and the management of IT in support of agency missions and business needs. The term comes from the Clinger–Cohen Act of 1996 and is generally used in relationship to IT management issues.[5]

Capital Planning and Investment Control (CPIC) Process: A process to structure budget formulation and execution and ensure that investments consistently support the strategic goals of the agency/organization.[8]

Capital Programming: It means an integrated process within an agency for planning, budgeting, procurement, and management of the agency's portfolio of capital assets to achieve agency strategic goals and objectives with the lowest life cycle cost and least risk.[5]

Chief Information Officer (CIO): The title often used for the executive in charge of information technology in an organization.

CIMOSA: CIMOSA defines a model-based enterprise engineering method that categorizes manufacturing operations into Generic and Specific (Partial and Particular) functions. These can then be combined to create a model that can be used for process simulation and analysis. The same model can be used on line in the manufacturing enterprise for scheduling, dispatching, monitoring, and providing process information.[5]

"City Planning": Refers to an analogy to a construction industry plan that lays out a broad set of rules and policies that fit the relevant urban needs, but does not define how a particular building must be built. It fits the definition of guidelines, policies, and rules.[1]

Clinger–Cohen Act of 1996: A law passed by the U.S. Congress that requires, among other things, that every federal department and agency have an enterprise architecture and a chief information officer responsible for all IT spending, personnel, and materials as well as its EA. Also see "Information Technology Management Reform Act."

Common-Systems Architectures: A TOGAF term referring to an architecture that is common to many (but not all) types of enterprises, in contrast to foundation architectures and industry architectures.[19]

Compliance: Concerns the degree to which a new system has been built in accordance with all appropriate guidelines and processes. Compliance must be determined—often by an architecture review board. The granting of exceptions may be part of the process. A high degree of compliance is necessary to gain the desired benefits from the architecture. Noncompliance may result in loss of funding, support, or other factors to encourage and motivate full cooperation. If compliance is only suggested or recommended, the benefits may be minimal.[1]

Component Reference Model (CRM): An FEA term that gives an IT view of systems that support business functionality.[19]

Composite Model: In the context of Zachman's Enterprise Framework, a model made of two or more primitive models. Multivariable, composite models are made up of components of several primitive models. Implementations, the creation of the end results, are the instantiation of composite, multi-variable models, that is, models comprised of more than one Abstraction (column) and/or more than one Perspective (row). An instantiation, by definition, is a "Composite."[25, 30] See also "Primitive Models."

Conceptual View: This architectural view of a system or application consists of the context, including the purpose, intent, and values relevant to the task.[1]

Data Architecture: The architecture of data assets, typically of an enterprise. Can also refer to a particular industry standard for data organization and structure, or that the product of a particular software vendor.

Data Architecture: Covers the sphere of managing data. Takes the same definitions (as-is, to-be, and guidelines) but applies them to information content, objects, databases, data warehouses, data access tools, information organizational principles, data extraction, data scrubbing, and so on.[1] See also "Architecture Domains."

Data Architecture: The architecture of the data (typically stored in databases) owned by enterprise.[19]

Department of Defense Architecture Framework (DoDAF): Defines a common approach for DOD architecture description development, presentation, and integration for both war-fighting operations and business operations and processes. The Framework is intended to ensure that architecture descriptions can be compared and related across organizational boundaries, including joint and multinational boundaries (from the *Executive Summary of the DoDAF*, version 1).

Design Objectives: Objectives, goals, or values important to the success of the enterprise that are reflected in its architecture. Examples of design objectives are: aligned, secure, low-cost, agile, fast to market, and flexible. Basically represented in the upper rows of column 6 in the context Zachman Enterprise Framework. See also "Business Drivers."

Enterprise: A unit of economic organization or activity such as a factory, a farm, or a mine, but especially a business organization.[29]

Enterprise: An organization supporting a defined business scope and mission. An enterprise is comprised of interdependent resources (people, organizations, and technology) that should coordinate their functions and share information in support of a common mission (or set of related missions).[2]

Enterprise Architect: An architect who specializes in enterprise architectures.[19]

Enterprise Architecture: The addition of the word *enterprise* extends the coverage of architecture to the business realm—including the mission, value chain, business strategy, business functions, and business processes, which together describe and define the role of the enterprise. Implies the entire breadth of the enterprise, as in enterprise-wide architecture.[1]

Enterprise Architecture: The set of primitive, descriptive artifacts that constitute the knowledgebase of the enterprise.[6]

Enterprise Architecture: A strategic information asset base, which defines the business, the information necessary to operate the business, the technologies necessary to support the business operations, and the transitional processes necessary for implementing new technologies in response to the changing business needs. It is a representation or blueprint.[4, 2]

Enterprise Architecture: All of the knowledge about the enterprise.[9]

Enterprise Architecture: An architecture in which the system in question is the whole enterprise, especially the business processes, technologies, and information systems of the enterprise.[19]

Enterprise Architecture: The organizing process for key business process and IT capabilities reflecting the integration and standardization requirements of the firm's operating model.[21]

Enterprise Architecture (as models): A holistic set of descriptions of an enterprise covering the perspectives of business, applications, data, and technical infrastructure, the relationships between those descriptions, and the principles and guidelines governing their design and evolution over time.[17]

Enterprise Architecture (as a practice): A business discipline of analytical tasks and techniques that use a business-centric approach to documenting and analyzing an enterprise in its current and future states from an integrated business and technology perspective.[17]

Enterprise Architecture: The holistic set of descriptions about the enterprise over time.[16]

Enterprise Architecture: The organizing logic for key business process and IT capabilities reflecting the integration and standardization requirements of the firm's operating model.[21]

Enterprise Architecture Framework: An organizing mechanism for managing the development and maintenance of architecture descriptions.[4]

Enterprise Architecture Framework: Provides an organizing structure for the information contained in an enterprise architecture. It does not contain the EA itself. Many organizations can use the same EA framework, but each EA is organization-specific. An enterprise architecture framework:

Identifies the types of information needed for the EA.

Organizes the types of information into a logical structure.

Describes the relationships among the information types.

Often the information is categorized into architecture models and viewpoints.[5]

Enterprise Architecture Policy: A statement governing the development, implementation, and maintenance of the enterprise architecture.[12]

Enterprise Architecture Products: The graphics, models, and/or narrative that depict the enterprise environment and design.[12]

Enterprise Engineering: A multidisciplinary approach to defining and developing a system design and architecture for the organization.[12]

Enterprise Engineering: That body of knowledge, principles, and practices having to do with the analysis, design, implementation, and operation of an enterprise. The enterprise engineer addresses a fundamental question: how to design and improve all elements associated with the total enterprise through the use of engineering and analysis methods and tools to more effectively achieve its goals and objectives.[5]

Enterprise Life Cycle: The integration of management, business, and engineering life cycle processes that span the enterprise to align IT with the business.[2]

Enterprise Service: An FEA term referring to a well-defined function that spans political boundaries, such as security management.[19]

Event Trace: An ordered list of events between different objects assigned to columns in a table.[5]

Exceptions: Permitted deviations from the use of guideline standards or processes that would normally apply. Typically involves a formal process whereby a request for an exception from the architecture guidelines is made to the architecture board or office.[1]

Federal Architecture Program EA Assessment Framework: A benchmark used by the OMB to measure the effectiveness of governmental bodies in using enterprise architecture.[19]

Federal Enterprise Architecture (FEA): An architectural description of the enterprise architecture of the U.S. federal government that includes various reference models, processes for creating organizational architectures that fit in with the federal enterprise architecture, and a methodology for measuring the success of an organization in using enterprise architectures.[19]

Federal Enterprise Architectural Framework (FEAF): A framework used in the U.S. federal government to describe both the process and products of EA at a fairly high level.

Federal Enterprise Architecture Framework (FEAF): A jointly developed overall framework for enterprise architecture created by the Federal CIO Council for shared use. It has continually evolved as legislation, regulation, knowledge, and practices have evolved. It accommodates the as-is and to-be, includes standards and process guidelines, and breaks the enterprise into business, data, application, and technical architecture subsystems.[1]

Federal Enterprise Architecture Framework (FEAF): An organizing mechanism for managing development, maintenance, and facilitated decision making of a federal EA. The Framework provides a structure for organizing federal resources and for describing and managing federal EA activities.[4]

Federal Enterprise Architecture Project Management Office (FEAPMO): The organization within the Office of Management and Budget that owns and administers the federal enterprise architecture.

Foundation Architecture: A term used by TOGAF to refer to the most generic of architectures that can be used by any IT organization.[19]

Framework: A logical structure for classifying and organizing complex information.[4]

Framework: A structure, usually rigid, serving to hold the parts of something together or to support something constructed or sketched over or around it. The basic structure, arrangement, or system.[5, 10]

Framework: A Framework is a schema, a classification scheme. It defines a set of categories into which various things can be sorted. It is a mechanism for simplification. For example, the Zachman Framework™ defines a set of categories for models, primitive models that are relevant for describing a complex object like an enterprise.[26] See also "Reference Model" and "Matrix."

Governance: This covers the process of making decisions and providing for their monitoring or enforcement. It includes who participates in the process, the basis of approval (voting or advisory), and the jurisdiction or scope of the decisions; it should also incorporate follow-through to verify that decisions are being implemented and that policies and rules are being complied with.[1]

Governance: The governance structure of an enterprise is concerned with the leadership, organizational structures, and processes that:

Set strategic enterprise goals.

Provide direction and strategy on achieving those goals.

Secure resources and allocate those resources to activities.

Establish measures for activities, results, and achieving goals.

Manage risks in achieving goals and operating the business.

Measure performance to ensure business value is achieved.[11]

Government Accountability Office (GAO): A branch of the U.S. government that is responsible for monitoring the effectiveness of different organizations within the U.S. government. Formerly known as the General Accounting Office, the mission of the GAO is: "To support the Congress in meeting its constitutional responsibilities and to help improve the performance and ensure the accountability of the federal government for the benefit of the American people. We provide Congress with timely information that is objective, fact-based, non-partisan, non-ideological, fair, and balanced." Sometimes known as "the investigative arm of Congress" and "the congressional watchdog." See http://gao.gov for additional information.

Guiding Principle: This represents an enduring value or belief that the organization wants to uphold and is used to guide decisions in daily operations and/or technology and organizational direction. It may be stated in the form of the principle, the rationale behind it, and the implications to the organization from observing it. A simple example is the belief that it is better to buy application packages than to build applications internally.[1] See also "Design Objective."

Industry Architecture: A TOGAF term that refers to an architecture that is common to most enterprises within an industry, in contrast to a "common-systems architecture" and an "organizational architecture."[19]

Information Architecture: The art and science of organizing information to help people effectively fulfill their information needs. Information architecture involves investigation, analysis, design, and implementation.[23]

Information Architecture: The art and science of organizing and labeling websites, intranets, online communities, and software to support usability.[24]

Information Architecture: Sometimes a synonym for the data architecture of an enterprise. See also "Data Architecture" and "Architecture Domains."

Information Technology (IT) Architecture: IT architecture is the organizing logic for applications, data, and infrastructure technologies, as captured in a set of policies and technical choices, intended to enable the firm's business strategy.[22]

Information Technology Management Reform Act: An act passed by the U.S. Congress in 1996 that requires all governmental organizations to use effective strategies and frameworks for developing and maintaining IT resources.[19] Also know as the "Clinger–Cohen Act of 1996."

Infrastructure Domain: The base foundation of capabilities in the form of computers, operating systems, and networks (not to mention the staff skills) that creates the environment for the development and use of applications that perform specific business functions, such as e-mail or customer relationship management. The term is subject to many interpretations, and architecture plays an important role in defining the current and future infrastructure.[1]

Integration Domain: The primary task of integration architecture is to establish sound guidelines for application-to-application sharing and the exchange of data. Driving forces in recent years have been enterprise resource planning, supply chain management, e-business, packages, outsourcing, and other drivers demanding intense sharing of information across various boundaries in a consistent and efficient manner.[1] (This basically describes postimplementation integration as it has been for many decades and what some might say is the result of not having done EA. – Editor)

IT architecture: The organizing logic for applications, data, and infrastructure technologies, as captured in a set of policies and technical choices, intended to enable the firm's business strategy.[22]

Legacy Systems: Those systems in existence and either deployed or under development at the start of a modernization program. All legacy systems will be affected by modernization to a greater or lesser extent. Some systems will become transition systems before they are retired. Other systems will simply be retired as their functions are assumed by modernization systems. Still others will be abandoned when they become obsolete.[2]

Legacy Systems: All systems and all of their components once they are implemented or deployed.

Logical View: Conceptually, the top three rows of Zachman's Enterprise Framework.

Logical View: This architectural view of a domain, system, or application that stresses the function or task to be performed. This may include activities, interactions, content, flow, and event timing.[1] (But it does not specify physical components and thus does not explicitly include information technologies. – Editor)

Matrix: A matrix is an intersection between two independent variables. A matrix could depict the relationship between two of any kind of independent variables. Some people would call a matrix a "model," just as some people would call a list a "model." A matrix is the relationship between two lists. The intent of a matrix is to depict relationships, not classifications.[26] See also "Framework" and "Reference Model."

Methodology: A documented approach for performing activities in a coherent, consistent, accountable, and repeatable manner.[2]

Migration Plan: Enterprises plan to move to new target architectures from the present or as-is environment.[1]

Migration Stages: When considering the migration process from as-is to to-be, the move will typically not come all at once but gradually in stages.[1]

Model: Representations of information, activities, relationships, and constraints.[2] See also "Artifact."

"Next Minute" Architecture: The collection of guidelines in the form of standards and processes to be followed when building new systems or capabilities. It includes reference models and practices that are intended to guide behavior during the design process. It becomes the method by which the transition is made from the as-is to the to-be. It is subject to regular change and updates.[1]

Office of Management and Budget (OMB): The part of the Executive Office of the President of the United States that assembles the President's budget proposal and provides executive oversight to federal process and agencies. "OMB's predominant mission is to assist the President in overseeing the preparation of the federal budget and to supervise its administration in

Executive Branch agencies. In helping to formulate the President's spending plans, OMB evaluates the effectiveness of agency programs, policies, and procedures, assesses competing funding demands among agencies, and sets funding priorities. OMB ensures that agency reports, rules, testimony, and proposed legislation are consistent with the President's Budget and with Administration policies. In addition, OMB oversees and coordinates the Administration's procurement, financial management, information, and regulatory policies. In each of these areas, OMB's role is to help improve administrative management, to develop better performance measures and coordinating mechanisms, and to reduce any unnecessary burdens on the public." (From http://www.whitehouse.gov/omb/.)

Organizational Architecture: A TOGAF term that applies to an architecture that is specific to a particular organization, in contrast to an industry architecture.[19]

Performance Reference Model (PRM): An FEA term that gives standard ways of describing terms related to measuring value.[19]

Physical View or Physical Architecture: Conceptually, the bottom three rows of Zachman's Enterprise Framework. See also "Technical Architecture."

Physical View: This architectural view of a system or application consists of where the work is performed—outlining the specific device, location, capacity, links, performance, backup, and support.[1]

Primitive Model: In the context of the Zachman Framework, the ontological, single-variable intersections between the Interrogatives (columns) and the Transformations (rows). Zachman contends that such single-variable models, that is, one Abstraction by one Perspective, are the raw material for doing Engineering. If you have no "Primitive" models, you have no raw material for doing Engineering and therefore, you are not doing Engineering (that is, you are not doing "Architecture").[25, 30] See also "Composite Model."

Principle: A statement of preferred direction or practice. Principles constitute the rules, constraints, and behaviors that a bureau will abide by in its daily activities over a long period of time.[2]

Principles: A component of the strategic direction. In terms of the federal enterprise architecture, the principles are statements that provide strategic direction to support the federal vision, guide design decisions, serve as a tie breaker in settling disputes, and provide a basis for dispersed, but integrated, decision making.[4]

Process: A repeatable unit of work with recognizable starting and stopping points, using personnel, materials, tools, and information to create products, services, and/or new information.[5]

Reference Model: A reference model is a model, by definition, an instance of some specific kind of model. Because models are applications of classification theory, they are technically classifications but tend to be relevant to a specific situation. A reference model tends to be an "industry-standard," generic representation for some specific industry. Reference models tend to be at a fairly high level of detail to accommodate all the models of their type for enterprises within the industry. Reference models tend to be "composite models" with either a strong process orientation or a strong technology orientation. The reference model is an instance of a model, not a classification of models. It is conceivable that you could have a (primitive) reference model for every cell of the Zachman Framework for every industry.[26]

Reference Model: Typically a set of standards for some aspect of an enterprise, technical and/or nontechnical. Applicable in the context of within a single organization as well as among organizations.

Repository: An information system used to store and access architectural information, relationships among the information elements, and work products.[2]

Road Map: The plan for migration of the enterprise, or some subsystems of it, from one state to another, as in from the as-is to the to-be state. The specifications of "where are we" and "where we are going." Sometimes applied in the context of a "Technology Road Map" to describe the development or evolution of a particular technological product category or sector.[1] See also "Sequencing Plan," "Technology Road Map," and "Transition Strategy."

Segment: An FEA term that refers to a major line-of-business functionality, such as human resources, that might be shared across organizations.[19]

Sequencing Plan: A document that defines the strategy for changing the enterprise from the current architectural state to some future target architecture. It schedules multiple, concurrent, and interdependent activities and incremental builds that will evolve the enterprise.[12] See also "Sequencing Plan," "Road Map," and "Transition Strategy."

Service-Oriented Architecture (SOA): An approach to implementation of information systems, SOA relies on composite models primarily for application development. Based on the principle of dividing business processes into a series of subunits or services that can then be assembled and linked together in a loosely coupled environment to perform a desired function. The services are defined at a level above that of the traditional view of components.[1] Instantiated composite components and information about them are the artifacts SOA.

Service-Oriented Architecture: Service-oriented architectures are component-based (i.e., object-oriented) and machine independent. In SOAs, services, data, and work flow processes are enabled, through object-oriented languages, XML protocols, and standards, shared across a distributed, interconnected set of users (more typically applications and/or their developers).[5]

Software Architecture: The structure of the components of a program/system, their interrelationships, and principles and guidelines governing their design and evolution over time.[13]

Spewak EA Planning Methodology: Formal methodology for defining architectures for the use of information in support of the business and the plan for implementing those architectures developed and published by Steven H. Spewak.[14]

Standard: A standard in general is an approved or accepted way of doing or buying something. It may exist in an industry or within a particular enterprise. It may be endorsed by a standards organization (a de jure standard), or it may have just arisen through wide use, but not endorsed (a de facto standard). Within one IS organization, this is usually applied to an IT component or characteristic of some type that has been approved for use and is on the approved-purchase list or "buy list" of the purchasing organization. It represents the selected or preferred choice, unless a specific exception has been granted. It acts as a primary guideline for implementation choices at the physical level (basically row 5 decisions in a Zachman Framework context). The use of standards can be beneficial in itself, such as the de facto use of HTML.[1, 30, 15]

Standards: A component of the FEAF. Standards are a set of criteria (some of which may be mandatory), voluntary guidelines, and best practices. Examples include:

    Application development
    Project management
    Vendor management
    Production operation
    User support
    Asset management
    Technology evaluation
    Architecture governance
    Configuration management
    Problem resolution[4]

Standards Information Base (SIB): A TOGAF term that refers to a collection of information about standards, particularly in the area of open source.[19]

System: A collection of components organized to accomplish a specific function or set of functions.[7]

System Management Domain: This is a subsection of the technical architecture that concerns itself with the many issues involved in designing the appropriate monitoring capability and operational practices to gain desired levels of service and reliability.[1]

Target Architecture: Representation of a desired future state or "to be built" for the enterprise within the context of the strategic direction. The target architecture is in two parts:

Target Business Architecture: Defines the enterprise future business needs addressed through new or emerging technologies.

Target Technical Architecture: Defines the future technologies used to support future business needs.[4]

Target Architecture: The set of products that portray the future or end-state enterprise, generally captured in the organization's strategic thinking and plans. It is commonly referred to as the "to-be" architecture.[5]

Taxonomy: A classification scheme or technique. The science or practice of classification.

Technical Architecture: Conceptually, the bottom three rows of Zachman's Enterprise Framework. See also "Physical View."

Technical Architecture: The generic term that applies to the collection of hardware and software components and processes. This is a complex arena further divided into several other areas or domains including: infrastructure, security, and system management.[1]

Technical Architecture: Usually refers to the architecture of the technical infrastructure within which applications run and interact.[19]

Technical Reference Model: An organizing structure for categorizing the various technical architecture standards and processes in a coherent manner to facilitate location and navigation. The model is organized according to a consistent taxonomy—a hierarchical structure of areas, domains, and elements using a specific vocabulary.[1]

Technical Reference Model (TRM): Part of TOGAF, a reference model that provides a common language for various pieces of IT architecture. This term is also used for a similar meaning within FEA.[19]

Technology Road Map: See "Road Map."[1]

The Open Group Architecture Framework (TOGAF): An architectural methodology for IT in organizations that is controlled and sold by The Open Group.[19]

Timing/Event Diagram: A model used to describe a particular dimension of architecture (basically column 5 information in terms of the Zachman Framework – Editor). It is a means of showing a sequence of actions that occurs in a system or process as a result of some initial trigger. It is often illustrated in a table or "swim lane" format.[1]

"To-Be" or "Tomorrow" Architecture: A description of the system(s) that are targeted to be in place in the future. It should be based on fulfillment of the business strategy. It may be used for the purpose of acting as a set of guidelines or design standards.[1]

"To-Be" Architecture: The target or future state of an enterprise and its architecture (see also "Target Architecture").[2]

Top-Down Architecture: This represents a strategy to initiate or organize an architectural effort that starts at the top or the business strategy and direction level, and then works down to business processes, business activities, and the subsequent layers of information, application, and integration architecture that employ the infrastructure, security, and system management architecture. The benefit of top-down architecture comes from making a series of choices that are directly traceable back to fulfilling the business needs and goals. This objective has been hard to accomplish because architects (who are usually technology oriented) are generally not good at perceiving the link to business results and performance.[1] See also "Bottom-Up Architecture." A descriptor for an architecture process.

Transition Strategy: According to OMB document A-130, a term sometimes used interchangeably with sequencing plan. However, the concept is broader and more inclusive.[5] See also "Sequencing Plan" and "Technology Road Map."

Transitional EA Components: Representation of a desired state for all or part of the enterprise for an interim milestone between the baseline architecture and the target architecture. A time-sliced set of models that represent one or more increments or stages in the sequence plan.[12]

Treasury Enterprise Architecture Framework (TEAF): The framework parallels the work done on the FEAF, but includes the particular computational demands that are critically important to U.S. Treasury operations and performance.[1]

Use Case: A narrative document that describes the sequence of events of an actor (an external agent) using a system to complete a process.[5] A composite modeling technique generally used to determine system requirements.

Value Chain: Disaggregates a firm into its strategically relevant activities to understand the behavior of costs and the existing and potential sources of differentiation (from other companies/products).[18] A high-level composite model of an enterprise.

Vision: A description or picture of where you want to be at some point in the future. It can be functional, technological, or organizational. The vision is represented in the "to-be" or "tomorrow" architecture.[1]

Zachman Framework: The Zachman Framework™ is a semantic model or schema represented in two dimensions as the intersection between two historical classifications that have been in use for literally thousands of years. The first is the fundamentals of communication found in the primitive interrogatives: what, how, when, who, where, and why. It is the integration of answers to these questions that enables the comprehensive, composite description of complex ideas. The second is derived from reification, the transformation of an abstract idea into an instantiation that was initially postulated by ancient Greek philosophers and is labeled: Identification, Definition, Representation, Specification, Configuration, and Instantiation. The Zachman Framework is a meta-model; it is not a methodology for creating the implementation (an instantiation) of the object. It is an ontology—a theory of the existence of a structured set of essential components of an object for which explicit expression is necessary. There are actually four frameworks as formally identified in Zachman's second (1992) *IBM Systems Journal* paper. Although the logic is identical for all, each framework is used for analyzing a different meta-level analytic target.[25, 27, 30]

Zachman Framework: Classic work on the concepts of information systems architecture that defined the concept of a framework and provided a semantic model or schema depicted as a 6 × 6 matrix of architecture views and perspectives with each intersecting cell containing a unique architectural artifact or product.[6] See Zachman's "Architecture is Architecture is Architecture" and "Concise Definition of the Zachman Framework" articles in Chapter 2.

Notes

1. Gartner Publication ID No. COM-20-2071, *Applying Enterprise Architecture*, September 2005, http://www.commonperu.com/html/eventos/2006/cio/ppt/gartner/GARTNER_Applying_Enterprise_Architecture.pdf.
2. *Treasury Enterprise Architecture Framework (TEAF)*, July 2000, http://www.eaframeworks.com/TEAF/teaf.doc.
3. DOD Joint Pub 1-02, April 2001, http://www.dtic.mil/doctrine/jel/new_pubs/jp1_02.pdf.
4. *Federal Enterprise Architecture Framework,* version 1.1, Federal Chief Information Officers Council, September 1999.
5. P. Hagan, ed., MITRE *Enterprise Architecture Body of Knowledge*, 2004, http://www.mitre.org/tech/eabok/.
6. J. Zachman, Society for Information Management Enterprise Architecture Working Group Meeting, 8–9 January 2008, University of North Texas, Denton.
7. IEEE STD 610.12, 1990, http://ieeexplore.ieee.org/xpls/abs_all.jsp?tp=&isnumber=4148&arnumber=159342&punumber=2238.
8. Office of Management and Budget, *Circular No. A-130*, http://www.whitehouse.gov/omb/circulars/a130/a130trans4.html.
9. L. Kappelman, Society for Information Management Enterprise Architecture Working Group Meeting, 8–9 January 2008, University of North Texas, Denton.
10. *Merriam-Webster's Unabridged Dictionary,* http://www.merriam-webster.com.
11. *Board Briefing on IT Governance,* IT Governance Institute, Information Systems Audit and Control Foundation, ISBN 1-893209-27-X, Rolling Meadows, IL 60008, 2001.
12. Federal CIO Council and U.S. GAO, *A Practical Guide to Federal Enterprise Architecture 1.0,* February 2001, http://www.gao.gov/bestpractices/bpeaguide.pdf.
13. D. Garlan and D. Perry, "Introduction to the Special Issue on Software Architecture," *IEEE Transactions on Software Engineering* 21, no. 4 (April 1995): 269–74.
14. S. H. Spewak and S. C. Hill, *Enterprise Architecture Planning: Developing a Blueprint for Data, Applications and Technology* (Wellesley, MA: QED Information Sciences, Inc., 1993).

15. *PC Magazine's Online Encyclopedia*, http://www.pcmag.com/encyclopedia/.
16. Society for Information Management Enterprise Architecture Working Group Meeting, 8–9 January 2008, University of North Texas, Denton.
17. E. Nassiff, Lockheed Martin Corp., at Society for Information Management Enterprise Architecture Working Group Meeting, 8–9 January 2008, University of North Texas, Denton.
18. M. Porter, *Competitive Advantage* (New York: Macmillan, 1985).
19. R. Sessions, "A Comparison of the Top Four Enterprise Architecture Methodologies," May 2007, http://msdn2.microsoft.com/en-us/architecture/bb466232.aspx. (The article provides useful descriptions but is conceptually frail in its attempt to compare ontologies, methodologies, processes, models, methods, and concepts, as if they are all of the same family. – Editor.)
20. IEEE Std 1471-2000, *IEEE Recommended Practice for Architectural Description of Software-Intensive Systems—Description*, 2004, http://standards.ieee.org/reading/ieee/std_public/description/se/1471-2000_desc.html.
21. J. W. Ross, "Stop Aligning IT with the Business," presentation at the Milwaukee SIM Chapter, 7 March 2007, https://www.simnet.org/Portals/0/content/Chapters/Wisconsin/Documents/Ross_Milwaukee_SIM_March_2007.pdf.
22. J. W. Ross, "Creating a Strategic IT Architecture Competency: Learning in Stages," *MIS Quarterly Executive* 21, no. 1 (March 2003): 31–43.
23. Kat Hagedorn, *Information Architecture Glossary*, March 2000, http://argus-acia.com/white_papers/ia_glossary.pdf.
24. Information Architecture Institute (2007). *What Is Information Architecture?*, 2007, http://www.iainstitute.org/documents/learn/What_is_IA.pdf.
25. J. A. Zachman, The Zachman Framework™: A Concise Definition, Zachman International, 2008, http://zachmaninternational.com/index.php/the-zachman-framework/26-articles/13-the-zachman-framework-a-concise-definition. Also see Zachman's "Concise Definition" article in Chapter 2.
26. J. A. Zachman, *Frameworks, Reference Models, and Matrices*, Zachman International, http://zachmaninternational.com. 2003.
27. J. A. Zachman, *Framework Standards: What's It All About?*, Zachman International, 2005, http://zachmaninternational.com/index.php/home-article/19#maincol. Also see Zachman's "Framework Standards" article in Chapter 2 and "Framework Standards" at link http://zachmaninternational.com/index.php/home-article/17#maincol.
28. GAO, *Enterprise Architecture: Leadership Remains Key to Establishing and Leveraging Architectures for Organizational Transformation*, GAO-06-831, August 2006, http://www.gao.gov/new.items/d06831.pdf.
29. *Merriam-Webster's Unabridged Dictionary*, http://www.merriam-webster.com/.
30. J. A. Zachman, *Architecture Is Architecture Is Architecture*, Zachman International, 2007, http://zachmaninternational.com/index.php/ea-articles/26-articles/68-architecture-is-architecture-is-architecture. Also see Zachman's article by the same name in Chapter 2.

Index

265